SHAKESPEARE SURVEY

SHAKESPEARE SURVEY

AN ANNUAL SURVEY OF
SHAKESPEARIAN STUDY & PRODUCTION

6

EDITED BY
ALLARDYCE NICOLL

Issued under the Sponsorship of

THE UNIVERSITY OF BIRMINGHAM

THE UNIVERSITY OF MANCHESTER

THE SHAKESPEARE MEMORIAL THEATRE

THE SHAKESPEARE BIRTHPLACE TRUST

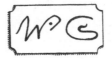

CAMBRIDGE
AT THE UNIVERSITY PRESS
1953

PUBLISHED BY

THE SYNDICS OF THE CAMBRIDGE UNIVERSITY PRESS

London Office: Bentley House, N.W. 1
American Branch: New York

Agents for Canada, India, and Pakistan: Macmillan

Printed in Great Britain at the University Press, Cambridge
(Brooke Crutchley, University Printer)

PREFACE

Within recent years the History Plays have been rapidly coming into their own. Keen appreciation of Shakespeare's purposes in the penning of such works as *Richard II* and *Henry IV* has gone along with what might almost be called the discovery of the stage interest of others formerly despised. Appropriately, therefore, the present volume of *Shakespeare Survey* takes consideration of these plays as its 'core'. The volume starts with a survey of critical attitudes adopted towards the Histories during the past fifty years, and this is accompanied by various contributions dealing with aspects of this theme, as well as by reviews of recent productions.

In the account of Elizabethan material preserved in the Henry E. Huntington Library appears the fifth of the articles devoted to analysis of collections rich in this field, while the notes on Spanish and Chinese translators' problems continue the series of contributions designed to give information concerning twentieth-century Shakespearian activities in diverse countries.

As in previous volumes, other articles have been selected for the purpose of presenting fresh documentary material and of relating study to stage. New facts appear here concerning theatrical activities shortly before Shakespeare came to London; evidence is brought forward to show his indebtedness to a contemporary 'French Without Tears'; the dramatist is shown at work on *Timon of Athens*; and the suggestion is made that in Daniel's *Cleopatra* is preserved an eyewitness description of the puzzling scene wherein Antony is hauled up to the monument. The analysis of a passage in *Othello* demonstrates how actor and scholar must collaborate in the task of interpretation.

Once more it is gratifying to reflect that, apart from the reports of its Correspondents, *Shakespeare Survey* has the privilege of presenting here, alongside articles by British and American scholars, essays from Austrian, Chinese, German, Israeli and Spanish contributors.

For the following volume, to appear in April 1954, the theme has been chosen of Shakespeare's Style and Language—another topic which of late has attracted much critical attention.

Contributions offered for publication in *Shakespeare Survey* should be addressed to:
The Editor, The Shakespeare Institute (University of Birmingham), Stratford-upon-Avon.

CONTENTS

[Notes are placed at the end of each contribution. All line references are to the 'Globe' edition, and, unless for special reasons, quotations are from this text]

LIST OF PLATES

SHAKESPEARE'S HISTORY PLAYS: 1900-1951

BY

HAROLD JENKINS

SOME NINETEENTH-CENTURY VIEWS

In contemplating the masterpieces of the past, each age imparts to them something of itself. In few fields of literary criticism is there a more striking contrast between the last century and this than in their interpretation of Shakespeare's history plays. Although we no doubt add some different alloy from our own prejudice, it is easy for us now to see that the nineteenth century's conception of them was in some measure the result of its predilection. For an age of industrial and commercial progress, of growing nationalisms and imperialist expansion, the most obvious thing about Shakespeare's history plays was their expression of a national spirit. Together they formed an 'immortal epic' of which England was the true protagonist. It would be foolish to look for a single originator of this common view, but it can be traced back especially to A. W. Schlegel's *Lectures on Dramatic Art and Literature*, delivered in 1808 and translated into English in 1815. Most of the German and many of the English critics followed Schlegel in regarding the ten histories as one great work of which *King John* was the prologue and *Henry VIII* the epilogue. An occasional sceptic found difficulty in accepting as a prologue something which gives no hint of the work to follow or of reconciling such a scheme with the belief, then usual, in the composite authorship of the first three or four plays. Nevertheless, it was the large vision of the romantic critics that showed us the broad historical pattern into which the plays fall. Schlegel himself strikingly anticipated recent critics when he saw that the dethronement of Richard II begins a cycle of revolts which continue until the curse is finally expiated in the overthrow of Richard III. What is more, in this pattern he discerned a "mirror for kings", reflecting the universal consequences of bad or weak rule. Later in the century Richard Simpson's essay on 'The Politics of Shakspere's Historical Plays' (*Transactions of the New Shakspere Society*, 1874) attempted to direct the mirror towards the political situations of Shakespeare's own day, but the parallels he drew between Prince Arthur and Mary Queen of Scots or Henry V and Essex were ill received. More congenial to his age, with its interest in character-portraits and its quest for a 'criticism of life', were those discussions of Shakespeare's kings as exemplars of royal strength and weakness which Dowden (*Shakspere: His Mind and Art*, 1875) garnished with quotations from Newman or analogies with George Eliot.

Separate studies of the history group were rather rare. The biggest, Courtney's *Commentaries on the Historical Plays of Shakspere* (1840), had the pedestrian aim of discovering how far they were "properly historical". Yet in its lucid statement of Shakespeare's deviations from fact and its incidental demonstration of Shakespeare's dependence on his sources this proved useful pioneering work. More detailed research on the chronicles was done in the second half of the century, which closed on the landmark of Boswell-Stone's *Shakspere's Holinshed* (1896). At the same time B. E. Warner's *English History in Shakespeare's Plays* (1894) illustrated only too well some characteristic defects of its period. It regularly confused the dramatic hero with his historical original, had no doubt that when Shakespeare deviated from the letter he was faithful to the spirit of the past, and supposed him to interpret it in the manner of J. R. Green, who was appropriately quoted in the conclusion. The theme of Shakespeare's histories was "the passing of feudalism and the rise of the common people". More detached critics were, however, beginning to perceive that Shakespeare looked at history with the interests of *his* age, and that it was natural for him to see in John's reign, for example, not Magna Carta, but the King's struggle with the Pope.

THE FIRST QUARTER OF THE CENTURY

The most perceptive writing on the histories round about 1900 was probably contained in the introductions to the single plays in a number of critical editions—in Herford's 'Eversley Shakespeare' (1899), for example, or such an excellent little 'Warwick' volume as Moore Smith's *King John* (1900). But though often freshly presented, most of the criticism was traditional. Furness's 'Variorum' *Richard III* (1908) and *King John* (1919) had little new to report. With the 'Arden' volumes, which sprinkled the first two decades of the century, it is perhaps significant that the histories were not usually allocated to the most distinguished editors. The exceptions were the *Henry VI* volumes of H. C. Hart (1909–10), which presented an unsifted mass of material on possible literary echoes and some complicated theories of collaboration and revision resting on a basis since shown to be fallacious. For the rest, the 'Arden' introductions weighed learned opinion on date or authorship, outlined Shakespeare's deviations from the chronicles, analysed—or at least described—the principal characters, and added perhaps a little on style or structure while avoiding spectacular conclusions. Monographs on Shakespeare in this period usually echoed the opinion that the histories were Shakespeare's national epic and some found room for character-portraits of at least the two Richards and Henry V. Occasionally the plays were combed for their expressions of patriotic sentiment or their references to the common people. Otherwise there was little disposition to isolate the problems of the histories or assess their collective importance. An exception here is G. P. Baker's *The Development of Shakespeare as a Dramatist* (1907), which, at the cost of some undervaluation and some violence to chronology, contrived to see them as a stage in the progress towards tragedy or the comedy of manners. Criticism was not yet ready to attempt the equivalent of Bradley's *Shakespearean Tragedy* (1904) or MacCallum's *Shakespeare's Roman Plays* (1910).

In the criticism of these years there are two questions which come fitfully into prominence. The first is that of genre. While some, like Baker, Raleigh, and Gregory Smith, denied that there was a genre of the history play at all, others were seeking to determine its distinguishing characteristics, and Schelling, in *The English Chronicle Play* (1902), had made the first elaborate attempt to trace the development of the type. Influenced by the nineteenth-century notion of a grand *épopée*, he found the essence of Shakespeare's histories in their "assertion of the national consciousness"; and, looking for a relation between form and content, he defended a structure—best exhibited, he thought, in *Henry IV*—which represented historical events with epic comprehensiveness instead of with dramatic concentration upon individual personalities. Epic unity was easier to assert than to demonstrate, but Courthope (1903) saw Shakespeare's histories to be animated by a "central poetical idea" based upon great moral laws. An important chapter in Tucker Brooke's *The Tudor Drama* (1912) showed Shakespeare moving away from the facile plan of the earliest chronicle plays towards a structure dependent less on particular events than on the historical process; and a similar concern with the development of an organic historical drama out of the chronicle-history informs W. D. Briggs's long introduction to his edition of Marlowe's *Edward II* (1914). A more theoretical 'Note on the History Play' by C. S. Baldwin (*Shaksperian Studies*, ed. Matthews and Thorndike, 1916) explained how historical drama grows out of history by giving to historical events and personages an ideal or archetypal quality.

Out of such discussions emerged a second question—that of the political significance of Shakespeare's histories, which earlier critics had minimized. Dowden of course had distinguished history from tragedy by its concern with man in his practical life rather than in his universal aspect, and Schelling noted in passing that the achievement of *Henry IV* was to represent "the whole range of human life...in its political and social relations". More specifically Tucker Brooke found that Shakespeare's histories set forth a philosophy of statecraft based upon a principle of kingly responsibility which was finally expressed in the ideal figure of Henry V. Among historians the orthodox view of A. F. Pollard that Shakespeare's plays were quite divorced from politics was presently challenged in Sir J. A. R. Marriott's *English History in Shakespeare* (1918) and by F. J. C. Hearnshaw (especially in the *Contemporary Review*, CXXIV, 1923). Marriott indeed, writing in the middle of a world war, found in the history cycle political messages for our age which he thought Shakespeare must have intended for his own. The need for national unity was the dominant theme and lesson. Judging therefore by non-literary criteria, he over-simplified the plays and begged some questions of first importance in criticism. But in compensation the historian's vision showed more clearly than had been done before the links Shakespeare had made between the "crooked ways" of usurpation in one play and the nemesis of fear and strife in those which followed. He also knew that the historical pattern came to Shakespeare from Hall. These were matters which would be explored in the following decades but of which the ordinary critic—if we may judge him from John Bailey's essay on 'Shakespeare's Histories' (*The Continuity of Letters*, 1923)—as yet suspected nothing.

There was in this period insufficient inquiry into the precise sources of the history plays. Malone's old notion that Shakespeare rarely went outside Holinshed was still commonly repeated; and though Boswell-Stone's *Shakspere's Holinshed* was a collection of illustrative passages more than an investigation of sources, it led many scholars, perhaps through some confusion in its title and plan, to assume that a task had been completed which in reality was just begun. Churton Collins's *Studies in Shakespeare* (1904) contained an essay based on Boswell-Stone explaining how Shakespeare "simply dramatized" Holinshed, and H. R. D. Anders, examining *Shakespeare's Books* (1904), thought the history plays had been "exhaustively investigated" already. Although the sounder scholars, including Boswell-Stone himself, referred to other chroniclers, an adequate examination of Shakespeare's debt to these, and especially to Hall, was postponed for thirty years. Ebisch and Schücking's standard *Shakespeare Bibliography* (1931) still described Boswell-Stone as a reprint of what "Shakespeare used".

There were, however, at the beginning of the century (particularly in the German *Palaestra* series) several useful studies of the legends which lay behind the Elizabethan chronicles. They included an excellent one by G. B. Churchill on the evolution of the Richard III saga (1900) and W. Baeske's discussion (1905) of the Oldcastle legends which Gairdner had shown to be part of the heredity of Falstaff. Further suggestions about Falstaff's historical origin were made by Alfred Ainger (*Lectures and Essays*, 1905), D. W. Duthie (*The Case of Sir John Fastolf*, 1907), and L. W. V. Harcourt (*Transactions of the Royal Historical Society*, 3rd series, IV, 1910). More valuably, the last of these contested the nineteenth-century disbelief in the tales of Prince Hal's wild youth. That they have some foundation in fact appeared probable from C. L. Kingsford's account of them prefixed to *The First English Life of King Henry the Fifth* (1911), and is now generally believed.

Something was also added to our knowledge of Shakespeare's subsidiary sources. Daniel's *Civil Wars*, long known to have resemblances with Shakespeare, was established as a source for *Henry IV* by F. W. Moorman (*Shakespeare Jahrbuch*, XL, 1904) and, after Hardin Craig's 'Tudor' *Richard II* (1912), for that play also. The relation of *Richard II* to Froissart and to the anonymous play of *Woodstock* attracted some attention, and finally P. Reyher, in some important 'Notes sur les Sources de "Richard II"' (*Revue de l'Enseignement des Langues Vivantes*, XLI, 1924), gave evidence for at least six authorities and thus changed our notions of how Shakespeare went to work. The study of his opposite practice in *King John*, with its single source in *The Troublesome Reign of King John*, was facilitated when this old play was again reprinted in Gollancz's 'Shakespeare Library' (1913) and in the 'Variorum' *King John*. This matter was well treated by F. Liebermann (*Archiv für das Studium der neueren Sprachen und Literaturen*, CXLII, 1921, and CXLIII, 1922); but the more complicated problem of Shakespeare's debt to *The Famous Victories of Henry the Fifth* could not be satisfactorily investigated until bibliographical scholarship had thrown more light upon its text.

TEXT AND CANON

This is not the place to discuss the new bibliographical criticism which has been the most striking feature of Shakespeare scholarship in this century. Yet reference must be made to its most important findings on the histories, and for this purpose the chronological survey here breaks off. *Henry V* was prominent from the first in the discussions of 'bad' Quartos, which reached a climax of interest in the 1920's. In spite of H. T. Price's argument for shorthand (*The Text of Henry V*, 1920), scholars accepted the view that the Quarto text is an abridgement in a memorized version supplied by pirate actors. Conclusions reached about the nature of bad Quartos in general helped to suggest that *The Famous Victories* is probably only a degenerate version of Shakespeare's actual source. They also illuminated the long-debated problem of the widely divergent Folio and Quarto texts of *Richard III*: for the theory that this Quarto too was an abridged version with actors' corruptions, though not necessarily a piracy, was ultimately established in the admirable study by D. L. Patrick (1936). The relation between Folio and Quarto for *2 Henry IV* was discussed at length in the 'Variorum' edition by M. A. Shaaber (1940). Some of the omissions in the Quarto, formerly regarded as theatrical cuts, are now, following the arguments of Schücking (*Times Literary Supplement*, 1930) and Alfred Hart (*Shakespeare and the Homilies*, 1934), more generally thought to have had a political motive.

A far more vital matter is the relation of *2* and *3 Henry VI* to the Quartos called *The Contention of York and Lancaster* and *The True Tragedy of Richard Duke of York*. Malone's view that Shakespeare was here revising two old plays so firmly held the field throughout the nineteenth century that when Halliwell-Phillipps asserted that these *Contention* plays, as it is convenient to call them, were "vamped...versions of the poet's own original dramas", Furnivall dismissed this as "a refuge for the brain-destitute"; and Thomas Kenny's demonstration of it (*The Life and Genius of Shakespeare*, 1864) was ignored. Yet when this view was put by Peter Alexander, first in the *Times Literary Supplement* in 1924 and then more elaborately in his book of 1929, so thoroughly had the way now been prepared by the new knowledge of bad Quartos that it won almost immediate acceptance. An independent investigation by Madeleine Doran (1928) gave confirmation, and that the *Contention* plays are in fact bad Quartos of *2* and *3 Henry VI* has been the scholarly opinion for the last twenty years. A promised study by C. T. Prouty, however, is understood to be reopening the matter.

The new textual theory about *Henry VI* demolished most older theories about its authorship. In the early years of this century most scholars, accepting Shakespeare as mainly a reviser, were still debating the respective shares of Marlowe, Greene and other supposed collaborators. Courthope was almost alone in attributing the whole trilogy to Shakespeare on the grounds of its single "comprehensive grasp". But the demonstration of the derivative character of the *Contention* plays removed the chief argument against Shakespeare's authorship of *Henry VI* at the same time as the whole trend of bibliographical scholarship, by vindicating the Folio editors, was strengthening the case in favour of it. Since about 1930 it has been usually accepted for Parts II and III; and, the tide now setting against the disintegrators, a growing belief in Shakespeare as the effective, if not the sole, author of all three parts has contributed immensely to the reorientation in the criticism of the histories as a whole. It has also, incidentally, changed the probabilities for the sequel, *Richard III*: whereas the 'Arden' editor (1907) showed considerable uncertainty before deciding this play to be "substantially Shakespeare's", it has not since the 1920's been seriously suspected. Yet *1 Henry VI*, which Malone long ago dismissed from the canon, has proved something of a stumbling-block. J. B. Henneman's theory that it is Shakespeare's adaptation of an older play on Talbot (*PMLA*, xv, 1900) was only the first of numerous excavations seeking to reveal different strata in its composition. But the full swing of the pendulum now finds H. T. Price praising its "severely controlled design" (*Construction in Shakespeare*, 1951) and L. Kirschbaum appealing to this in defence of Shakespeare's single authorship (Stratford Conference, 1951, in a paper since printed in *PMLA*, lxvii, 1952). This is still an undecided question; and Dover Wilson gives warning that his edition of *Henry VI*, now in the press, will maintain the presence of more than one hand in all three parts.[1]

The effect of crediting Shakespeare with the *Henry VI* plays was enhanced by the addition to the canon at the same time of the insurrection scene in the play of *Sir Thomas More*. First claimed for Shakespeare by Simpson and Spedding eighty years ago, this scene attracted intense interest only after Maunde Thompson's examination of *Shakespeare's Handwriting* (1916) had favoured Shakespeare's authorship. A. W. Pollard and a group of other scholars presented a strong case in *Shakespeare's Hand in the Play of Sir Thomas More* (1923); and R. W. Chambers afterwards developed further—especially in *Man's Unconquerable Mind* (1939)—his powerful argument from the presence in More's great speeches of characteristic Shakespearian sequences of thought. Most scholars, like R. C. Bald in the most recent review of the matter (*Shakespeare Survey*, 2, 1949), are now disposed to accept the scene as Shakespeare's.

The biggest problem in the canon now is *Henry VIII*. This, since a famous paper by Spedding in 1850, has usually been held to be partly Fletcher's work; but after Baldwin Maxwell had questioned the stylistic evidence (*Manly Anniversary Studies*, 1923), Shakespeare's undivided authorship was asserted by Alexander (*Essays and Studies*, XVI, 1931) and Wilson Knight (*Criterion*, XV, 1936). Knight's subsequent profound study of the play in *The Crown of Life* (1947) demonstrated its spiritual unity with Shakespeare's other work. It is true that a recent essay by A. C. Partridge (1949) reassembles the linguistic evidence for Fletcher, but there is now more willingness to ascribe the whole play to Shakespeare than there has been for a century.

THE NEW ORIENTATION

The changed perspective of the canon has thus had the effect of bringing the history plays into much greater prominence. But it did not so much initiate as accelerate the new development in their study. Signs have been noted of a willingness, already before 1920, to discover in Shakespeare's histories some political significance; and it may be that this loomed larger for a generation which had witnessed a world war and great social revolutions. Marriott again affirmed Shakespeare's faith in "order and degree; national unity; social solidarity and selfless patriotism" (*Cornhill*, new series, LXIII, 1927). Yet he still expected his mere title, 'Shakespeare and Politics', to provoke objections from idealistic critics. And indeed Tucker Brooke, notwithstanding his earlier insight on the history genre, was describing Shakespeare as an unworldly dunce in "politics, or religion...or current affairs" (*Shakespeare of Stratford*, 1926); while even Stoll, who had so firmly linked Shakespeare with the theatrical traditions of his time, believed him to express no "convictions or principles" that one can easily make out (*Shakespeare Studies*, 1927). Charlton showed the newer trend in a lecture on *Shakespeare, Politics, and Politicians* (1929), which, in a searching, if slightly contrived, attempt to clarify the old critical problem of their genre, maintained that the histories were political plays. He traced Shakespeare's progress from the chronicle drama of *Henry VI* and the tragedies of the Richards, through the crucial experiment of *King John*, where the political interest was dominant over the dramatic, to the later histories, in which political issues were built into the dramatic structure. About this time a group of articles in the *Shakespeare Jahrbuch* (W. Keller, LXIII, 1927; Agnes Henneke, LXVI, 1930; W. Clemen, LXVIII, 1932) discussed Shakespeare's conception of kingship; and his expression of Elizabethan doctrines on allegiance and rebellion was among the topics covered by R. V. Lindabury's *Patriotism in the Elizabethan Drama* (1931). Belief was growing that the histories drew vitality from the political convictions of their author and his age. Most critics thought them concerned only with the more general principles of political conduct; but it was perhaps inevitable that there should be attempts to demonstrate specific correspondences with Elizabethan happenings. G. B. Harrison (*Times Literary Supplement*, 1930) plausibly discovered topical significances in the relations between English and French depicted in *King John*: others less plausibly identified Shakespearian characters with Elizabethan personalities. Extreme examples occur in the articles by Evelyn M. Albright (*PMLA*, XLII, 1927; XLIII, 1928; XLVI, 1931; XLVII, 1932), who saw Elizabeth's actions reflected on in those of Richard II and John, and took *Henry V* to be the climax of Shakespeare's persistent propaganda on behalf of Essex. Such theories were easily rejected; but they showed the prevailing wind, and a comparable

Essex theory was incorporated in Dover Wilson's "biographical adventure", *The Essential Shakespeare* (1932).

The belief that Shakespeare's histories reflected contemporary political thinking was but one aspect of that newer scholarship which sought illumination on his work from the intellectual background of his time. In particular it was shown that Shakespeare held the traditional view of earlier English history. Previous hints about the crucial influence of Hall's Chronicle were now elaborated by Kingsford in an important essay on 'Fifteenth-Century History in Shakespeare's Plays' (*Prejudice and Promise in XVth Century England*, 1925), which led in turn to a pregnant passage in E. A. Greenlaw's *Studies in Spenser's Historical Allegory* (1932). It became customary to interpret Shakespeare's cycle of plays according to the pattern imposed on history by Hall: the tragic story of York and Lancaster was a consequence of Bolingbroke's crime and a warning to England of the dangers of civil strife, which the accession of the Tudors had blissfully terminated. Alfred Hart drew attention to the surprisingly neglected influence of the Tudor homilies (1934), showing how they asserted political order to be an aspect of universal order and how they preached, with historical illustrations, the iniquity of rebellion as a crime against God to be punished by a curse on generations to come. Shakespeare's debt to Hall was now explored in some detail. Its importance for *Richard III* was shown by Edleen Begg (*Studies in Philology*, XXXII, 1935), and for *Henry VI* in some notable articles by Lucille King (*Philological Quarterly*, XIII, 1934; *PMLA*, L, 1935 and LI, 1936). And the whole matter was well brought into focus by W. G. Zeefeld (*E.L.H.* III, 1936), who not only discussed Hall as a source for particular passages but showed Shakespeare's dramatic power building on the interest in character and conduct which Hall derived from Polydore Vergil and the habit of Renaissance thought.

When scholarship had once demonstrated that the historical material reached Shakespeare already shaped into a large cyclic unity, embracing cause and effect, connecting political crime with retributive civil war, it was easier for literary criticism to detect in the sequence of the plays themselves a unity more organic than was inherent in the old idea of a national epic. And although this unity was latent in the material, the feeling grew that its realization in the plays was to be attributed to a single capacious imagination. This chimed with the new textual theory which established Shakespeare as the responsible author of *Henry VI*, and in these early plays, formerly dismissed as prentice patchwork, there came to be recognized, however fumbling in execution, a dramatic undertaking on the grand scale. This had various important consequences. First, enthusiasts leapt to the notion of a master planner projecting two historical 'tetralogies'; and even on the more reasonable assumption that the finally emergent pattern gradually evolved as one play succeeded another, the history sequence now appeared as the major achievement of the first half of Shakespeare's career. Secondly, the long-repeated theory of Shakespeare's debt to Marlowe was now revised. Charlton and Waller, editing *Edward II* (1933), made the almost revolutionary suggestion that Marlowe's history play was influenced by Shakespeare; and by 1940 Hazelton Spencer, in *The Art and Life of William Shakespeare*, could say that the notion of Shakespeare "stumbling along at Marlowe's heels is, though still orthodox, in process of being discarded". Finally, *Henry VI* was examined with new gravity and itself revealed an unsuspected gravity of tone. In a British Academy lecture (1937) R. W. Chambers emphasized its vital portraiture of evil men and its powerful sense of doom, and accordingly attacked the popular theory of a gay Elizabethan Shakespeare unanticipatory of mature Jacobean glooms. The new estimate of Shakespeare's early work was clearly apparent here and in Alexander's *Shakespeare's Mind and Art* (1939), where the awful significance of the early histories was illuminated by the famous image, from the Shakespearian scene of *Sir Thomas More*, of men without ordered government as ravenous fishes feeding on one another.

RECENT ACTIVITY

The last fifteen years or so have seen more attention given to Shakespeare's history plays than ever before. At the beginning of this period came the important 'Variorum' editions of *Henry IV* by S. B. Hemingway (Part I, 1936) and M. A. Shaaber (Part II, 1940), while *Richard II* is presently to follow. By a happy chance the progress of his 'New Cambridge' edition brought Dover Wilson to the histories just when scholarship on them was at a crucial stage. Accepting the view that they were firmly rooted in the political concepts of their day, he had the acumen to see the need for that thorough reconsideration of them which his vigorous prefaces and commentaries are carrying out. After examining in *King John* (1936) Shakespeare's handling of the conflict between monarchy and papacy, he turned to the disruption of the political order which is shown beginning in *Richard II* (1939) and causing instability and rebellion in *Henry IV* (1946). The excellent study of *Richard II* explained how the play, while drawing strength from the traditional medieval themes of the fall of a prince and the helplessness of man on Fortune's wheel, has its centre in the conflict between two Elizabethan political principles—the preference for the good ruler and the sacredness of a God-appointed king. A similarly large view praised in *Henry V* (1947) the delineation in speech and action of an Elizabethan ideal of heroic virtue. And this ideal was shown as integrally related to that moral and dramatic pattern in *Henry IV* which was so skilfully analysed in *The Fortunes of Falstaff* (1943).

By this time the history plays were seen to draw their inspiration from a wider sphere than history and politics. Middleton Murry, for example (*Shakespeare*, 1936), perceived how Shakespeare's interest in these things led him to a grand conception of order transcending the political and expressive of the aspirations of a people united in a spiritual bond. To the belief in order as a principle of creation increasing significance was attached. Research continued active on Elizabethan ideas, of which an able synthesis was made by Hardin Craig in *The Enchanted Glass* (1936). For our purpose the most important discoveries were those which showed the Elizabethan conception of the state, with its divinely appointed ruler and its hierarchic structure, to be part of a philosophic system embracing all things from the vegetable kingdom to the planetary universe. Interest in this system was immensely stimulated by such a work as Lovejoy's *The Great Chain of Being* (1936), and the application to Shakespeare was specifically made in *Shakespeare and the Nature of Man* (1942), by Theodore Spencer, who suggested that the action of the history plays always involved the violation and restoration of the "vast in-clusive pattern of order" which governed throughout nature. His sense of their profound reverberations led him to regard the histories as Shakespeare's most significant work before the great tragedies. A similar awareness of the correspondence between the state and the cosmos led Tillyard to expound *The Elizabethan World Picture* (1943) as a prelude to the study of the history plays themselves. In Wilson Knight's *The Olive and the Sword* (1944) Shakespeare's faith in order, manifest alike in his "royalistic doctrine" and in his sense of man as a part of creation, assumed a more mystical character; but this was less a study of the histories than an exploitation of them to provide a "gospel" for Britain at war.

A brief account of Tillyard's *Shakespeare's History Plays* (1944) may serve to bring into sharper focus the questions by which recent work on these plays has been dominated. Though its conclusions are less new and more tentative than is always made clear, this book, in a many-angled approach, shrewdly recognizes the significant clues revealed by modern research and shows imaginative energy in following them up in the most comprehensive study the history plays have yet received. It deliberately sets out not only to enforce the new perspective but to make use of it for literary criticism. Accepting without question the authenticity of *Henry VI*, as no one twenty years before could do, Tillyard makes the first considered appraisal of it. He shows the importance of the early group of histories and continues scepticism of Marlowe's influence. He expounds the Tudor myth of English history and, strengthening the tendency to esteem Hall above Holinshed, he shows Shakespeare's observance of Hall's moral pattern: "As by discord great things decay and fall to ruin, so the same by concord be revived and erected." This notion of history's ordered processes he merges in the sixteenth-century conception of a universal order, which he demonstrates in an account of the cosmic background. In the later histories he finds a theory of monarchy in which political and educational ideals blend, so that the whole series thus becomes a version of the Elizabethan "pattern of culture". This fits well with the modern reaction against the view of an unlearned Shakespeare, and in fact Tillyard allies Shakespeare with Chapman, Daniel, Raleigh and "the best educated writers" of the age. There is probably an overstatement here and the author's enthusiasm may lead to others. He favours the notion of a grand plan for a series of histories, of which the first tetralogy at least was written "academically". Under the need to explain why the second half of the plan was executed first, he too lightly throws out the suggestion that the *Henry V* group might have had an earlier sketch. His zest for lofty doctrine belittles the tradition of the chronicle play in order to elevate that of the Moralities. The demand for a moral structure may lead to an underestimate of *Henry V*. But there is an admirable demonstration of the harmonious variety within the epic dimensions of *Henry IV*, and the general effect of Tillyard's criticism is to reveal in the whole cycle a richness and complexity not fully appreciated before.

Overlapping Tillyard's work chronologically were a number of more specialized essays relevant to Shakespeare's handling of particular political or historical topics. For example, Gertrude C. Reese (*University of Texas Studies in English*, XXII, 1942) showed how the drama reflected throughout the reign the Elizabethan preoccupation with the problem of the succession and the idea of hereditary right. Ruth L. Anderson (*Studies in Philology*, XLI, 1944) discussed further the questions of sovereignty, allegiance and rebellion. W. A. Armstrong (*Review of English Studies*, XXII, 1946 and XXIV, 1948), in an examination of the concept of the tyrant, illuminated the complex of political and literary traditions behind such plays as *Richard III*. Brents Stirling (*Modern Language Quarterly*, II, 1941; *Huntington Library Quarterly*, VIII, 1944–5) collected anti-democratic utterances of Elizabethan writers and preachers in order to throw light on *The Populace in Shakespeare* (1949). He surely misjudged Shakespeare in calling him a conservative "spokesman" and probably exaggerated the "dangerous mass tensions" in Elizabethan society; but there was importance in his discovery that Jack Cade, like Richard II in another context, was a stock example in Elizabethan exhortation. The fullest study that we have of the historical background of *King John* was written by a French historian, C. Petit-Dutaillis (1944). A more comprehensive French work, Reyher's *Essai sur les Idées dans l'Œuvre de Shakespeare* (1947), though it suffered from the author's lack of contact with English and American research during the war years, soundly extracted from the history plays Shakespeare's views on the authority and responsibilities of a king, and once more went over the moral-political pattern of usurpation, suffering and expiation which Shakespeare drew from history and Hall.

As early as 1935 the study of the traditional interpretation of English history was being extended by Lily Campbell, editor of the *Mirror for Magistrates*, to an inquiry into the aims and functions of Elizabethan historical writing (*Tudor Conceptions of History and Tragedy in 'A Mirror for Magistrates'*, 1936; *Huntington Library Quarterly*, 1, 1937–8). Her verdict that an historian set out to add moral judgement to factual record is confirmed in L. B. Wright's *Middle-Class Culture in Elizabethan England* (1935) and L. F. Dean's *Tudor Theories of History Writing* (1947). Her big work on *Shakespeare's 'Histories'* (1947) conclusively demonstrates that history was expected to give examples of God's justice, to use the past to illuminate the present, and thus to offer to princes a mirror of policy. She therefore strongly supports the modern hypothesis that Shakespeare's histories intend to dramatize political issues; but it is a defect of the book that no clear connexion is ever established between theories of history and the practice of the stage. The assumption of an overriding didactic intention leads in some instances to positive misinterpretation of the plays, and many analogies thought to be intended between the situations of history and of Shakespeare's day seem irreconcilable with any view of Shakespeare as a playwright with a living to make and a censor to beware of. Nevertheless, the most learned of all those who have thought Shakespeare used history to "teach politics", Miss Campbell adds much to our knowledge of matters treated in the plays. There is, to take one example, a most informative discussion of Elizabethan theory on military ethics and methods in relation to *Henry V*. The military background has also been explored by G. G. Langsam (*Martial Books and Tudor Verse*, 1951).

In literary criticism Lily Campbell's work strengthened the view that the political motive in the history play is the distinguishing mark of the genre; and this problem continued to evoke considerable interest and some difference of opinion. It was ably handled by Una Ellis-Fermor in *The Frontiers of Drama* (1945), where a chapter significantly called 'Shakespeare's Political Plays' combined the old notion that the history cycle formed an epic drama with the new perception of a preciser unity in its "central matter". This, defined less in its historical than in its poetic aspect, was an emergent image of the perfect ruler to which each of the protagonists was related but which no one of them embodied. It was partly the recognition of such an ideal figure that had led Dover Wilson and Tillyard to detect the influence of the Morality play tradition; and A. P. Rossiter, in his edition of the anonymous *Woodstock* (1946), went on to develop the concept of a "moral history" as an Elizabethan dramatic type. Such a theory gives a sharp reorientation to literary history and has been undeniably fruitful in criticism; but it fits our age's taste for moral symbolism so perfectly as to prompt a hint of scepticism. J. F. Danby (*Shakespeare's Doctrine of Nature*, 1949) studied the moral idea less as a principle of form than as an index of Shakespeare's own moral development, tracing in the histories successive stages in Shakespeare's approach to a dominant problem—that of the good man in the bad society—which was to come to solution in *King Lear*. John Palmer's *Shakespeare's Political Characters* (1945) sidestepped moral and formal questions alike, and ignoring too the Elizabethan "frame of reference", as it is called, looked a little odd in this decade. Its old-fashioned method of the character-study was nevertheless adapted to the modern theory of the histories as political plays; and its spirited commentaries usefully emphasized those traits which Shakespeare's princes share with public men of all times. Alfred Harbage (*As They Liked It*, 1947) more deliberately reminds us that the essential frame of reference is "human nature as it still appears", and he again illustrates a critical reaction when, acknowledging the bondage of the history play to fact, he accepts in consequence a formal fragmentariness less apt for moral patterns than are the fabulous kinds of drama. Modern theories of genre seem well synthesized by Hardin Craig when he agrees that the history play has "no rigid formal structure", but holds that it was nevertheless guided in its course by an Elizabethan philosophy of history (*An Interpretation of Shakespeare*, 1948).

Through the key position of the histories in the period of Shakespeare's maturing, attention has also been focused on them in the study of the development of his style. Some recent conclusions, it is true, were anticipated at the beginning of the century: Herford had noted the emergence of Shakespeare's mature dramatic verse in *Henry IV*, and Sarrazin associated significant developments of metaphor and syntax particularly with Part II (*Aus Shakespeares Meisterwerkstatt*, 1906); Hardin Craig distinguished two styles in *Richard II* (1912) and found Shakespeare moulding his verse to the needs of an historical action. Investigation of such matters was stimulated by the critical interest which the 1930's took in imagery and the 1940's extended to devices of rhetoric. With the acceptance of the authenticity of *Henry VI* it was possible for such critics as Clemen, Middleton Murry, Van Doren and Tillyard to reveal in Shakespeare's early historical writing a process both of conscious experiment and of artistic growth; and there has been corresponding interest in those formal speech patterns of *Richard III* which the nineteenth century found tedious. A. P. Rossiter (*Durham University Journal*, xxxi, 1938) exhibited in this play a "ritual technique". By the analysis of 'Imagery in *Richard II* and in *Henry IV*' (*Modern Language Review*, xxxvii, 1942) Madeleine Doran described one aspect of Shakespeare's development; and among several recent papers on *Richard II*, an excellent one by R. D. Altick (*PMLA*, lxii, 1947) showed how the poetic imagery gave a dramatic unity. Most significantly, Hardin Craig has worked out how the progressive modification of rhetorical elements in Shakespeare's style may be related to his evolution of the history play (*J. Q. Adams Memorial Studies*, 1948).

Such interest in the workmanship was not perhaps accompanied during the 1940's by as much fresh scrutiny of the chronicles as the reorientation of the 1930's had seemed likely to herald. But Dover Wilson's editions gave regular attention to the sources and he shed new light on *Henry V*, while J. Elson went into the chronicles underlying *The Troublesome Reign of King John* (*J. Q. Adams Memorial Studies*, 1948). Alan Keen's suggestion that a copy of Hall's Chronicle in his possession might contain Shakespeare's own annotations (*John Rylands Bulletin*, xxiv, 1940) seems to have been a red herring. Dover Wilson had supposed the numerous sources of *Richard II* to have been predigested in some lost play; but M. W. Black inferred wide, if rapid, reading on Shakespeare's part (*J. Q. Adams Memorial Studies*, 1948). There are signs that this problem may stimulate further inquiry—recently both C. A. Greer (*Notes and Queries*, cxcv, 1950) and R. A. Law (*University of Texas Studies in English*, xxix, 1950) have compared *Richard II* against Holinshed in search of further clues to Shakespeare's method—and the whole question of the sources, now that it has proved less simple than used to be supposed, is in need of fresh survey and synthesis.

Some Particular Critical Problems

It remains to touch very briefly on some twentieth-century changes in the interpretation or evaluation of individual plays or characters.

Whereas our age has been on the whole less kind to those theatrical elements which gave *Richard III* its long popularity, *Richard II* has gained remarkably in esteem since the nadir reached in Swinburne's abusive essay (*Three Plays of Shakespeare*, 1909). Good nineteenth-century democrats had thought Richard a tyrannical rascal given to unmanly 'maunderings', and all the older misgivings about the play were embalmed in the 'Arden' edition (1912). But, following the eulogy by Pater (*Appreciations*, 1889), this view of Richard's character had already been powerfully challenged by Yeats, who interpreted his downfall as the tragedy of the sensitive, contemplative mind (*Ideas of Good and Evil*, 1903). This no doubt equally subjective judgement at least led to a more sympathetic approach, but was accompanied by a denigration of the contrasted figure of Henry V. A romantic imagination, repelled by practical efficiency and the material prosperity of the nineteenth century, saw all success as vulgar; so that the "king without a flaw" became now a "vessel of clay", and Richard a "vessel of porcelain". While academic critics sought to balance the opposite views of these two kings, the execration of Henry mounted with the publication of Shaw's *Dramatic Opinions* (1906) and Masefield's *William Shakespeare* (1911). He was rough, callous, and stupid; Philistine, blackguard, and brute. It became unthinkable that Shakespeare could have approved of him, and the recoil from war after 1914 precipitated the extreme of misinterpretation when Gerald Gould (*English Review*, xxix, 1919) explained *Henry V* as a satire on war, imperialism and monarchy. Others followed Masefield in extending condemnation to Henry's father. But that all this merely reflected our own changed conceptions of war and kingship appeared from the corrective arguments of Cunliffe (*Shaksperian Studies*, ed. Matthews and Thorndike, 1916) and an introduction to *Henry V* by Stoll (1922). John Bailey (*Shakespeare*, 1929) made a sane defence of Prince Hal against the judgement of a pacifist and egalitarian age. But this group of plays has provided occasion for some of those critical aberrations to which the enlightened modern mind is prone when it combines a dislike of Shakespeare's political ideals with a search for ironies alien to the temper of his art. L. C. Knights interpreted *Henry IV* as a comedy satirizing honour and state-craft (*Scrutiny*, I, 1932–3); D. A. Traversi as a study of "futility", "the real meaning of the battle of Shrewsbury" (*Scrutiny*, xv, 1947–8); H. M. McLuhan as a representation of a "corrupt" court surrounding a "treacherous" king (*University of Toronto Quarterly*, xvii (January 1948), 152–60). The more general opinion at present, led by Tillyard and Dover Wilson, has not only replaced Hal on his pinnacle but given him a more solid base in Elizabethan ideals of courtesy and political morality. This is sometimes qualified, however, by the hypothesis, which Granville-Barker was one of the first to frame (*From Henry V to Hamlet*, 1925), that Shakespeare's own perception of his hero's limitations was in some way connected with the coming transition from history to tragedy.

Much criticism of Shakespeare's prince has always centred on his rejection of Falstaff, whom Hazlitt taught Hal's detractors to see as "the better man of the two". Morgann's famous denial of Falstaff's cowardice, traditional through the nineteenth century, was reinforced at the beginning of the twentieth in a brilliant lecture by Bradley (1902, printed in *Oxford Lectures in Poetry*, 1909).

This extolled Falstaff as an emancipated spirit transporting us from morality, earnestness and law into a world of joy and freedom, and held that since his necessary overthrow was therefore a violation of our sympathies, Shakespeare had "overshot his mark". Though Augustine Birrell pronounced Falstaff "terrible" in his "corruption" ('Renaissance' edition, 1908), the popular orthodoxy of the following decades—as might be illustrated by Priestley's *English Comic Characters* (1925)—took it for granted that we sympathize with the rejected rascal rather than with the newly crowned king. Bradley's continuing influence contributed also to the interpretations of Falstaff by Charlton (*John Rylands Bulletin*, xix, 1935) and Murry (*Shakespeare*, 1936), who both, in different ways, perceived some incompatibility between Shakespeare's apparent theatrical aims and the deeper impulses of his imagination. As late as 1940 an editor of the standing of Kittredge still maintained that Falstaff was no coward. But some, like John Bailey (*A Book of Homage to Shakespeare*, ed. Gollancz, 1916), had long before suspected that such opinions derived from a sentimental or hypersubtle criticism; and more particularly Stoll had begun in 1914 (*Modern Philology*, xii) a thirty years' war against the whole Morgann-Bradley tradition. Characteristically insisting on a dramatic and not a psychological interpretation, and taking up the work of German scholars on the *miles gloriosus*, Stoll demonstrated Falstaff's kinship with the cowards of the Elizabethan stage. He allowed too little for Shakespeare's creative originality and did not at first appreciate how complex the theatrical tradition was, but it was part of his achievement to prompt many other studies which amplified his own. A number of scholars[2] helped to show in Falstaff traditional elements of the clown, the jester, the Vice, the Glutton, and the soldier of the European stage as well as a realistic Elizabethan captain. Enid Welsford related Falstaff to the medieval and Renaissance buffoon, "the conscious fool" who delighted to "show himself up" (*The Fool*, 1935), Willard Farnham to the grotesque tradition in medieval art (*J. Q. Adams Memorial Studies*, 1948). The immense richness of such a heritage has been admirably brought out by Dover Wilson (*The Fortunes of Falstaff*, 1943) and Tillyard, who present Falstaff as an archetype of disorder and misrule. In a further synthesis by J. I. M. Stewart (*Character and Motive in Shakespeare*, 1949) Falstaff combines the realistic and archetypal roles and has also the symbolic significance of a sacrificial victim.

With the critical shift away from psychological naturalism some former problems have disappeared. But in the most satisfying interpretations of Falstaff something of Bradley survives; though incorporating many traditional figures, he is yet an original creation expressing with the utmost exuberance a universal principle of human nature in which we may properly delight. But that Shakespeare would finally submit this principle to order and rule is suggested not merely by the sort of traditions he made use of but by all those studies which, ceasing to view Falstaff in isolation, would reabsorb him into the dramatic structure of *Henry IV*. This process perhaps began with Quiller-Couch's hint of a Morality pattern (*Shakespeare's Workmanship*, 1918). It developed with A. H. Tolman (*PMLA*, xxxiv, 1919), J. W. Spargo, R. A. Law (*Studies in Philology*, xxiv, 1927) and especially, of course, Dover Wilson. And so long as we avoid the danger of imposing on the play too rigid a scheme, modern criticism suggests that this richest of all Shakespeare's characters may have his deepest meaning within the history framework where, after all, his creator placed him. Tingling throughout his vast bulk with a vigorous individual life, he is none the less the tempter whom the virtuous gentleman of Renaissance courtesy first indulges and then subdues; the private will impeding public good; the riotous disorder which the wise ruler must bring under control.

Such a judgement offers a clear instance of what the new attitude to the history plays means in literary criticism. For it reverses the opinion general at the beginning of the century that the comic and historical parts of *Henry IV* were very loosely integrated, and directly contradicts the statement of Sir E. K. Chambers ('Red Letter' edition, 1906, and *Shakespeare: A Survey*, 1925) that the play lacks "the dynamic unity of an emotional issue set and resolved in the course of the action". But there is still no agreed solution of the problem which before the century opened was already long debated and clearly diagnosed by Herford: while Part I presumes a sequel, to end in the death of the King and the overthrow of Falstaff, Part II reduplicates as much as continues the action of Part I. Tucker Brooke had many supporters for his theory that a two-part play was not premeditated, and Kittredge always maintained that each part was complete in itself. But in the last ten years the opposite view, though cogently disputed by Shaaber (*J. Q. Adams Memorial Studies* (1948), 217–27),[3] has been confidently spread by Tillyard and especially Dover Wilson, who discovers the usual curve of a dramatic action neatly distributed over the ten acts. This controversy is of course part of the larger one about Shakespeare's planning of the whole history cycle. With the new emphasis on the historical pattern which emerges from eight plays, the theory of two deliberately designed and linked tetralogies has been widely popularized. But difficulties are raised by what we know of the conditions of Elizabethan dramatic authorship and conceivably by the plays themselves. So that even while a Stratford theatre-programme in 1951 announced it to be "generally agreed" that the four plays beginning with *Richard II* "were planned by Shakespeare as one great play", some scholars at a Stratford Conference were taking leave to doubt it.

CONCLUSION

This, then, is one of a number of matters upon which opinion is still fluid. What can no longer be doubted is that, whether by design or not, the history plays have a collective unity, deriving from an Elizabethan view of history and a common fund of ideas and ideals about the ordering of man's society. In this larger sense, if not in the narrower topical one, they must be accepted as political. They not merely presented an epic of England's past but dramatized issues of great moment for Shakespeare's contemporaries. That the remarkable revival of interest in them still continues seems clear when a popular volume by a Shakespeare scholar, G. I. Duthie (*Shakespeare*, 1951), gives to the major history group more space than to either 'Comedy' or 'Tragedy'. Among the latest books, this adopts the current views about the histories, while the relevant chapters of Muriel C. Bradbrook's *Shakespeare and Elizabethan Poetry* (1951) suggest in addition some questions which an informed scepticism may raise. They echo, for example, the doubts about the master plan, correct the overemphasis on the Morality tradition, and hint at the variety which crowds into the later histories to complicate the outlines that have been perhaps of late too sharply drawn. Much detail still needs sifting, some new theories re-examining; research has left criticism with some leeway to make up. It is none the less the achievement of the last twenty-five years to have shown far more clearly than before what the important centres of interest in these plays are.

NOTES

1. Published 1952. (This edition seeks to re-establish the view that Shakespeare was the reviser of originals by Greene.)

2. J. Monaghan (*Studies in Philology*, XVIII, 1921), J. W. Spargo (*Washington University Studies*, Humanistic, IX, 1922), E. C. Knowlton (*Journal of English and Germanic Philology*, XXV, 1926), J. W. Draper (*Review of English Studies*, VIII, 1932; *Modern Language Quarterly*, VII, 1946), J. W. Shirley (*Philological Quarterly*, XVII, 1938), D. C. Boughner (*Journal of English and Germanic Philology*, XLIII, 1944).

3. And now also by H. E. Cain (*Shakespeare Quarterly*, III, 1952).

THE UNITY OF *2 HENRY IV*[1]

BY

CLIFFORD LEECH

It should perhaps be made clear that this is not a contribution to the debate on Shakespeare's original planning of the Prince Henry plays. It has been argued by Dover Wilson in *The Fortunes of Falstaff* and in his New Cambridge edition, and by E. M. W. Tillyard in *Shakespeare's History Plays*, that the two parts of *Henry IV* constitute one long play, envisaged at least in its main outlines from the very beginning of Part I. M. A. Shaaber, on the other hand, has put a case for regarding Part II as a sequel, outside Shakespeare's original plan, brought into being through the remarkable success of Part I.[2] Whichever of these views is correct, it is possible for Part II to have its own characteristic mood and structure, its separate dramatic impact, and my concern will be to demonstrate that this is indeed the case. The only assumption I shall make, which I think will be readily granted to me, is that Part II was written after Part I.

In writing the series of eight plays which give an outline of English history from the reign of Richard II to the accession of Henry VII, Shakespeare can hardly at the beginning have seen the scheme as a whole. If he had, it would be odd to start with the troubles of Henry VI. The mention of Prince Henry near the end of *Richard II* suggests it was then that Shakespeare began to think of plays in which he would be the central figure, plays which would close the gap between Bolingbroke's usurpation and the funeral of Henry V. But clearly the plays in the sequence already written had been markedly different from one another in structure and atmosphere. This was partly, of course, because Shakespeare's grasp of play-making and dramatic language was rapidly becoming more secure, but partly too it was because the action of each play had demanded a specific handling. There are recognizable distinctions in material and manner between the three *Henry VI* plays, and when Shakespeare continued the story with *Richard III* he employed a new massiveness and formality of structure in his presentation of a strong man who abused his sovereign power in the wanton exercise of his own will: Richard of Gloucester, the Samson in the devil's cause who brought down the temple upon himself, demanded a play in which all his followers and adversaries were reduced almost to a choric function, until Henry of Richmond came, as a god from over sea, to confront him. The play of *Richard II*, because Shakespeare saw the King as a man too conceited for scruple, complacent in his royalty, and yet with an exquisite taste in suffering, had necessarily a quieter tone, a more human presentation of the usurper, an elegiac note because this play marked the beginning of England's trouble. So, later on, with *Henry V*, the glorious interlude which had its centre in Agincourt was to be punctuated only with marks of exclamation, those chorus-passages directed at keeping the mind alight: the only conflict was that of arms, and for once it is not the sickness of the commonwealth that we are asked to consider, but the success of a foreign campaign. In describing these plays, I have of course simplified their effects. There are quieter, elegiac moments even in the grim ritual of *Richard III*; national glory is for a little, when Gaunt dies, the theme of *Richard II*; and there are passages in *Henry V* which demonstrate that the strife and intrigue of the previous reign are by no means done. Yet there is a dominant tone in each drama. Similarly, each of the two parts of *Henry IV* makes its characteristic and distinct impression on us.

When Shakespeare began to write of the youth of Prince Henry, he had indeed a subject that called for lightness of heart. Here was a young man, having his fun, yet not compromising himself so far that he could not later shine in council and on the field of battle. The civil troubles of his usurping father could not be shirked, but at least these troubles were manageable and might even afford some apprenticeship for the growing Prince. Coleridge has described *Romeo and Juliet* as a play given unity of feeling by the youth and springtime that permeate every character and moment: even its old men, he says, have "an eagerness, a hastiness, a precipitancy—the effect of spring".[3] That might almost be our judgement too of *1 Henry IV*. There is a graver note in the portraits of the King and old Northumberland, but the dominant feeling is young, excited, good-hearted. The Prince must not forget his future, must not think exclusively in terms of personal glory, as Hotspur does, must not think only of the moment's pleasure, as Falstaff does: but he can and should value these things, while recognizing their subordination to the obligations and opportunities that will come to him with the golden round. When seeing Part I, we may prefer the company of either Hotspur or Falstaff to that of the Prince, but we are not out of sympathy with him, and esteem him when he shows respect for Hotspur and liking for Falstaff. At the end of Part I, he has overcome Hotspur in single combat, an incident not found in Holinshed: he has revealed himself as the good and honourable fighter needed for the play of Agincourt.

In arguing that Part II was an "unpremeditated addition", which need not concern us here, R. A. Law[4] has emphasized the morality characteristics of that Part, the placing of Prince Henry between the personified representations of order (in the Lord Chief Justice) and disorder (in Falstaff). This account of the play's structure has been elaborated by Tillyard, though of course he disagrees with Law on the play's origin. It does indeed now seem beyond question that the Prince, no longer on the field of battle, is exhibited as slowly abandoning his old associations with disorder and becoming ultimately at one with its opposite. Not that we have a 'conversion', as in the old moralities, but rather a manifestation of a hitherto concealed adherence. This part of the play's substance becomes most noticeable towards its end, when Falstaff is ready to steal any man's horses because his "dear boy" is on the throne, and Doll and the Hostess are taken to prison for being concerned in a man's death. To demonstrate this second phase in Hal's apprenticeship is the overt intention of this Part, as we may say that the overt intention of *Macbeth* is to demonstrate the ills that come upon a man and his country when he murders his King and steals the crown. But just as we may think that there is a secondary intention to *Macbeth*, to hint at a protest against the very frame of things, so in this Second Part of *Henry IV* we may feel that the dramatist, in giving us the preparation for Agincourt, hints also at a state of dubiety concerning basic assumptions in the great historical scheme. He shows us the new King adhering to political order, yet makes us half-doubt whether that order is worth its price, whether in fact it is of the deepest importance to men. And with this element of doubt, the poet's awareness of mutability grows more intense.

Whether Part II was a new play or a continuation of one already begun, the battle of Shrewsbury had marked the end of a phase. Shakespeare, returning to his subject, and to a more sober aspect of that subject (for law has not the manifest attractiveness of chivalrous encounter), was bound to approach his task with less light-heartedness, with a cooler and more objective view. Just as Marlowe in *Tamburlaine* appears to see his hero with less enthusiasm in Part II than in Part I, recognizing his excess as such and not keeping him immune from ridicule, so here Shakespeare weighs his characters more carefully and questions even the accuracy of his balance.

This note in the play is, I think, struck in the Induction itself. Clearly Shakespeare needed an introductory speech here, both to remind his auditors of what had happened at Shrewsbury and to make plain the irony of the false news brought to Northumberland in the first scene of the play. But he is not content with a simple Prologue. His speaker is a quasi-morality figure, and no pleasant one. Rumour expresses scorn for the credulity of men, and even—though irrelevantly —for their love of slander. The scorn is brought home when Rumour calls the audience he addresses "my household". In tone this Induction is similar to the Prologue to *Troilus and Cressida*: there too the speaker was in a costume appropriate to the mood of the play—"A Prologue arm'd...suited in like conditions as our argument"—and there too the tone was not gentle.

In the play we at once meet Northumberland, who has not gained much of our affection in either of the two earlier plays in which he appeared. Here he is the first of a series of old and sick men that we are to encounter. Falstaff and Justice Shallow, King Henry IV and the Lord Chief Justice, are all burdened with their years, and the only one in full command of his wits and his body is the character given no personal name and conceived almost as a morality-presentment of the Justice which he executes. Dover Wilson has drawn our attention to the way in which our attitude to Falstaff is made to change in the course of this Second Part,[5] though in concentrating on the figures of Prince Hal and the Knight he does not perhaps fully relate this change to the new atmosphere in the drama as a whole. When we first meet Falstaff in I, ii, his talk is at once of his diseases, and he reverts to this at the end of the scene when, like Ancient Pistol in *Henry V*, he asserts his readiness to "turn diseases to commodity". There is, of course, plenty of gaiety in this talk of disease, as there is in the scene with Doll at the Boar's Head: we delight in the comedy of it, but the frailty of ageing flesh is grotesque as well as amusing. Before we see "Saturn and Venus in conjunction", we are told by the Drawers of how Falstaff was once "anger'd...to the heart" when the Prince jested rudely on his age. The comedy here and in Gloucestershire has a sharper savour because we are never allowed to forget the evidence of decay. Justice Shallow, wrapping his thin frame in a fanciful tapestry of wild youth, is comedy of the rarest sort, but "Jesu, the days that we have seen!" is a line with a barb in it for us all. And the King, in his different way, belongs with these men. When we first meet him in Act III, he is longing for the sleep denied him; he cannot rid himself of guilt, ever more and more pathetically he talks of the crusade he will never make; and when he is dying he asks to be carried to the chamber called Jerusalem, so that the prophecy may be fulfilled and he may derive consolation from submitting to what has been decreed.

Along with the Falstaff scenes and the scenes at court, we have other parts of this play where a rebellion is launched and destroyed. This enterprise is contrasted sharply with the rebellion in Part I. There is no Hotspur to give dash and gaiety to it. His father is once more "crafty-sick", and the leadership of the revolt is in the grave hands of the Archbishop of York. He is not presented as a man scheming for advancement but as one who gives a measure of sanctification to the rebels' cause. Yet when they come together for the planning of their campaign, their language is hesitant, cautious, argumentative, as if they would talk themselves out of a situation from which there is no escape. At the end of I, i there is little hope in Northumberland's voice as he bids

> Get posts and letters, and make friends with speed:
> Never so few, and never yet more need.

And Hastings's concluding cry in I, iii—"We are time's subjects, and time bids, be gone"—has a fatalistic ring. It is no surprise to us when Northumberland's defection is shown, and it seems appropriate that these rebels, so given to sober talk, should be vanquished by a verbal trick before a blow is exchanged. In Holinshed it is not Prince John of Lancaster but the Earl of Westmoreland who dupes the rebels:[6] Shakespeare uses Westmoreland as an ambassador of Prince John, but gives to the King's son all the doubtful credit of the action. The change can, I think, only be explained by the assumption that Shakespeare wanted to bring this line of conduct more closely home to the royal house. Because Prince John is the King's son and Hal's brother, the stain of the exploit falls partly on them. Perhaps some will claim that such conduct was justified in the cause of law and order, that an Elizabethan would simply admire the skill of it. Yet is it possible not to find irony in John's concluding speech in the scene of Gaultree Forest?

> I promised you redress of these same grievances
> Whereof you did complain; which, by mine honour,
> I will perform with a most Christian care.   (IV, ii, 113–15)

In the mouth of the astute Prince John the word "Christian" has an effect gross and palpable. When he proceeds to claim "God, and not we, hath safely fought to-day", we seem to recognize blasphemy. If this is not plain enough, one can turn to the next scene, where Falstaff demands from Prince John recompense for taking Sir John Colevile prisoner: he will otherwise, he says, see to his own glorification in ballad and picture: if that does not come to pass, he tells Prince John to "believe not the word of the noble". A few lines before we have seen the value of a noble's word in Gaultree Forest, and there is therefore strong irony in Falstaff thus exhorting Prince John. Nor should we overlook Shakespeare's reminder that Prince John's adroit handling of the situation is but a momentary trick. Hastings has told him that, if this revolt is put down, others will rise against the House of Lancaster:

> And though we here fall down,
> We have supplies to second our attempt:
> If they miscarry, theirs shall second them;
> And so success of mischief shall be born,
> And heir from heir shall hold this quarrel up,
> Whiles England shall have generation.   (IV, ii, 44–9)

To that John replies:

> You are too shallow, Hastings, much too shallow,
> To sound the bottom of the after-times.

It is Hastings who is right: John is too vain to see the total situation.

I have said that Shakespeare's substitution of Prince John for Westmoreland in the Gaultree affair brings the taint of it nearer to the King and Hal. When the play ends, and the new King has banished his old followers, the stage is empty except for Prince John and the Lord Chief Justice. Before mentioning the talk of French wars, Prince John spares a moment to praise his brother: "I like this fair proceeding of the king's", he says. It is surely not enviable to be praised by such men as Prince John. It is like Flamineo in *The White Devil* praising Brachiano's hypocritical display of grief for Isabella's death. Praise like that is a burden for a man to carry. We need not dispute that it was necessary to banish Falstaff if England was to be for a time secure and Agincourt won. But we are made to realize that there is a heavy price to pay for political success. Indeed, we are reminded of it in the succeeding play, when, during the battle itself, Fluellen refers to the rejection of the fat knight whose name he has forgotten.

In Shakespearian drama there is often a condition of tension between the play's overt meaning and its deeper implications. The gaiety of *Twelfth Night* is enriched by the thread of sadness that runs through it, but we cannot say that the baiting of Malvolio is in easy accord with the play's surface texture. In *Macbeth* the enfolding of the tragic idea within a morality pattern leaves us with a feeling of suspended judgement in which we resent Malcolm's concluding reference to "this dead butcher, and his fiend-like queen". So in this Second Part of *Henry IV* the deeper, more disturbing implications impinge directly on the main action of the drama, and then, as in *Macbeth*, the writer appears to strain for the re-establishment of the original framework. We get this feeling in the harshness of the words that Henry V uses to Falstaff, for we have come to wonder a little whether there is ultimately much to choose between Falstaff and Prince John, and indeed we greatly prefer Falstaff's company. And the same feeling emerges, I think, in the often praised scene where Hal is reconciled to his father. Justifying his taking of the crown when he believed his father dead, he says:

> I spake unto this crown as having sense
> And thus upbraided it: 'The care on thee depending,
> Hath fed upon the body of my father;
> Therefore, thou best of gold art worst of gold.
> Other, less fine in carat, is more precious,
> Preserving life in medicine potable:
> But thou, most fine, most honour'd, most renown'd,
> Hast eat thy bearer up.' Thus, my most royal liege,
> Accusing it, I put it on my head,
> To try with it, as with an enemy
> That had before my face murder'd my father,
> The quarrel of a true inheritor. (IV, v, 158–69)

The elaborateness of the imagery is notable: the burden of the crown is a devouring monster, its gold is contrasted to *aurum potabile*, it is a murderer with whom the dead man's son must wage a blood-feud. In this scene and in the new King's rejection of Falstaff, the note of sternness and sobriety is heavily, almost clumsily, pressed down, in an attempt to silence the basic questions that so often in the play demand to be put. And perhaps, when he had done, Shakespeare realized that this close was altogether too ponderous for a play that had taken us to the Boar's Head and into Gloucestershire, and altogether too assured for a play persistently though not obtrusively concerned with change and ineradicable frailty. So he gave us the dancer's epilogue, in tripping prose, with its casual half-promise that Falstaff would come again in the next play: the banishment was to be merely from the King, and not from us. Later he was to change his mind again, perhaps because he realized that Sir John was no longer a figure of delight: around him had grown a small forest of disturbing thoughts, which might well choke the brief glory of Agincourt. *Henry V* was not the climax of a series, but rather an interlude, a holiday-play, in which for a while disaster was kept remote. Its epilogue does make plain that by this time Shakespeare had come to see his eight-play sequence as a whole, and within that sequence the Agincourt play must be predominantly sun-lit. He had to avoid, not too much gaiety with Falstaff, but too little. It is all the more remarkable that the questioning mood of *2 Henry IV* does show itself here and there in the succeeding play—with the intrigues of Canterbury and Ely; the frank presentation of many unchivalrous details of the war, from Bardolph's stealing of a "pax" to the King's twice-given order that every man shall kill his prisoners; the repeated reminder that a war-maker must have a just cause. But these things on the whole are kept in their place, and an audience for *Henry V* is not much disturbed in its dream of glory. In *2 Henry IV*, on the other hand, an audience is rarely at its ease.

In Law's paper on *Henry IV*, to which I have already acknowledged a debt, the darker side of Part II is in no way brought out. But Law does draw attention to the comic echoing of serious things in the play: Henry IV's sick memories of his early life are immediately followed, he points out, by Justice Shallow's maunderings on his deeds in the same period; Davy's petition to Shallow that "a knave should have some countenance at his friend's request" reminds us of Prince Hal's vigorous intercession for Bardolph with the Lord Chief Justice. There are a number of other ironic echoes in the play. At the end of the Boar's Head scene, when "a dozen captains" come to summon Falstaff to court, the Knight rises to the occasion, putting his rest from him:

Pay the musicians, sirrah. Farewell Hostess; farewell Doll. You see, my good wenches, how men of merit are sought after: the undeserver may sleep, when the man of action is called on. (II, iv, 403–6)

It is immediately after this that Henry IV has his famous utterance on the sleeplessness of kings. We are the less inclined to contemplate the ills of greatness with awe, because Falstaff has taken them to himself already. We have noted the way in which Falstaff's "believe not the word of the noble" comes immediately after the scene in Gaultree Forest, but in III, ii there is an echo at Falstaff's expense. In Part I he has this exchange with the Prince when the battle of Shrewsbury is about to begin:

> *Fal.*   I would 'twere bed-time, Hal, and all well.
> *Prince* Why, thou owest God a death.
> *Fal.*   'Tis not due yet; I would be loath to pay him before his day.   (v, i, 125–9)

Then there follows the 'catechism' on 'Honour'. In Part II the despised Feeble has a moment of splendour when, unlike Bullcalf and Mouldy, he does not attempt to escape from impressment:

By my troth, I care not; a man can die but once: we owe God a death: I'll ne'er bear a base mind: an't be my destiny, so; an't be not, so: no man is too good to serve's prince: and let it go which way it will, he that dies this year is quit for the next. (III, ii, 250–5)

There is of course an absurdity in these words of bravery poured from so weak a vessel, yet they demand respect. Bardolph's reply, "Well said; thou'rt a good fellow", cannot be wholly ironic, and the impressiveness of the effect is only mitigated, not destroyed, when Feeble comes out again with his "Faith, I'll bear no base mind". The interplay of feelings in this Second Part is so complex that our sympathy resides securely nowhere. Falstaff can be used to direct our feelings, as he does with Prince John, and often through the play we prefer his gross and witty animality to the politic management of the Lancastrians. But just as the dramatist makes no attempt to disguise his age and sickness or even a churlish arrogance in him, so here he is put down by Feeble's curious, inverted echo of his own words in the First Part. I am of course not suggesting that Shakespeare could expect an audience to note the echo: for us, however, it seems to indicate a trend of feeling in the writer's mind.

The remarkable degree of objectivity in the presentation of the characters reminds us of certain later plays of Shakespeare, those that we call the 'dark comedies'. It is not merely through our latter-day squeamishness, I believe, that we are made uneasy by the presentation of the Duke and Isabella in *Measure for Measure*; and in *Troilus and Cressida* Shakespeare's own Prologue warns us that the expectation of armed strife is "tickling skittish spirits, On one and other side". And *2 Henry IV* is close to these plays also in the peculiarly acrid flavour of certain generalized utterances. On his first appearance in the play, the King sees the process of time in geological change and in the pattern of a human life, and there is no comfort in the vision, only a desire to have done:

> O God! that one might read the book of fate,
> And see the revolution of the times
> Make mountains level, and the continent,
> Weary of solid firmness, melt itself
> Into the sea! and, other times, to see
> The beachy girdle of the ocean
> Too wide for Neptune's hips; how chances mock
> And changes fill the cup of alteration
> With divers liquors! O, if this were seen,
> The happiest youth, viewing his progress through,
> What perils past, what crosses to ensue,
> Would shut the book, and sit him down and die. (III, i, 45–56)

And when he is himself dying and he believes that his son has greedily seized the crown in advance of his right, he speaks of the human greed for gold, a theme no Elizabethan could long avoid, and how each generation is impatient for possession:

> See, sons, what things you are!
> How quickly nature falls into revolt
> When gold becomes her object!
> For this the foolish over-careful fathers
> Have broke their sleep with thoughts, their brains with care,
> Their bones with industry;
> For this they have engrossed and piled up

> The canker'd heaps of strange-achieved gold;
> For this they have been thoughtful to invest
> Their sons with arts and martial exercises:
> When, like the bee, culling from every flower
> The virtuous sweets,
> Our thighs pack'd with wax, our mouths with honey,
> We bring it to the hive, and, like the bees,
> Are murdered for our pains. This bitter taste
> Yield his engrossments to the ending father. (IV, v, 65–80)

This is not far from what the Duke has to say to the condemned Claudio in *Measure for Measure*. Though he wears a friar's habit, he gives no religious consolation, but bids him see the vanity of existence, the impossibility of any sure possession, the cold impatience of an heir:

> Friend hast thou none;
> For thine own bowels, which do call thee sire,
> The mere effusion of thy proper loins,
> Do curse the gout, serpigo, and the rheum,
> For ending thee no sooner. (III, i, 28–32)

It seems probable that *2 Henry IV* was written some three years before *Troilus*, some six before *Measure for Measure*, yet here Shakespeare anticipates that objectivity of manner, fused with a suggestion of deep and personal concern, which is characteristic of these two later plays. The sequence of the histories depends on the cardinal assumption that order in a commonwealth is a prime good: it is not altogether surprising that, as his task came towards its conclusion, and with the additional effort required in writing a second play on a young king's apprenticeship, Shakespeare should have reached a condition of dubiety, should have felt less secure in his assumptions. The 'dark comedies' come during the tragic period, and in their way give evidence of a similar slackening of grasp. The basic assumption made by the tragic writer is that a personal goodness, inexplicable and apparently futile, can nevertheless be realized. But, unless the writer has the sense of a direct revelation, this assumption can be maintained only by strong effort: in the 'dark comedies' the mind is not kept tragically taut.

So far from demonstrating "the unity of *2 Henry IV*", it may appear that I have shown only a clash of feelings within the play, an overt morality intention, a preoccupation with the effects of time, and a latent scepticism. That I would acknowledge, while maintaining that such a contradiction persists in all the major plays of the Elizabethan and Jacobean years. The tragic figures of the time are of great stature, compelling our awe, but we are not spared realization that they can be petty and grotesque and villainous as well. They are made to seem free agents in their choice of good or evil, yet simultaneously we are made certain, from the beginning of the play, that destruction will be theirs. So, in the best comedy, the gay march from wooing to wedding, from pretence to its merry discomfiture, is counterpointed with a low murmur of regret. Elizabethan dramas are rich in implication because they have emotional, but not logical, coherence. We travel two roads, or more, at once. We arrive at no destination. But, home again once more, we feel that—if we could but speak effectively of such things—we should have travellers' tales to tell.

But it has been apparent, I think, that *2 Henry IV* differs from Part I in its dominant tone. Of course, there are sharp incidental things in the earlier play, but they do not weigh heavily on the spectator's mind. Falstaff abuses the press in both Parts, but his activities in this direction are shown at closer quarters in Part II. And there is broad merriment in the later play, but it is worked into a pattern where good humour is not the main theme. Towards the end of Part II there is, indeed, a strong measure of simplification. From the Prince's last interview with his father to the rejection of Falstaff, Shakespeare strives to make the morality-element all-pervading, until we have the curious spectacle of Henry V urging repentance on his old companions: banishment was, of course, required, but he is an odd preacher to men whom kingship did not call to the disciplined life. And, as we have seen, the prose epilogue pretends that, after all, merriment is the prime concern of this play and the one to come. But, until Henry IV's death-scene, the delicate balance between the two layers of meaning is skilfully maintained.

When one is interpreting a Shakespeare play, one is always in danger of being reminded that Shakespeare was an Elizabethan, that his assumptions and standards of judgement were therefore different from ours. Tillyard has commented thus on Prince Hal's treatment of Francis in Part I:

The subhuman element in the population must have been considerable in Shakespeare's day; that it should be treated almost like beasts was taken for granted.[7]

But is not this to overlook the fact that Shakespeare can make us resent the ill-treatment of any human being, and respect the most insignificant of creatures, a Feeble or a servant of the Duke of Cornwall? In *Measure for Measure* he reminds us even that an insect shares with us the experience of death and corporal suffering. He was an Elizabethan certainly: he made assumptions about kingship and 'degree' and incest and adultery that perhaps we may not make. But he was also a human being with a remarkable degree of sensitivity: it is indeed for that reason that he can move us so much. If he merely had skill in 'putting over' characteristic Tudor ideas, we could leave him to the social and political historians. Because his reaction to suffering, his esteem for good faith, his love of human society, his sense of mutability and loss, his obscure notion of human grandeur, his ultimate uncertainty of value, are not basically different from ours—though more deeply felt and incomparably expressed—he belongs supremely to literature. We do him, I think, scant justice if we assume that he could write complacently of Prince John of Lancaster, and could have no doubts about Prince Hal.

NOTES

1. This article is based on a paper read at the Shakespeare Conference, Stratford-upon-Avon, in August 1951.
2. 'The Unity of *Henry IV*', *Joseph Quincy Adams Memorial Studies*, 1948, pp. 217–27. Since this article was written, H. Edward Cain has supported Shaaber's case in 'Further Light on the Relation of *1* and *2 Henry IV*', *Shakespeare Quarterly*, III (January 1952), 21–38.
3. *Coleridge's Shakespearean Criticism* (ed. Raysor, 1930), II, 265.
4. 'Structural Unity in the Two Parts of *Henry the Fourth*', *Studies in Philology*, XXIV (1927), 223–42.
5. *The Fortunes of Falstaff* (1943), pp. 93–8.
6. *The Historie of England* (1587), III, 529–30.
7. *Shakespeare's History Plays* (1944), p. 277.

ANTICIPATION AND FOREBODING IN SHAKESPEARE'S EARLY HISTORIES

BY

WOLFGANG H. CLEMEN

It is strange that the role of anticipation and foreboding in Shakespearian drama has so far not received adequate attention and treatment. For here we find an important feature of Shakespeare's dramatic art which is closely connected not only with the dramatist's technique of preparation, but also with his art of characterization. It bears, too, on the composition and structure of his plays, since the peculiar function of anticipation and foreboding often consists in establishing subtle correspondences between earlier and later utterances or situations in the drama, or in binding together various threads of the action. Until now, however, the only aspect under which foreboding in Shakespeare's drama has been studied connectedly seems to have been Shakespeare's use of the supernatural.[1] But the role played by foreboding is, with Shakespeare, in no way exhausted by his use of omen, prophecies and other portents which could be classified as more or less supernatural. And it is this very extension of the device of foreboding beyond the traditional realm of prophecy, omen, dream, etc., which makes a study of this particular feature so interesting and displays Shakespeare's superiority over his contemporaries and predecessors in such a singular manner. For although we find anticipation and foreboding in all great dramatists, in Sophocles and Euripides as well as in Calderón and Ibsen, it can safely be said that with no other dramatist has this feature been turned to so manifold use and developed into such a refined and subtle instrument of dramatic art as with Shakespeare.

Anticipation rests for its effect on the interplay between the audience and the actor on the stage; as a rule it is to be felt by both audience and the characters in the play. It is the dramatist's business to build up within us the right state of expectation and tension, by which we are to take in the inner or outward events which form the play's centre of climax. This building up is a gradual process, a process of preparation by which our attention, our curiosity, is turned in a certain direction. And in thus preparing us the great dramatist must always strike a balance between the certainty of foreknowledge and the uncertainty of ignorance, between the restlessness of our inquiring mind and mental composure, between a vague presentiment and an assured expectation. At the same time the dramatist must therefore unveil and veil, promise and again withdraw his promise; he must proceed rather by "hints and guesses" than by obvious and obtrusive signs. Indeed, the dramatic effect will largely depend upon this balance between varying states of mind. There is, of course, no law to lay down to what extent the anticipation felt by the audience must be shared by some of the characters or must be expressed by other means in the play itself. For Shakespeare also makes powerful use of the contrast existing between the growing anticipation on the part of the audience and the entire lack of such presentiment in the hero and in those around him.

It is natural that in the three parts of *Henry VI* we mostly find that kind of foreboding which was already established as a traditional convention in the pre-Shakespearian chronicle plays and tragedies and of which he also read in Holinshed and Hall:[2] prophecies,[3] omens and dreams.

Thus Exeter, whose role in *1 Henry VI* often consists in uttering the objective truth, twice recalls prophecies made by or under Henry V (III, i, 195; v, i, 30), and in *2 Henry VI* Gloucester and Suffolk make or remember prophecies (I, i, 146; IV, i, 34; III, i, 152). In *3 Henry VI* we find the king himself acting as a divining prophet, in the medieval manner laying his hand on the young Earl of Richmond's head whom he foresees as proving "our country's bliss" (IV, vi, 68). In this connexion it is interesting to note that the only time an omen is actually seen occurring 'on the stage' is in *3 Henry VI*, II, i, where Edward and Richard observe in the sky three suns which soon afterwards join and embrace, suggesting the union of three sons of Richard Plantagenet. The two instances we have in *Henry VI* of conjuring 'spirits' who are to disclose the future are a further example of this perseverance of medieval elements which, through the revival of magic beliefs in the Renaissance, are to be found in Elizabethan drama (*1 Henry VI*, v, iii, 2–23; *2 Henry VI*, I, iv, 18–42). The comparison of these two scenes with, for example, the witches in *Macbeth* will easily show how, in this early phase, the device is used without dramatic skill and without any deeper relation to character and plot, its potential meaning for the future progress of the action being not yet discovered. The same applies to the way in which those characters who are to die foreknow their death, or are told their impending death by others (*1 Henry VI*, IV, ii, 35; *3 Henry VI*, I, iv, 25; v, ii, 9). This is done such a short time before their death and in such an explicit manner, that we need only think of Antony, Macbeth, Othello or Caesar to feel the difference. Here we can see that Shakespeare's early manner of explaining and announcing as much as possible to his audience, as though they were pupils 'who must be told twice', makes genuine anticipation of dramatic impact impossible. Even where we have, instead of prophecy, the more subjective form of prescience, as in York's words "I foresee with grief The utter loss of all the realms of France" (*1 Henry VI*, v, iv, 111), or in Exeter's words at the end of *1 Henry VI*, IV, i, we cannot help feeling that these utterances are too obtrusive, too explicit, to fill us with a genuine sentiment of anticipation.[4] They fit, however, into the pattern of these early histories in so far as they will serve Shakespeare's purpose of linking up the present with the happenings of the future and of thus making clearer and more intelligible the concatenation of events the mass of which, in *Henry VI*, is apt to give us a confused impression. As Paul Reyher has shown,[5] this is a procedure the reverse of that of the chroniclers who prefer looking back into the past instead of forward into the future. Moreover, whereas in Hall we find frequent passages where the chronicler denounces prophecies as a "diabolical device" to lead people astray, Shakespeare, in his histories, takes them, save for a few exceptions, seriously, attaching a great significance to them.

The forms of foreboding occurring in *Henry VI* persist in *Richard III* but appear now with a greater structural significance. Not only do the prophecies, curses and warnings uttered mostly against Richard III occur at important points of the dramatic action, considerably contributing to the scene's tension and portentous tone, they are also remembered at later moments of the play when becoming fulfilled, thus emphasizing, as Moulton has pointed out,[6] the nemesis pattern of the plot. They constitute a sort of unifying factor in the tissue of the play, binding together earlier and later scenes by a common motive.[7] Thus Margaret's curses pronounced in I, iii are recalled by Rivers and Grey in III, iii, 15–18, by Queen Elizabeth in IV, iv, 79, by

Buckingham in v, i, 25.[8] This third scene of the first act indeed derives part of its gloomy effect from Margaret's power to curse and to utter abusive and threatening imprecations, a power against which not even Richard can stand up, so that Margaret may continue her curses for a while in spite of Richard's efforts to interrupt her. A similar use of malediction and execration evoking, in connexion with ever-renewed laments, a dense atmosphere of evil foreboding and of impending catastrophe is to be found in IV, iv, where Queen Margaret, Queen Elizabeth and the Duchess of York unite in uttering their melodramatic complaints and woes. This scene, rich in anticipating phrases, opens with Queen Margaret's lines

> So, now prosperity begins to mellow
> And drop into the rotten mouth of death.

Shakespeare has now found a new kind of bold imagery to express the abstract issues of anticipation and foreboding. It is also not without significance that, in the first of these two scenes, he twice emphasizes the effectiveness of curses, so that, in the beginning of the play, we are made to feel that all this is not mere rhetoric, but will come true later on. Buckingham's sceptical remark "for curses never pass The lips of those that breathe them in the air" is answered by Margaret's

> I'll not believe but they ascend the sky,
> And there awake God's gentle-sleeping peace,   (I, iii, 287–8)

these words linking up with an earlier utterance of Queen Margaret.[9]

These curses, imprecations, prophecies and warnings, frequent though they be in *Richard III*, are, however, only one means of arousing anticipation. There is the feeling of fear and uncertainty running like a keynote through almost all the scenes of the play and finding expression in various characters and ways. As early as I, iii Queen Elizabeth says

> Would all were well! but that will never be:
> I fear our happiness is at the highest.   (I, iii, 40–1)

Far more intensely is the atmosphere of fear and dark presentiment brought out in the next scene, where Clarence, before being murdered, relates his dream to Brakenbury, introducing his narrative of the dream by some general remarks on the horrors and oppressive sights of the preceding night: "So full of dismal terror was the time", and ending it by the portentous "My soul is heavy, and I fain would sleep". The intermediate description of his dream-experience is a fine example of how differently the dream-device is handled here by Shakespeare compared with previous instances. Clarence's narrative is in accord with the actual nature of dream-experience. And, whereas in earlier literary treatment of dreams we usually find emphasis on the rational meaning of the dream, with focus on the explication and interpretation of its significance, here almost nothing is given in the way of explanation; the dream itself, with its bold and powerful visions, its sombre and terrible scenery, is to affect us. And it does affect us more deeply than a clear exposition of its portent could ever do, acting rather on our subconscious feeling, on our imagination, than on our rational comprehension.

In the second act this atmosphere of fear and impending evil envelops the anonymous citizens who meet in a London street.[10] We have here a 'choric scene' without particular relevance to plot and character, a scene without dramatic tension or contrast, its main purpose being to reflect this general mood of alarm, premonition and imminent catastrophe. It was Shakespeare who developed this type of atmosphere-creating mirror scene[11] for which we find no clear models in the drama before him.[12] The note of fear, menace and ominous anticipation is first struck by the Second Citizen in

> I fear, I fear, 'twill prove a troublous world (II, iii, 5)

and is then summed up in a series of so far separately-used premonitory images by the Third Citizen:

> When clouds appear, wise men put on their cloaks;
> When great leaves fall, the winter is at hand;
> When the sun sets, who doth not look for night?
> Untimely storms make men expect a dearth.

Compared with this scene the other references to 'fear' and 'dread' spread all over the play are of minor importance, some of them being, however, particularly effective, as for example the end of III, i, where, after an ambiguous and significant play on the word "fear", the young Prince announces his intention of going to the Tower "with a heavy heart" (III, i, 149).

In the sequence of the scenes a subtle variation in degree as well as in method of expressing foreboding may be traced. Thus, for example, after the choric scene II, iii, where anticipation was uttered, in more general terms, regarding the whole country's fate, we find in the following scene Queen Elizabeth, more concretely, foreseeing "the downfall of our house", whereas in the next scene (III, i), as we have just seen, anticipatory phrases come even from the mouth of a child.

Up to the last act, Richard himself seems to be exempt from this feeling of fear and insecurity.[13] But then, in the great scene v, iii, after the ghosts of his murdered victims have appeared to him in his sleep, he wakes up shaken by terror, and henceforth the word 'fear' occurs again and again in his speech. His fragmentary reply to Ratcliff: "O Ratcliff, I fear, I fear—" echoes the Second Citizen's phrase from II, iii and the words then following reveal that the powers at which so far Richard has scoffed have now gained ascendancy over him. But this sudden intrusion of 'fear' into Richard's soul and speech is not even the dramatically most effective means of arousing a foreknowledge of the near end. At the beginning of the scene, by an interplay of gestures, short answers and significant reactions, Shakespeare gives us, in Richard, the picture of someone who has lost his balance and is filled with a dark presentiment. His helmet seems to him "easier than it was", and he "will not sup to-night"; he admits he has not "that alacrity of spirit, Nor cheer of mind, that I was wont to have". He utters abrupt and disconnected orders and sentences, his whole language is confused. There is, in these passages, no definite 'foreboding phrase', but this new way of expressing anticipation by behaviour rather than by language is striking and noteworthy. The impression thus created in the first part of the scene is ironically set off by the contrast of Richard's later defiant effort to refute the bad omen of the not-shining sun,[14] noticed first by himself: "A black day will it be to somebody"

> Not shine to-day! Why, what is that to me
> More than to Richmond? for the selfsame heaven
> That frowns on me looks sadly upon him. (v, iii, 284–6)

The subjective or double interpretation of omen is a device which Shakespeare was to develop and expand in later plays.[15] Compared with these subtle and original forms of foreboding the presages and curses pronounced alternately to Richard and Richmond by the Ghosts[16] of Richard's victims are more in the traditional and obvious manner, making use of symmetry and parallelism.

Passages of dramatic irony are particularly frequent in this play and also help to build up this dense tissue of foreboding hints. There are too many examples of this to be quoted here.[17] It is particularly effective in Hastings's behaviour, whose deceptive feeling of security and confidence stands in ironic contrast to what is actually going on and, being a kind of warning, creates anticipation in the audience. Act III, scene ii is built on this contrast,[18] while III, iv with Hastings's waking up to realities, shows us, at the same time, his waking up to the capacity of prophecy and to a realization of those presages which he formerly ignored.[19] Another interesting way of using dramatic irony as a means of contrast and foreboding is offered by the repetition of Gloucester's ironic "God will revenge it" (II, i, 138) in the following scene, only sixteen lines later, by the Boy (II, ii, 14), both echoing King Edward's preceding words

> O God, I fear thy justice will take hold
> On me, and you, and mine, and yours for this!   (II, i, 131–2)

The same thought appearing in three different shades of meaning! Richard, of course, as a master of irony, cannot escape using it against himself, as for example in IV, iv, when he retorts to Queen Elizabeth

> All unavoided is the doom of destiny.

There is a similar dramatic irony linked up with anticipation in his words to Elizabeth later on in the scene:[20]

> Heaven and fortune bar me happy hours!
> Day yield me not thy light nor, night, thy rest!
> Be opposite all planets of good luck
> To my proceedings.   (IV, iv, 400–3)

Ironic, too, though not in the sense of dramatic irony, is his use of proverbs, said 'aside', in III, i to give expression to his foreknowledge.

Sometimes, it is by one word only that anticipatory effects are achieved. In IV, i Brakenbury, expecting Gloucester's imminent coronation, refers to him, by a slip of his tongue, as "the King", which leads to an angry retort from Queen Elizabeth and to his own apology. Or, to quote only one example of Shakespeare's anticipatory use of ambiguity in one single word, we may recall the overconfident remarks made by Hastings before his fall: "the boar will use us kindly" (III, ii, 33), where the second meaning of 'kindly' will come true later on.

Compared with other plays there is a great deal of anticipation and foreboding in *Richard III*, more than, at first sight, seems to be actually demanded by the exigencies of plot and character. The impression of excess is, however, modified by the great variety of means to which Shakespeare resorts. On the other hand, the play's total effect as well as its main idea necessarily imply from the very beginning an atmosphere charged with disaster, a haunting sense of impending terror and increasing gloom. Moreover, what A. P. Rossiter[21] has called the "cyclical structure" of *Richard III*, its "repetitiveness" and "ritual" pattern, finds expression in a wealth of cross-references, of correspondences and echoes which further enhance the effect of foreboding and anticipation.

Richard II, besides offering further examples of the use of prophecy, warning and dramatic irony, displays some new and interesting types of anticipation. Act II, scene ii presents the Queen, who feels some inexplicable sadness which, although she cannot give any reason for it, appears to her as something quite real and irrefutable. The idea that the farewell from Richard may be the reason for her grief does not satisfy her:

> yet again, methinks,
> Some unborn sorrow, ripe in fortune's womb,
> Is coming towards me, and my inward soul
> With nothing trembles: at some thing it grieves,
> More than with parting from my lord the king. (II, ii, 9–13)

Nor can Bushy's endeavours to explain away this grief with clever arguments convince her:

> It may be so; but yet my inward soul
> Persuades me it is otherwise: howe'er it be
> I cannot but be sad; so heavy sad,
> As though on thinking on no thought I think
> Makes me with heavy nothing faint and shrink. (II, ii, 28–32)

We have quoted fully these strange utterances of the Queen because here we have the first example in Shakespeare of anticipation which cannot and does not name its object, finding expression merely in unfounded melancholy and depression. Speedy answer is given to this feeling in the same scene through Green's bad news and the Queen confesses: "Now hath my soul brought forth her prodigy." The atmosphere of impending disaster then steadily increases, first by York's appearance, then by the servant's news of the duchess's death, making York exclaim

> what a tide of woes
> Comes rushing on this woeful land at once! (II, ii, 98–9)

and lastly by the ominous parting of the three accomplices of the king

> Farewell: if heart's presages be not vain,
> We three here part that ne'er shall meet again. (II, ii, 142–3)

the whole scene ending on the significant note of

> *Bushy*   Well, we may meet again.
> *Bagot*   I fear me, never.

If of this scene it can be said that its purpose consists to a considerable extent in arousing forebodings, this holds true even more of II, iv, which seems wholly to be built upon anticipation transformed into a dramatic situation. York's last words of the preceding scene are still in our ears: "Things past redress are now with me past care", when we hear a Welsh captain announcing to Salisbury the discharge of his troops because there were "no tidings from the king". In his reply to Salisbury's futile entreaty, the Captain links up this lack of tidings (in itself a bad omen) with a series of other ominous signs—

> 'Tis thought the king is dead; we will not stay.
> The bay-trees in our country are all wither'd,
> And meteors fright the fixed stars of heaven,
> The pale-faced moon looks bloody on the earth,[22]   (II, iv, 7–10)

The foreboding brought out by these omens of various description is, in Salisbury's concluding words, transposed into an inner vision of a mind clearly foreseeing the coming end:

> Ah, Richard, with the eyes of heavy mind
> I see thy glory like a shooting star
> Fall to the base earth from the firmament.
> Thy sun sets weeping in the lowly west,
> Witnessing storms to come, woe and unrest.[23]

The actual omen has been turned into metaphor; anticipation is being expressed on two different levels. Foresight based on portentous natural phenomena bordering on the 'supernatural' is followed by foresight due to a realistic and intuitive insight into the situation.

The other types of foreboding and anticipation occurring in *Richard II* have already appeared in earlier plays and can therefore be summed up here shortly. The prophecies[24] pronounced by Gaunt and Carlisle have an important position in the play, they are more subtly prepared for, and by situation[25] and diction, by rhythm and imagery, set off to impress us and make us listen to the manifold implications and predictions they contain. The woe-sorrow-grief-care theme running like a *leitmotif* through the whole play[26] contributes considerably to "clouding the sky" and consequently to creating a dark presentiment. "For sorrow ends not when it seemeth done" the Duchess exclaims as early as I, ii, 61. Warnings uttered to Richard from various quarters stand in sharp contrast to his own deafness for these voices. Over the first two acts numerous hints are spread suggesting Richard's impending failure (e.g. "Reproach and dissolution hangeth over him", II, i, 258). But from Act III on, Richard's own speech becomes tinged with a dark foreknowledge of his end; his references to death, to "Richard's night", to the grave, and, increasingly, to grief, care, woe, sorrow should be examined in this connexion. Now he himself becomes prophetic (III, iii, 85–100; v, i, 55–68). On the whole, *Richard II* shows a more subtle, less obtrusive and explicit use of anticipation and foreboding. The strong lyrical quality of the play and its reflective note demand means of expression different from those we found in *Richard III*.

Compared with *Richard III* and *Richard II* there are surprisingly few foreboding passages in the first two acts of *King John*. It is only from Act III onwards that anticipation is stirred on a larger scale, being mainly connected with young Arthur's fate. And there is a further difference; the feeling of impending evil and gloom is far more strongly awakened by the appearance and behaviour of certain characters than by brief utterances. Thus, in III, i Constance's "sad and passionate" appearance (II, i, 544), her railing and wailing, the magnificent picture of her sitting down on the ground "here I and sorrows sit", the ironic contrast of her desperate and gloomy vein to the false conciliatory mood between the French and the English kings—all this is more powerful and more effective in making us feel that this new peace will not hold than any single lines or allusions could be. Of these, of course, a few may be quoted in this connexion, as, for example, Constance's reaction to King Philip's sonnet-like[27] glorification of the present day (III, i, 75–82), beginning "A wicked day, and not a holy day!" and ending with

> This day, all things begun come to ill end,
> Yea, faith itself to hollow falsehood change! (III, i, 94–5)

her invocation to "the heavens" which "ere sunset" ought to "Set armed discord 'twixt these perjured kings" (III, i, 111). All this, we know, comes true even in the course of the same scene, and Blanche's words "The sun's o'ercast with blood: fair day, adieu!" (III, i, 326)[28] will refute King Philip's complacent references to the auspicious "splendour" of the "glorious sun" in the beginning of the scene (III, i, 77). When, therefore, Constance appears again in III, iv, "a grave unto a soul", invoking Death and filled with a fearful foreknowledge of young Arthur's death, we are apt to believe her after what has happened in III, i. Pandulph's effort to attribute her foreknowledge to "madness" (III, iv, 43) leads only to a still more effective assertion of her fatal prescience

> I am not mad; too well, too well I feel
> The different plague of each calamity,

and in her next speech she even has a vision of her son looking "as hollow as a ghost, As dim and meagre as an ague's fit, And so he'll die..." (III, iv, 84–6).

A fine and subtle contrast is then brought out by Pandulph's speeches in the same scene; he also anticipates Arthur's death, not prompted, however, by passionate feeling and instinct, but rather by the cool calculation of a cunning observer who by rational arguments foretells that Arthur must die, foreseeing that this event will bring about political revolt which will fit into his own game.[29] The cool cynicism with which he thus utilizes the coming tragedy of Arthur's death is also evident in his prediction that the common people, terrified by this cruel act, will then interpret all sorts of quite natural phenomena as "meteors, prodigies and signs, Abortives, presages and tongues of heaven"—another instance of the very different way these omens are made use of and believed in in Shakespeare's later histories. We shall remember this forecast when, in IV, ii, Hubert tells King John of the five moons which were observed the preceding night,[30] or when the Bastard relates how he found the people "strangely fantasied". But compared with the early histories these omens and prophecies[31] have become a less important means of foreshadowing events. In the next scene, the same Bastard gives a far more suggestive and forcible expression to foreboding[32] in his pregnant lines

> and vast confusion waits,
> As doth a raven on a sick-fall'n beast
> The imminent decay of wrested pomp.
> Now happy he whose cloak and cincture can
> Hold out this tempest. (IV, iii, 152–6)

Fully to appreciate these lines it is necessary to understand the character of the Bastard and the role assigned to him in this play. This is only one example of how, in the plays of Shakespeare's middle and later period,[33] the kindling of anticipation and foreboding will be closely linked up with other issues which cannot be grasped by quoting certain passages but demand a consideration of several other aspects, sometimes, in fact, an interpretation of the whole play. Thus, in *Romeo and Juliet*, an enumeration and appreciation of the well-known anticipatory lines spoken by Romeo, Juliet and Friar Laurence will not suffice to demonstrate the subtle effects of foreboding in this play unless the specific conception of fate, chance and tragedy in this drama of the "star-crossed lovers" is understood and illustrated by simultaneous reference to plot, character and situation. In *Julius Caesar* the foreboding lines spoken alternately by Brutus, Caesar, Cassius and Casca derive their full significance only from the different temper and role of these characters, from the specific kind of dramatic irony used, for example, in Caesar's speech, and from the peculiar atmosphere in the respective scenes. In *Macbeth* the very core of the play depends upon the element of anticipation and foreboding, and a discussion of these elements in its structure would demand a special and a lengthier study.

NOTES

1. Cf. J. Paul, S. R. Gibson, *Shakespeare's Use of the Supernatural* (Cambridge, 1908); Cumberland Clark, *Shakespeare and the Supernatural* (London, 1931). Studies on dramatic irony in Shakespeare will also often refer to passages being at the same time ironic and anticipating. But this anticipatory function is not singled out for special examination. Cf. G. G. Sedgewick, *Of Irony Especially in Drama* (Toronto, 1948); A. R. Thompson, *The Dry Mock, A Study of Irony in Drama* (Berkeley and Los Angeles, 1948).

2. Foreboding plays a larger part in Holinshed and Hall than is usually recognized, partly because many omens occur in passages which have not been directly used by Shakespeare as source material. These omens appear to fall into the following main divisions: tempests and catastrophes brought about by natural causes (floods, earthquakes, fires), heavenly apparitions only partly natural (comets, planets, prolonged darkening of the sun, appearance of five moons, three suns, etc.), miraculous and strange happenings (fiery spirits in likeness of birds, a fiery dragon, appearance of strange animals), semi-normal occurrences in our every-day life to which superstition has attributed an ominous significance (the stumbling of a horse, the crying of birds, etc.), prophecies either true, or false because uttered by deceivers. The many miracles and monstrosities reported in the chronicles are by no means always portents, but in a few instances they are (as, for example, Holinshed's *Chronicles of England* (London, 1807, II, 287, 829; III, 264)). This category Shakespeare seems to have deliberately avoided; he prefers the first and second class of omens above quoted, developing especially the tempest-omen but making less use of the other natural catastrophes cited above. With regard to heavenly apparitions it is only in the early histories that we find such extraordinary portents as the three suns (*3 Henry VI*) or the five moons (*King John*).

3. On Shakespeare's use of prophecies seen before the background of contemporary belief and on their significance for Shakespeare's fundamental concepts, cf. the excellent study of Paul Reyher, *Essai sur les idées dans l'œuvre de Shakespeare* (Paris, 1947), pp. 232 ff.

4. We therefore exclude from our survey those passages, especially numerous in the early histories, where characters announce their plans, unveil their intentions, and make their decisions as to the future. Similarly obvious and therefore not examined here in detail is anticipation roused by the gloomy face or deject appearance of messengers or other bearers of ill tidings. The bad news in turn often incites a feeling of foreboding.

5. Cf. Reyher, *op. cit.* p. 233.

6. R. G. Moulton, *Shakespeare as a Dramatic Artist* (Oxford, 1892), p. 115.

7. On the structural significance of the curses in *Richard III* see E. M. W. Tillyard, *Shakespeare's History Plays* (London, 1948), p. 212 and A. P. Rossiter, 'The Structure of Richard III', *Durham University Journal*, XXXI (1938–9), 44–75.

8. Similarly Anne remembers in IV, i, 72–85 the curses she pronounced in I, ii, 26 against Gloucester's future wife. Other prophecies not, however, previously pronounced in the play are remembered by Richard in IV, ii, 108, by Buckingham in V, i, 12 (a curse directed against himself) and by Gloucester in I, iii, 174, this curse having been

pronounced by Richard, Duke of York, in *3 Henry VI*, I, iv, 164. It is significant that in the play's first scene it is Gloucester who makes use of the people's belief in "drunken prophecies" by enraging the King against Clarence. This stands in ironic contrast to the very effective and serious part played by the prophecies uttered by, for example, Margaret later in the play. The source for the story about the "drunken prophecies" is in Hall's Chronicle (*Edward IV*, fol. 50). Cf. also Holinshed, vol. III, p. 346.

9.   Can curses pierce the clouds and enter heaven?

                Why, then, give way, dull clouds, to my quick curses!   (I, iii, 195)

This passage should be compared with IV, iv, 124–31 (on the relative power of words). Reyher interprets these passages in a different sense and connexion (*op. cit.* p. 238).

10. For this premonitory scene there is a parallel in the following passage in Thomas More's *History of King Richard the thirde* (ed. J. Rawon Lumby; Cambridge, 1924, p. 43), "...yet began there, here and there about, some maner of muttering amonge the people, as though al should not long be wel, though they neither wist what they feared nor wherfore; were it that before such great thinges mens hartes of a secret instinct of nature misgiveth them, as the sea without wind swelleth of himself somtime before a tempest; or were it that some one man, happely somewhat perceiving, filled mani men with suspicion though he shewed few men what he knew".

11. Cf. Hereward T. Price, 'Mirror Scenes in Shakespeare', *Joseph Quincy Adams Memorial Studies* (Washington, 1948), pp. 101–13. Cf. too, III, vi, especially the Scrivener's last words (ll. 13–14).

12. A certain parallel is given by III, ii of *The Raigne of King Edward the Third* (*The Shakespeare Apocrypha*, ed. C. F. Tucker Brooke; Oxford, 1908), where anonymous French citizens meet indulging in similar premonitory phrases and images as in *Richard III*, II, iii. But it is probable that this scene was influenced by *Richard III*.

13. His words to Buckingham in IV, ii, 5 cannot be safely interpreted as a sign of anticipation as they are meant to provoke a definite reaction on the part of Buckingham. They are, however, ambiguous and bear dramatic irony.

                But shall we wear these honours for a day?

                Or shall they last, and we rejoice in them?

14. The purple, veiled or not-shining sun, darkness, gloom, clouds, mist, night are among the numerous images and symbols Shakespeare uses to forebode evil and misfortune. The complete material is examined and collected in a forthcoming Munich dissertation by Paulita Veit, *The symbol of darkness and light in Shakespeare*. In Holinshed's *Chronicle* Shakespeare could find a few instances where the clouding of the sky is taken as portentous as in, for example, the following passage: "On the ninth of Julie the sunne seemed darkened with certaine grosse and evill favoured clouds comming betwixt it and the earth so as it appeared ruddie, but gave no light from noone till the setting thereof. And afterwards continuallie for the space of six weeks, about the middest of the daie, clouds customablie rose, and sometimes they continued both daie and night, not vanishing awaie at all. At the same time, such a mortalitie and death of people increased in Northfolke and in many other countries of England..." (Holinshed, II, p. 818).

15. In Holinshed and Hall omens are generally believed in unreservedly. The typical attitude is expressed in Holinshed, II, p. 291 (A.D. 1204): "Neverthelesse, of all uncouth and rare sights, speciallie of monstruous appearances we ought to be so farre from hauing little regard; that we should rather in them and by them obserue the euent and falling out of some future thing, no lesse miraculous in the issue, than they be woonderfull at the sudden sight. This was well noted of a philosopher, who to the purpose (among other matters by him touched) hath spoken no lesse pithilie than crediblie, saieng;

                Nec fieri aut errore aut casu monstra putandum,

                Cum certas habeant causas, ut tristia monstrent,

                Unde illis nomen, quare et portenta vocantur."

16. The Ghost prompting to vengeance and simultaneously foreboding the future is frequent in Seneca-influenced tragedy. Cf. *Locrine*, V, iv, 1–30 (*The Shakespeare Apocrypha*).

17. There are new and illuminating remarks on the use of irony in *Richard III* in A. P. Rossiter's article 'The Structure of *Richard III*'.

18. See, for example, his rejection of the warning given by Stanley's dream, III, ii, 25. Compare his words

                And we will both together to the Tower

                Where, he shall see, the boar will use us kindly   (ll. 32–3)

with young York's "I shall not sleep in quiet at the Tower" (l. 142), both passages containing dramatic irony. The audience's foreknowledge is particularly enhanced by the juxtaposition of Hastings's security with warnings pronounced by other people (Catesby, Stanley). Cf., for example, ll. 83–4 with 85–9. Buckingham's aside at the end of the scene "And supper too, although thou know'st it not" (l. 123) is the last link in this chain.

19. Cf. his acknowledging the significance of Stanley's dream (l. 84) and of his horse's stumbling (l. 86, a feature to be found already in Holinshed). Cf. also ll. 94, 105, 82.

20. In earlier scenes Shakespeare also made certain characters utter curses or imprecations which, in fact, as shown by the following events, were directed against themselves (Anne, I, ii, 26; Buckingham, II, i, 32).

21. A. P. Rossiter, *loc. cit.*

22. J. Dover Wilson points out (*Richard II* in the 'New Cambridge Shakespeare', p. 180) that these omens are taken partly from Holinshed and partly from Daniel's *Civil Wars*. It is, however, characteristic of Shakespeare's use of omen, that he does not take over the miraculous apparitions like Daniel's "Red fiery dragons in the aire doe flie".

23. As in all Shakespearian plays the tempest-imagery plays an important role in foreshadowing coming disaster; cf. G. Wilson Knight, *The Shakespearian Tempest* (Oxford, 1932). As early as II, i we hear Northumberland exclaim:

> But, lords, we hear this fearful tempest sing,
> Yet seek no shelter to avoid the storm;
> We see the wind sit sore upon our sails,
> And yet we strike not, but securely perish.

For this, however, Shakespeare had merely to turn to Holinshed (see p. 33 above).

24. Gaunt's prophecy and warning cover almost half the scene (II, i, 1–138). Carlisle's great speech is in IV, i, 114–49. With this should be compared Richard's prediction in III, iii, 85–8 and his words to Northumberland in V, i, 55–68. It should be noted that almost all of these prophecies stretch beyond the frame of the play, whereas in *Richard III* the prophecies are fulfilled within the play.

25. The dying Gaunt carried on to the scene and introducing his predictions by solemn and lyrical phrases cast into a quatrain (II, i, 9–12) is a fit medium for a prophecy; so is Bishop Carlisle who, in Westminster Hall, is the only person who can raise his voice against Bolingbroke (IV, i).

26. Cf. R. D. Altick, 'Symphonic Imagery in *Richard II*', *PMLA*, LXII (1947), 339–65.

27. The 'Arden Edition' (Ivor B. John) compares Sonnet XXXIII.

28. Cf. V, v, 1 Lewis's "The sun of heaven methought was loath to set".

29. III, iv, 126. The difference between this rationalized and sober prophecy of Cardinal Pandulph and the exalted and solemn prophecies in *Richard II* and *Richard III* should be noted.

30. In *The Troublesome Reign of King John* the five moons (occurring also in Holinshed, III, 163) are represented as seen on the stage, whereas Shakespeare mentions them in a merely casual way. Dover Wilson says "what is in *Troublesome Reign* an elaborate stage-effect becomes with Shakespeare a mere detail of the general atmosphere of rumour and fantasy in the land" (*King John*, ed. J. Dover Wilson, p. 164).

31. In IV, ii the Bastard appears with Peter of Pomfret, a popular prophet, whose prophecy that King John will abdicate before "the next Ascension-day at noon" (l. 151) will come true and will be remembered by the king himself in V, i, 25.

32. Cf. the present author's *The Development of Shakespeare's Imagery* (London, 1951), p. 85.

33. As to the later histories *Henry IV*, *Henry V* and *Henry VIII* there is little that is new with regard to Shakespeare's use of foreboding along the lines pointed out in this article. It was therefore thought fit to conclude this study with an examination of *King John*.

MIDDLE-CLASS ATTITUDES IN SHAKESPEARE'S HISTORIES[1]

BY

KARL BRUNNER

Shakespeare's attitude to history has been dealt with exhaustively by E. M. W. Tillyard in his *Shakespeare's History Plays*. He has shown that Shakespeare's basic conception of history corresponds with that of the Tudor historians, who themselves followed medieval ideas. The Universe was considered to be a unity, in which everything had its definite place, and it was the perfect work of God. Since any imperfection was regarded as the work not of God, but of man, the varied history of the civil wars appeared as evils caused by human sinfulness. Mortal sins, such as murder, worldly ambition, revenge, were the cause of the disorder. Henry VII favoured such ideas in official historiography, for he could use them for supporting his title to the crown: by uniting the claims of the two houses of York and Lancaster his ascent to the throne brought the disastrous rivalry to an end. This 'official' outlook was entirely different from that of later Renaissance authors. Machiavelli, for example, looked upon the natural state of man as disorder which only a clever ruler could restrain by using his wit and power.

With two exceptions (*King John* and *Henry VIII*) Shakespeare's history plays deal with the period of the civil wars. This period was apparently congenial to him because it offered the best example for his conception of history. Other dramatists of the time did not in general deal with it, or if they did, they did not show the same conception of history. Sometimes they merely presented historical facts, without regard to any philosophy of history, as the author of the early play on King John (*The Troublesome Reign of King John*); sometimes they sought only to amuse their audiences by anecdotes very loosely attached to history, as Peele in his *Edward I* or the author of the old play on Henry V (*The Famous Victories of Henry V*); sometimes they tried to find a tragic plot in the story of the downfall of a weak monarch who neglected his duties for worthless flatterers, as Marlowe in his *Edward II*, or the author of *Woodstock*. Later dramatists tended to follow the Renaissance conception of history, dealing with ruthless princes whose tragic ends were caused by counter-intrigues against their cruel behaviour, as Massinger in *The Duke of Milan*.

Shakespeare's presentation of the medieval conception of history could not have been the result simply of his finding it in the chronicles. Other dramatists had read them as well. Nor was this conception universal at his time. Even if Elizabethan educationalists recommended the study of the historians to young gentlemen as a training for future careers in public life, those gentlemen themselves, in their actual conduct, did not show much profit by this study. They preferred to follow Machiavelli and the Renaissance ideas. The medieval conception, on the other hand, undoubtedly made a special appeal to the conservative elements in the population—the old landowners, the well-to-do citizens—just the class from which Shakespeare came. As a son of a Stratford landowner and business man, who had grown up and had many friends in the small but prosperous town, he must have gained the impression that peace and quiet develop-

36

ment helped the mass of the middle class to which he belonged. Successful as he himself was in business, he showed clearly his own middle-class interests when he used his savings to buy New Place. When he procured a coat of arms for his father, and thus incidentally for himself, he revealed once more his consciousness of tradition. He remained content to be a 'gentleman from Stratford', as his friends the Quineys did and various others. They wanted peace and order at home, a thrifty government, freedom from interference by rival aristocratic factions—just the opposite of what had happened during the civil wars, which were not so far remote that they could not be remembered by the older generation.

This general conception of history is clearly shown in *Henry VI*. At the very beginning of Part I it is expressed by the Duke of Bedford:

> Henry the Fifth, thy ghost I invoke:
> Prosper this realm, keep it from civil broils, (I, i, 52–3)

and shortly afterwards by the Messenger:

> Awake, awake, English nobility!
> Let not sloth dim your honours new-begot. (I, i, 78–9)

But the English nobles in the play do not act accordingly. Their discord first brings defeat in France, and later the dreaded civil wars. The King, pious and well-meaning though he is, is not able to bring them to terms. He is not even able to mitigate his beloved wife's thirst for revenge.

The force of middle-class attitudes and predilections may be suspected even in those incidents wherein Shakespeare deviates from or expands upon the chroniclers' material. Thus, for example, when we look at the bold Talbot we are compelled to recognize that the scenes in which he appears are coloured not merely by what the dramatist found in his history books but, more significantly, by the tints of medieval romance. Talbot in France is conceived in a manner not unlike that in which the Middle Ages conceived Richard Cœur de Lion among the Saracens. Now the important thing to observe here is that just such narratives as the *Cœur de Lion* romance were widely read among the middle classes, and one is tempted to believe that Shakespeare may have had these works, unconsciously at least, in his mind, when formulating the Talbot scenes.

Similar examples are to be found in the treatment of Jack Cade and the Mayors of London and of York. In the chronicles much is made of the fact that Cade was instigated by the King's opponents: Shakespeare tones this down as though he wished to emphasize instead the disruptive, vaguely communistic ideas and slogans of the crowd and the disasters which may come from a weak and divided government. On the opposite side stand the Mayor of London and the Mayor of York, both eminently sensible men, the former becoming a kind of chorus intended to express sound public opinion and the latter representative of the bewilderment of worthy citizens when confronted by the civil confusion they feared.

What can be observed in these scenes of *Henry VI* may perhaps help us to understand Shakespeare's aim in the later *Henry IV*. Falstaff there has always been a rather puzzling and perplexing figure. Are we, as some believe, to see this Falstaff as a relic, gloriously elaborated, of the Prince's loose companions who are mentioned in the chronicles and whom the author of the older play, *The Famous Victories of Henry V*, uses at length to amuse his audience? Or shall we, with Tillyard, see in the play the old morality pattern, with the Prince representing 'Mankind' set between the evil forces 'Sloth' and 'Vanity', represented by his bad companions, and the good forces, 'Chivalry' and 'Honour', represented by the King and by his brothers? Does Percy Hotspur represent excess in military qualities and Falstaff defect in them, while the Prince stands in the middle and thus represents Aristotle's medium way of life? Perhaps there is something else in Falstaff, in Percy Hotspur, in the comic and political scenes. Falstaff is a knight, not a commoner. He is a likeable companion, he is witty, but otherwise certainly not an ideal representative of his class. His old friend from his student days in the Inns of Court, Justice Shallow, and the latter's fellow-justice, Silence, are undoubtedly the most stupid persons in the whole large gallery of Shakespeare's characters. Falstaff's companions, Pistol, Nym, Bardolph, are not ideal soldiers; they belong to the rabble of soldiery which good citizens must have despised and even feared. In *Henry V* they are clearly contrasted with the upright soldiers Fluellen, Gower and MacMorris. Thus, perhaps, Shakespeare wanted to make his audience realize what sort of persons might be bred by times of disorder and civil war, and even entice the heir to the crown into their companionship. It is not unlikely, too, that Percy Hotspur is similarly conceived. Although personally likeable, he is depicted in the play as a figure who must politically be condemned—the man for whom fighting rules out all those other human activities in which the middle classes believed and on which they depended. Henry, as a prince and still more as a king, is in contrast with those characters—and perhaps also with his father and his brothers—the true general, liked by his subordinates with whom he converses in disguise before the decisive battle. He is the kind of king the commoners liked: the chroniclers, of course, describe him as such, but Shakespeare has given added vitality and urgency to their suggestions.

NOTE

1. Excerpts from a paper read at the Shakespeare Conference, Stratford-upon-Avon, 1951.

A RECONSIDERATION OF *EDWARD III*

BY

KENNETH MUIR

Since 1760, when Capell claimed that *Edward III* was written by Shakespeare, its authorship has been discussed by numerous critics. In the nineteenth century, Tennyson, Ward and Fleay believed that the Countess scenes were Shakespearian, while Swinburne, Saintsbury, Symonds and Moore Smith denied their authenticity. In the present century, Tucker Brooke, while admitting that these scenes were much more Shakespearian at first sight than the rest of the play, came to the conclusion that they were by the same author as the remaining scenes, and that this author was George Peele.[1] F. W. Moorman argued that Shakespeare revised the play between 1590 and 1596, and that he completely rewrote the Countess scenes.[2] R. M. Smith showed that Froissart provided the main source of the play, and that the Countess episode was derived from this source as well as from Painter's *Palace of Pleasure*.[3] Smith, however, went beyond the evidence when he concluded that the whole play must have been written "at one time by one playwright", and that this playwright could not have been Shakespeare. At about the same time, Platt argued that as "Lilies that fester smell far worse than weeds" and "scarlet ornaments" were both more appropriate to their contexts in the *Sonnets* than to those in the play, the unknown author must have seen some of the sonnets in manuscript.[4] Sir Edmund Chambers cautiously supported the view that Shakespeare wrote not only the Countess scenes, but also IV, iv.[5] Finally, Alfred Hart, by means of vocabulary tests, came to the conclusion that the whole play must be either by Shakespeare or by some author unknown—not by Peele, Greene, or Marlowe.[6]

Such is the present state of the controversy in which Swinburne has argued most persuasively against the attribution of the play to Shakespeare,[7] and Hart has presented the most 'scientific' case for his authorship. Swinburne relied entirely on aesthetic arguments. He thought the author was "a devout student and humble follower" of Marlowe; that the faults of the play were due, not to haste or carelessness, but to "lifelong and irremediable impotence" of a "conscientious and studious workman of technically insufficient culture and of naturally limited means"; that although there are stray lines reminiscent of Shakespeare, "the structure, the composition, is feeble, incongruous, inadequate and effete"; and that resemblances to Shakespeare are due to the fact that in his early plays "the style of Shakespeare was not for the most part distinctively his own". Swinburne then devoted some twenty pages to an analysis of the Countess scenes. He thought that the speech containing the Shakespearian phrase, "scarlet ornaments" (II, i, 1–24) is "but just better than what is utterly intolerable"; that Warwick's lines (II, i, 443–7) "vaguely remind the reader of something better read elsewhere"; and that the passage containing the other quotation from the *Sonnets* (II, i, 447 ff.) appears more like "a theft from Shakespeare's private store of undramatic poetry than a misapplication by its own author to dramatic purposes of a line too apt and exquisite to endure without injury the transference from its original setting". Swinburne's intimate knowledge of Elizabethan drama gives more weight to his opinion than Tennyson's; but, as we shall see, some of his arguments are questionable.[8]

On the other side of the controversy, some of Hart's vocabulary tests appear to be inconclusive.[9] His most significant test deals with the use of Compound Participial Adjectives. If we modify his figures so that they represent the use per 1000 lines of different kinds of adjectival compounds, we get the following table:

	Compound Adjectives	Participial Adjectives	Noun+ Participle
Shakespeare	21	12	3.6
Marlowe	10.6	5.1	0.86
Greene	7.4	4.4	0.48
Peele	9.4	3.6	0.14
Edward III	23	14.8	3.6

Unless the author of *Edward III* was experimenting in a different style from his usual one, it is reasonable to assert that the play was not written by Marlowe, Greene, or Peele; and the figures suggest that Shakespeare may have been the author.

Another of Hart's tests, which he does not himself apply to *Edward III*, is that of the occurrence of words not before used in Shakespeare's plays. In the last five plays there is (approximately) one unused word every twelve lines. Hart does not give figures for the early plays, but he mentions that the proportion of new words is highest in *Hamlet* and *King Lear*. The following table gives the figures for the allegedly Shakespearian parts of the play (A: i.e. I, ii, 90 ff. and II; IV, iv) and for the remainder of the play (B)—if it was written in 1597 (before *1 Henry IV*), or in 1596 (before *King John*), or in 1594 (before *Richard II*). The second half of the table corrects the figures by taking the poems into consideration:

	1597		1596		1594	
	New words	$\frac{\text{Lines}}{\text{Words}}$	New words	$\frac{\text{Lines}}{\text{Words}}$	New words	$\frac{\text{Lines}}{\text{Words}}$
A	68	13	78	12	91	10
B	62	26	70	23	79	20
A	61	15	70	13	78	12
B	54	29	61	26	67	24

The fact that the incidence of new words is twice as frequent in the former scenes suggests a difference of authorship; and the figures for those scenes are not incompatible with Shakespeare's authorship, assuming the play was written 1594-6.

A study of the imagery of *Edward III* reveals some interesting results.[10] First, there are about twice as many images, in proportion to the number of lines, in the scenes ascribed to Shakespeare as in the other scenes—one image every 3·8 lines compared with one every 7 lines. This may, perhaps, be due to the difference of subject-matter. Secondly, there appears to be iterative imagery in the play, which will be analysed below. Thirdly, there are a number of images which resemble those in Shakespeare's plays, and some of them are linked together by quibbles, as Shakespeare's often are.[11]

The iterative imagery is particularly apparent in the scenes which have been ascribed to Shakespeare (A), though there are traces of it in the other scenes (B). In the following table of selected groups of images it should be remembered that the number of lines in the B scenes is about twice as many as those in the A scenes:

Field	Total	A	B
Clothes, Masking, Disguise	28	17	11
Metals, buying and selling	36	30	6
Sun, Moon and Stars	23	22	1
War	23	14	9
Poison	10	7	3
Crime, Punishment, Law	16	14	2

These seem to be the most significant groups of images, for the nature images (83) and those drawn from books (10) have no particular, or interpretable, dramatic function. The first of the groups tabulated brings out the contrast between appearance and reality, and between true beauty and false:

These ragged walles no testimonie are,
What is within.... (I, ii, 157)

And trueth hath puld the visard from his face.... (I, i, 77)

Apparaled sin in vertuous sentences.... (II, i, 410)

Decke an Ape
In tissue, and the beautie of the robe
Adds but the greater scorne vnto the beast. (II, i, 444)

Away, loose silkes of wauering vanitie.... (II, ii, 94)

And euery ornament that thou wouldest praise.... (II, i, 86)

my passion,
Which he shall shadow with a vaile of lawne.... (II, i, 55)

And with the strumpets artifitiall line
To painte thy vitious and deformed cause,
Bee well assured, the counterfeit will fade,
And in the end thy fowle defects be seene.... (III, iii, 81)

Clothing and disguise images are used for much the same purpose in *Much Ado about Nothing*.

The images taken from the precious metals symbolize the value of love and also the counterfeit nature of adultery, thus linking up with the previous group:

For she is all the Treasure of our land.... (II, i, 45)

And be enriched by thy soueraignes loue.... (II, i, 75)

Whie dost thou tip mens tongues with golden words
And peise their deedes with weight of heauie leade.... (II, i, 303)

But soft, here comes the treasurer of my spirit.... (II, i, 184)

Of her, whose ransackt treasurie hath taskt
The vaine indeuor of so many pens.... (II, ii, 196)

41

He that doth clip or counterfeit your stamp
Shall die, my Lord; and will your sacred selfe
Comit high treason against the King of heauen.
To stamp his Image in forbidden mettel,
Forgetting your alleageance and your othe?   (II, i, 255)

When thou conuertest from honors golden name....   (II, i, 456)

        like a Country swaine,
Whose habit rude and manners blunt and playne
Presageth nought, yet inly beautified
With bounties, riches and faire hidden pride.
For where the golden Ore doth buried lie,
The ground, vndect with natures tapestrie
Seemes barrayne....   (I, ii, 145)

The images from the sun, moon and stars, as in Elizabethan sonnet sequences, including Shakespeare's, are used to symbolize love and beauty:

Now, in the Sunne alone it doth not lye,
With light to take light from a mortall eye....   (I, ii, 131)

For here two day stars that myne eies would see
More then the Sunne steales myne owne light from mee.   (I, ii, 133)

thy presence, like the Aprill sunne....   (I, ii, 141)

What is she, when the sunne lifts vp his head,
But like a fading taper, dym and dead?   (II, i, 145)

And, being vnmaskt, outshine the golden sun....   (II, i, 148)

Say shee hath thrice more splendour then the sun,
That her perfections emulats the sunne,
That shee breeds sweets as plenteous as the sunne,
That she doth thaw cold winter like the sunne,
That shee doth cheere fresh sommer like the sunne,
That shee doth dazle gazers like the sunne;
And, in this application to the sunne,
Bid her be free and generall as the sunne,
Who smiles vpon the basest weed that growes
As louinglie as on the fragrant rose.   (II, i, 156)

        like an humble shaddow
Yt hauntes the sunshine of my summers life....   (II, i, 232)

      alas, she winnes the sunne of me,
For that is she her selfe.   (II, ii, 69)

But loue hath eyes as iudgement to his steps,
Till too much loued glory dazles them.   (II, ii, 72)

The images from war, natural to the battle scenes, symbolize in the love scenes the attack on the Countess's chastity:

Vnnaturall beseege !	(II, i, 412)
A lingring English seege of peeuish loue....	(II, i, 23)
What bewtie els could triumph ouer me....	(II, i, 97)
The quarrell that I haue requires no armes But these of myne....	(II, ii, 63)
My eyes shall be my arrowes, and my sighes Shall serue me as the vantage of the winde, To wherle away my sweetest artyllerie.	(II, ii, 66)
My follies seege against a faithfull louer....	(II, ii, 209)
Giue me an Armor of eternall steele ! I go to conquer kings; and shall I not then Subdue my selfe?	(II, ii, 98)
thy soule is all too proud To yeeld her Citie for one little breach.	(IV, ix, 44)

The images from poison, and from crime and punishment, emphasize the corruption of unlawful passion:

Which shoots infected poyson in my heart....	(I, ii, 129)
a poison-sucking enuious spider To turne the iuce I take to deadlie venom....	(II, i, 284)
What can one drop of poyson harme the Sea, Whose hugie vastures can digest the ill And make it loose his operation?	(II, i, 401)
And giue the bitter potion of reproch A sugred, sweet and most delitious tast....	(II, i, 405)
That poyson shewes worst in a golden cup....	(II, i, 449)
O periurde beautie, more corrupted Iudge ! When to the great Starre-chamber ore our heads The vniuersall Sessions cals to count This packing euill, we both shall tremble for it.	(II, ii, 164)

One characteristic of Shakespeare's use of imagery is the presence of what Edward A. Armstrong calls image-clusters, groups of unconsciously associated words which reappear in play after play. He has argued that these clusters can be used as a test of authorship,[12] though traces of them have been found in Marlowe. One of the clusters he analyses, that of the Eagle and the Drone, appears in *Edward III*, where in the first scene (ll. 94 ff.) we have *drone, eagle, creeping, stealth, nightingale, voluntary* (music), and *grudging* (mood). In *2 Henry VI* (IV, i, 102–9) we find *drone, eagle, crept, suck,* and *rob*. (In the *Edward III* context there is mention of a storm, and in *Henry VI* of thunder.) In *Henry V* (I, ii, 170–204) we get *drone, eagle, sneaking, sucks, thieves, weasel, cat, music*, and *surly*. As we should expect from a study of such clusters, the *Edward III* example is larger than that in *Henry VI*, which was written earlier, and smaller than that in the later play, *Henry V*. But we cannot take this as a proof of Shakespeare's authorship since he did not believe that drones robbed eagles' nests, and the author of *Edward III* apparently did. In any case, the passage occurs in a scene that few critics have ascribed to Shakespeare.

There is, however, one other cluster—not one of those analysed by Armstrong—which is to be found in *Edward III* (II, i, 146–72). The key-word, *blot*, is accompanied by *heaven, night, moon, constancy, disguise* (mask), *sovereign, eye, winter* and *sun*. All these words, except *constancy* and *disguise* appear also in a passage in *Love's Labour's Lost* (IV, iii, 220 ff.); five of them, including *inconstancy, constant* and *disguise*, appear in *The Two Gentlemen of Verona* (V, iv, 107 ff.); seven of them in *Richard II* (I, iii, 202 ff.); six of them in *Venus and Adonis* (ll. 773–816), and five in another passage in the same poem (ll. 154–93). There are traces of the same cluster in ten other plays and in *Lucrece*.

Apart from image-clusters appearing in several plays, many other passages in *Edward III* have multiple links with single passages in Shakespeare. The pun on *apparelled* and *suit* (II, i, 410–11) reappears in *As You Like It* (IV, i, 88); and in both contexts the pun is closely followed by a mention of a *solicitor* or *attorney*. A few lines later (418–24), the author of *Edward III* has a passage containing *leprous, die, envenometh, dug, blood*, and *sin*. This may be compared with the speech of the ghost in *Hamlet* (I, v, 64–75), which contains *leperous distilment, blood, milk* (cf. *dug*) and *sin*. In the same scene a reference to Sara (II, i, 254) is followed by allusions to *chaplains, desire, death*, and *marriage*. In *Richard III* (IV, iii, 29–38) a reference to Sara's husband, Abraham, is preceded by a mention of *chaplain* and the other three words.

A few examples may be given of less-extended parallels. The pun on *habit*, whether intentional or not, in the line (I, ii, 146):

> Whose habit rude and manners blunt and playne

may be compared with the juxtaposition in *Hamlet* (I, iv, 29–30):

> by some habit that too much o'er-leavens
> The form of plausive manners;

with that in *Love's Labour's Lost* (V, ii, 365–8), where the same quibble occurs:

> My Lady, to the manner of the days,
> In courtesy gives undeserving praise.
> We four indeed confronted were with four
> In Russian habit;

and with that in *Twelfth Night* (III, iv, 80–1)

> the manner how;...in the habit of some sir of note.

The comparison of a face to a book (IV, iv, 128–9; V, i, 3) and the juxtaposition of *face, matter* and *printed* in the lines (IV, v, 26–8):

> that verie feare in deed,
> Which is so gastly printed in thy face:
> What is the matter?

may be compared with several passages in Shakespeare:

> Although the print be little, the whole matter
> And copy of the father, eye, nose, lip,
> The trick of's frown...   (*Winter's Tale*, II, iii, 98–100)
>
>   Why, what's the matter,
> That you have such a February face...
> Tush, fear not....   (*Much Ado about Nothing*, v, iv, 40–4)

In this passage, as in the third from *Edward III*, the word *fear* is found in the same context. The following lines (IV, iv, 97–8), containing, perhaps, a quibble on *ore*:

> For I will staine my horse quite ore with bloud,
> And double guild my spurs

may be compared with "double gild his treble guilt" (*2 Henry IV*, IV, v, 129), and with Lady Macbeth's determination to gild the faces of the grooms. A description in the same scene of *Edward III* (IV, iv, 20–2):

>   pendants cuff the aire
> And beat the windes, that for their gaudinesse
> Struggles to kisse them

looks forward to a passage in *Macbeth* (I, ii, 49–50):

> Where the Norweyan banners flout the sky
> And fan our people cold

and to the famous description of Cleopatra's first meeting with Antony (II, ii, 197–201):

> Purple the sails, and so perfumed that
> The winds were love-sick with them; the oars were silver,
> Which to the tune of flutes kept stroke, and made
> The water which they beat to follow faster,
> As amorous of their strokes

and here, as in the *Edward III* passage, there is a lavish use of gold and silver.[13]

There remain to be considered the relationship between three Shakespearian plays and *Edward III*. The resemblances between the Countess scenes and the Lady Grey scene in *3 Henry VI* may be due to the fact that the author of *Edward III* was deliberately imitating Shakespeare's early play. The resemblances between the battle scenes of *Edward III* and those of *Henry V* may be explained as the imitation by Shakespeare of a play he had seen, read, or performed.[14] But Angelo's temptation of Isabella offers more substantial grounds for believing that Shakespeare had a hand in the Countess scenes. In both plays a virtuous woman preserves her chastity against the assaults of a ruler. Both heroines attack the abuse of authority. Warwick's 'sentence' about the ape, already quoted above:

> An euill deed, done by authoritie,
> Is sin and subbornation: Decke an Ape
> In tissue, and the beautie of the robe
> Adds but the greater scorne vnto the beast   (*Edward III*, II, i, 443–6)

45

appears to have suggested:

>   proud man,
> Drest in a little brief authority,
> Most ignorant of what he's most assured,
> His glassy essence, like an angry ape,
> Plays such fantastic tricks before high heaven
> As make the angels weep.   (*Measure for Measure*, II, ii, 117–22)

Warwick tells his daughter:

> That sinne doth ten times agreuate it selfe
> That is committed in a holie place

and Angelo asks himself:

> Shall we desire to raze the sanctuary
> And pitch our evils there?

Warwick declares that:

> The freshest summers day doth soonest taint
> The lothed carrion that it seems to kisse:

and Angelo cries:

>   but it is I,
> That, lying by the violet in the sun,
> Do as the carrion does, not as the flower,
> Corrupt with virtuous season.

The Countess speaks of "the dangerous reigne of liberty"; Angelo tells Isabella:

> And now I give my sensual race, the rein   (II, iv, 160)

and Claudio declares that his restraint comes from too much liberty. Finally, the Countess compares counterfeiting coins with adultery:

> He that doth clip or counterfeit your stamp
> Shall die, my Lord; and will your sacred selfe
> Comit high treason against the King of heauen,
> To stamp his Image in forbidden mettel,
> Forgetting your alleagance and your othe?   (II, i, 255–9)

Angelo similarly declares:

>   It were as good
> To pardon him that hath from nature stolen
> A man already made, as to remit
> Their saucy sweetness, that do coin heaven's image
> In stamps that are forbid.   (II, iv, 42–6)

Of this last parallel Swinburne declared that "men of Shakespeare's stamp...do not thus repeat themselves". Certainly Shakespeare, having written the *Measure for Measure* passage, would not later produce the inferior version of *Edward III*; but if, as is generally agreed, the passage in *Edward III* was written first, it would be in accordance with Shakespeare's usual custom for him to refine on a passage he had written earlier. Hundreds of examples could be given of similar recurrences in plays whose authenticity no one disputes; and in nearly every case the second version is more pregnant and impressive than the first. Sometimes, as here, the earlier passage reveals the process by which Shakespeare evolved the later image. In the same way the speeches of Audley and Prince Edward seem to contain the germ of the Duke's great speech (III, i) and of Claudio's reply:

> For, from the instant we begin to liue
> We do pursue and hunt the time to die:...
> If, then, we hunt for death, why do we feare it?...
> I will not giue a pennie for a lyfe,...
> Since for to liue is but to seeke to die,
> And dying but beginning of new lyfe.   (IV, iv, 135 ff.)

>   merely, thou art death's fool;
> For him thou labour'st by thy flight to shun,
> And yet runn'st toward him still...
> To sue to live, I find I seek to die;
> And, seeking death, find life.   (III, i, 11 ff.)

Of course, even if these parallels are valid, Shakespeare might conceivably be echoing and improving on a play by another dramatist, in which perhaps he had himself acted. But if this were so, it would be unique in his career; for even where he was using a play as a direct source, as he did in writing *King Lear*, there are comparatively few verbal echoes.

The tests we have applied to *Edward III* are not, perhaps, conclusive. Hart's two vocabulary tests indicate that the whole play may have been written by Shakespeare. The presence of iterative imagery tends to show that the play was written by Shakespeare, or by some dramatist unknown;[15] and its distribution in the different scenes suggests, but does not prove, that the hand of Shakespeare is more apparent in the Countess scenes and IV, iv than in the rest of the play. The presence of image-clusters is one of the strongest arguments for Shakespeare's authorship, and most of these are in the scenes usually ascribed to Shakespeare. Other parallels to which attention has been called show that the author of *Edward III* seems to have possessed some of Shakespeare's characteristic mannerisms. The resemblances between the play and *Henry V* and *Measure for Measure* show that if Shakespeare was not the author, he was at least intimately acquainted with, and deeply influenced by, *Edward III*. One theory which would cover all the facts is that Shakespeare, as in *Pericles*, was hastily revising a play by another dramatist, certain scenes being entirely rewritten and the remainder being left with comparatively few alterations.[16]

NOTES

1. *The Shakespeare Apocrypha* (1908; ed. 1929), pp. xx–xxiii.
2. *The Cambridge History of English Literature*, v, p. 246.
3. *Journal of English and Germanic Philology*, x (1911), 90–104.
4. *Modern Language Review*, vi (1911), 511–13.

5. *William Shakespeare* (1930), I, p. 515.

6. *Shakespeare and the Homilies* (1934), pp. 219–41.

7. *A Study of Shakespeare* (1879; ed. 1918), pp. 231–75.

8. Swinburne illustrates the incompetence of the author by the phrase "helly spout of blood", which is certainly a misprint for "Hellespont of blood". Some of Swinburne's arguments fall to the ground if it is accepted that *Measure for Measure* was written after *Edward III*, for the author of the latter play could not have imitated an unwritten play of Shakespeare's. The real problem is whether Shakespeare was echoing his own work only or that of another dramatist.

9. The following tests seem not very conclusive: The average number of words used in five of Shakespeare's Histories is not very different from the average number of words used in three of Marlowe's plays, and neither average is very different from the number used in *Edward III*. The percentage of vocabularies common to *Edward III* and to five of Shakespeare's Histories ranges from 51·7 to 56·4. The percentage common to *Edward III* and to two of Marlowe's plays is 47·4 and 45·4. The percentage common to four pairs of Shakespeare's Histories ranges from 50·9 to 59; the percentage common to two pairs of Marlowe's plays ranges from 50 to 58·5. The use of certain prefixes and suffixes ranges from 28 (per 100 lines) to 36 in five of Shakespeare's Histories, 24 to 31 in three of Marlowe's plays, and the figure is 36 for *Edward III*.

10. Caroline Spurgeon apparently left no notes on the play.

11. Cf. Kenneth Muir, 'The Uncomic Pun', *The Cambridge Journal*, May 1950.

12. *Shakespeare's Imagination* (1946), p. 184.

13. Cf. also the following: I, ii, 78–80 and *King Lear*, II, iii, 11 ff. (*faceless-outface, weather-winds, bare arms*); III, ii, 56–71 and *King John*, II, i, 227–41 (*tread, march, fire, reeking-smoke, son, wives, cities*); I, i, 44–6 and *Hamlet*, V, ii, 266–8 (*fiery, ignorance, rakt-stick*); I, i, 67 (*occasion laughes*) and *Hamlet*, I, iii, 54 (*occasion smiles*); IV, iv, 9 (*eielesse terror of all ending night*) and *King John*, V, vi, 12 (*eyeless night*). Parallels with the *Sonnets* and early plays have been omitted as they might be imitations by the author of *Edward III*.

14. Cf. M. C. Bradbrook, *Shakespeare and Elizabethan Poetry* (1951), p. 209; E. Phipson, *New Shakespere Society Transactions* (1889), pp. *58 ff. and Kittredge's notes on the following passages in *Henry V*: I, i, 43–4; I, ii, 245; II, iv, 57; III, vii, 163; IV, Prologue, 26.

15. S. R. Golding, *Notes and Queries*, CLIV, 313, argues that *Edward III* was written by the same author as *A Larum for London*; but only one of his parallels (III, i, 26–7, 123–4; *A Larum*, 180 ff.) is at all impressive, and may be explained as the imitation of one dramatist by the other.

16. For many of the parallels quoted in this article I am indebted to a comprehensive collection placed at my disposal by Louise Eickhoff. V. Østerberg, in his *Gravinden af Salisbury og Marina* (Copenhagen, 1926), argues by means of a large number of parallel passages that the Countess scenes are by Shakespeare. He suggests that it would be odd for Shakespeare to have gone on echoing these scenes all his life if he had not himself written them. The most striking of the parallels, however, are with poems and plays which may have been written before *Edward III*. I am indebted to Mr H. A. Koefoed for a summary of Østerberg's arguments.

ON PRODUCING *HENRY VI*

BY

SIR BARRY JACKSON

[The Birmingham Repertory Theatre produced *2 Henry VI* on 3 April 1951, and *3 Henry VI* on 1 April 1952. The latter was taken to the Old Vic on 21 July 1952. *Editor.*]

Over a lengthy period of playgoing it is inevitable that certain productions of the classics make more lasting effect than others. This may be due to superlative rendering or, and I think more probably, the frame of mind of the spectator, who by some chance happens to be in a receptive key or mood to receive the play's message. Of the whole chronological sequence of Shakespeare's histories given at Stratford-upon-Avon by F. R. Benson in 1906, it was the unknown Second Part of *King Henry VI* that made the greatest impression on my mind. To see all the histories in succession was the experience of a lifetime, and, under present conditions, very unlikely to be repeated. Benson and his company had all the histories excepting the three parts of *Henry VI* in their repertoire: no existing company of artists can claim so much, and it was of unimaginable help in presenting the entire cycle to have only the Trilogy to rehearse and prepare from scratch. To embark upon the project with a blank sheet would prove a superhuman task. Nowadays, the only practical method, as with Benson, would be to build up the histories over a course of years with a permanent company. As modern theatrical activities are, in the main, opposed to team work, the chances of ever witnessing the entire chronology in order must remain beyond possibility.

Ambition is inherent to all of us, and my own is that the Birmingham Repertory Theatre shall share with the Shakespeare Memorial Theatre and Old Vic the honour and duty of having given its public the whole Shakespearian canon. During its thirty-eight years, the number presented at the Birmingham Repertory Theatre is now twenty-seven, many of which have had more than one production. The conditions of the theatre, an intimate-sized auditorium with a company of young artists, who make up in zest and loyalty for what they may lack in their more publicized comrades, is to me the ideal line of attack required for the poet's plays. They all demand youthful vigour and drive. Some of the subtleties, the results of age and experience, may be missing, but I willingly sacrifice these for forthright exposition. There comes a time when subtleties of production and star mannerisms grow to such proportion that the main theme vanishes into oblivion. When all is said and done, the plays were written at speed and speedily put before their public. That the lines have such profound significance is the accident of sheer inspiration. It has been my good fortune to hear some of the most famous of bygone actors in their interpretation of Hamlet. Every possible shade of thought was expressed. All that was lacking was the author's explicit direction that Hamlet was an undergraduate and, in appearance, precisely like Rosencrantz and Guildenstern. The tragedy had become a vehicle for the exploitation of an artist of quality and no longer the unfolding of the interplay of passionate story-telling— that inherent demand of the public which is the magical touchstone of the drama in all its diverse forms.

Here we have the main reason for the neglect of the Trilogy. That the work is ill-shaped, lacking the cohesion brought of practice, a spate of events viewed from a wide angle, may be added cause for neglect, but there is little doubt in my mind that the basic reason is the omission of one or two star roles and the inclusion of a number of interesting ones. Typical is the fact that when Charles Kean decided to present the play he seized upon one character, the Duke of York, extracted everything appertaining to that one role, making it a 'star' part, and pieced the various bits together in the hope of moulding one complete historical play in which he alone could shine. The result, as might be expected, was dire failure, as indeed I think must be the fate of any attempt, no matter how skilful, to boil down or condense the Trilogy for dramatic presentation.

The dissection of the text and the implication that it is not entirely Shakespeare's I must leave to the scholars in their cloistered nooks, but what is as clear as daylight from the practical view of stage production is that the author was a dramatist of the first rank, though perhaps immature. If the author was not Shakespeare, I can only regret that the writer in question did not give us more examples of his genius. In short, *Henry VI* is eminently actable.

Whilst Charles Kean detected the importance of the incidents connected with York, why has no major actress ever discovered the tremendous character of Margaret of Anjou, surely one of the greatest feminine roles in the whole gallery? In quantity, if not in quality, she surpasses her direct successor, Lady Macbeth, who has no such torrents of venomous rhetoric with its reiteration of simile to the tempestuous sea. (Incidentally, do not these references, so different from any previous ones, hint at Shakespeare's personal knowledge of the equinoctial gales at sea?) Margaret emerges as a gigantic character and her appearance to curse again in *Richard III* is made a hundredfold more comprehensible with the knowledge of her place in the forerunning plays. It is by no means easy to imagine the groundlings accepting her railings in *Richard III* without any clue to the reasons which inspired them. And then there is the slight reference in Part III to Warwick's daughter, the Lady Anne, who becomes so important in the later play. It is dubious whether the ordinary playgoer of to-day, seeing *Richard III*, knows whose burial rites she is attending. I mention these two instances to suggest that the original audiences were made aware of the Plantagenet sequence as a whole.

The histories, other than the Trilogy, are fairly well known. It has fallen to the lot of the Birmingham Repertory Theatre with its limited—in some views, fortunately limited—resources to revive interest in Parts II and III after too many years of neglect, years in which the main concern with the plays has been the question of authorship in scholarly circles. The experiment, as I have already indicated, proved beyond doubt that the author was a dramatist of no mean stature. The primary duty of the playwright, to portray events to his audience and show the reaction of his characters to such events, is demonstrated again and again. It is in incidents known to the spectator, but unknown to the characters, that the attraction of drama lies. In preparing the texts of *2* and *3 Henry VI* for modern performance, certain practical and, indeed, physical aspects have to be taken into consideration. An audience can become at least physically, if not mentally, wearied if it is asked to sit much longer than an hour or so. Intervals are, therefore, essential, as presumably they were in the poet's day, though present-day technique of breaking the thread of a play with an eye to eager anticipation has also to be considered when fixing them. In Part II, the limitations of the Birmingham Repertory Theatre enforced one interval after

PLATE I

A. *Henry VI, Part III*, Birmingham Repertory Theatre, 1952.
Production by DOUGLAS SEALE; Setting by FINLAY JAMES.
"WHY WHISPER YOU, MY LORDS, AND ANSWER NOT?"

B. The Henry E. Huntington Library and Art Gallery

PLATE II

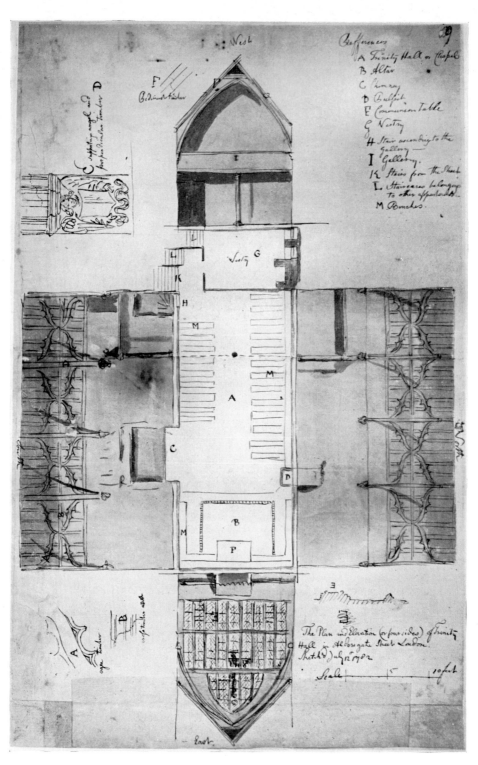

Plan and Elevation of Trinity Hall, Aldersgate-street, London.

Act III, scene iii, the death of Beaufort, and, regretfully, following Act IV, scene i. To have opened the latter half with the execution of Suffolk would have entailed a much larger company of players than the theatre could afford. Beyond the omission of this scene, no drastic alterations were necessary. In Part III, the sequence of short scenes, including the fights—so baffling to all producers—which form the greater part of Act IV, were blue-pencilled and some lesser passages omitted. Regardless of such cuts and excluding the usual interval times, Part II played for 2 hours and 43 minutes, and Part III for 2 hours and 41 minutes, despite the intimate character of the theatre. The conveyance of sound in a large auditorium always takes longer than in a smaller. I repeat, the impact of Shakespearian drama in an intimate house is intensified beyond belief.

Although Shakespeare was too experienced a man of the theatre to make demands which cannot be fulfilled, the histories offer a few puzzles to the modern stage. The greatest of these problems is the presentation of the endless "alarms, excursions and battles". I have little doubt that originally these were very rough and ready affairs as the apology for "the vasty fields of France" in *Henry V* denotes. But as the artists, like all men of their time, were accustomed to the use of weapons, the duels must have been exhibitions of skill, a tradition that appears to have obtained up to the early nineteenth century. On the presentation of battles, there is much to be said for the small stage, since the bigger the acting area the more unwieldly the problem. Numbers, inevitably limited in any case, merely add to the complications. The disposal of the fallen, too, is no easy matter; so the fewer the better. Decapitations are best committed to the shadows, though in the Cade scenes of Part II, the stage direction respecting the head of Lord Say being brought in adds considerably to the dramatic tension. Nevertheless, as with the battles, the line between the risible and the serious is of such infinitesimal breadth that the reaction of the audience can never be foretold. Part III contains two stage directions which created problems for the producer. Although the author directs that York shall be crowned with a paper crown, there is not the slightest indication as to its origin. Paper crowns are not usually part of the impedimenta of battlefields. Where and how was it obtained? Eventually, the producer, Douglas Seale (the Wakefield scenes having been drawn into one) gave young Rutland an accompanying boy jester wearing a paper crown. The boy is killed at the same time as Rutland and, his body being left on the stage, Margaret takes the crown from his head. The other direction is the entrance of a son who has killed his father and a father who has killed his son. Though we know that family cleavages of such a tragic nature occurred in Germany during our own life-time and that the parricides were not even accidental, Shakespeare's directions, when read, easily raise a smile. Rather than run the risk of a laugh in the audience, we discussed omitting the incident altogether. The poet's infallible intuition, however, proved right. The scene was retained, but treated as a static tableau: it shone out away and above the violent episodes with which it is surrounded and threw more light on the horror of civil war than all the scenes of wasteful bloodshed. The still figures of the father and son speaking quietly and unemotionally, as though voicing the thoughts that strike the saintly, sad King's conscience, presented a moment of calm and terrible reflection. The final scene also presented a problem. It is a very sketchy affair on which to end an almost melodramatic play. In an effort to strengthen it and, at the same time, to hint at things to come, after Edward's final couplet ending: "And here I hope begins our lasting joy", Richard was left on the stage to deliver the first lines of the opening soliloquy of Richard III, his voice being finally submerged by the fanfares and bells marking his brother's supposedly permanent triumph.

Perhaps the most important aspect of staging the Trilogy is the textual arrangement. We admit that cuts are essential so that the conventions of timing, required and expected by modern audiences, can be fulfilled. My own experience proves that having made such deletions as are deemed necessary, the proposed acting text should be submitted to a mind trained in academic study. Such approval will prevent irreparable blunders which can only draw obloquy on the producer's head. This has been a personal rule throughout my career, and guidance and advice have always been forthcoming, service for which I now record most grateful thanks. A young producer should be wary of incurring academic wrath by high-handed treatment of the classical works. The scholars will always respond with enthusiasm; they will never let him down and he will avoid many pitfalls.

The neglect of the Trilogy in present-day performance may well be due to a not infrequently expressed opinion that the public has little interest in the Shakespearian histories beyond those affording star roles. The rarity of revivals of Parts II and III may possibly account for the undeniable success achieved with the Birmingham public and those who came from afar to witness them. There is small doubt in my mind, however, that other revivals will follow elsewhere. How their undeniable theatricality has escaped attention is as perplexing as it is surprising, but I myself and my company at Birmingham regard it as an honour to have rescued at least these two plays from what was seemingly oblivion.

THE HUNTINGTON LIBRARY

BY

GODFREY DAVIES

The Huntington Library is dedicated to the study of Anglo-American civilization. Outside its chosen fields it is confined in the main to works which a scholar concentrating in one of these fields may wish to consult in order to learn what was happening elsewhere or at other times. For the Middle Ages it has no more than a fair representation of the original and secondary materials, though the presence of sets like *Acta Sanctorum* compensates to some extent for the absence of many smaller works. The purchase of the late T. F. Tout's books provided a good, working library for the medievalist. Though the Library contains the largest number of individual titles (but not of volumes) of incunabula in any collection in the Americas (listed in *Incunabula in the Huntington Library* by H. R. Mead, 1937), and has several thousand books in European languages, it is comparatively weak in Continental works. In general, the Continental authors represented, often by translations, are those known to have influenced Anglo-Saxondom.

The Library's great strength develops with the Renaissance and, so far as Great Britain is concerned, declines gradually after 1641 until 1800. After the latter date there are, for English literature, many first editions of classics and much correspondence of their writers, together with some authors' manuscripts. For English history there are the standard works and lives and letters of foreign secretaries and diplomats concerned with Anglo-American relations, together with a fair sampling of the descriptions of the United States written by English travellers. American history and literature are very strongly represented until about 1900, after which time the concentration is upon the Southwest to the comparative neglect of the rest of the United States.

The Founder,[1] Henry Edwards Huntington (1850–1927), was a self-made man. His only formal education was at local, private schools. By choice he started at the bottom of the ladder as a porter in an ironmonger's in New York, but his industry earned him promotion within a few days. His uncle, the famous railway magnate, Collis P. Huntington, entrusted him with several enterprises of increasing importance, the last taking him to the Pacific coast where his eagle eye detected the great future of southern California. He settled there in 1902, constructed an inter-urban, electric railway system, reorganized the Los Angeles street railways, and engaged in many other business enterprises in the vicinity while retaining and increasing his interests in the East. He is said to have sat on sixty boards of directors. Between 1908 and 1910 he gradually 'retired', though he could never divest himself of all responsibility for the management of his many businesses. From 1910 onward he had for the first time an opportunity to devote himself wholeheartedly to other interests he had long cherished, as his early purchases of books and pictures prove. At his estate in San Marino he created botanical gardens, an art gallery and a library, to-day collectively known as 'Henry E. Huntington Library and Art Gallery' or, for short, 'The Huntington Library'. All three have an international reputation, but this article is restricted to the third.

Naturally, the Founder, when becoming a collector after forty years' experience of business methods, employed them to enable him quickly to accumulate what he wanted. He made *en bloc* purchases to an extent to justify the phrase, "a collection of collections or a library of libraries". In addition to buying whole libraries already formed he not infrequently bought up all the lots to be offered for sale at auction. A hundred of these *en bloc* purchases are described in the first issue of the *Huntington Library Bulletin* (1931) by George Sherburn, assisted by the staff. An account of the separate lots bought at auctions—which, taken together, sometimes rivalled in importance the leading *en bloc* purchases—is yet to be written. Nearly twenty-five thousand items were bought at four hundred auctions. Many individual items were called to Huntington's attention by their owners, or, more often, discovered in catalogues and acquired.

For Shakespeariana, the four most important purchases were the Church, Devonshire, Halsey and Bridgewater. The library of Elihu Dwight Church was Huntington's first really extensive acquisition, and was very rich in early editions of Shakespeare, including twelve Folios and thirty-seven Quartos, mostly Locker Lampson copies, and of Spenser and Milton. George Watson Cole, when employed by Church, prepared an elaborate catalogue of the 2,133 items in seven volumes, of which two are devoted to English literature. The Devonshire purchase was the most notable of all so far as the drama is concerned.[2] The sixth Duke of Devonshire (1790–1858) had bought from the actor, John Philip Kemble, some 3,500 to 4,000 plays and ninety-two volumes of playbills. The Duke added to the collection so that it contained over 7,500 plays and 111 volumes of play-bills (for about a third of the play-bills see *Drury Lane Calendar* by Dougald MacMillan; the Covent Garden play-bills are not yet listed). Of the plays, about 700 were printed before 1641, 950 before 1701, 1,200 before 1751, 2,200 before 1801, and 2,500 before the Duke's death. Shakespeare is represented by four Folios and fifty-seven Quartos, including the first and second Quartos of *Hamlet*, dated 1603 and 1604 respectively. Kemble dismembered most of his plays, inlaid each leaf in a sheet of paper, and then had them rebound, half a dozen to a volume. Huntington had the volumes of the more valuable plays broken up, and the plays rebound individually by Macdonald in morocco.

Frederick Robert Halsey had amassed some twenty thousand volumes, including rarities of nearly all the notable English writers from Shakespeare (Folios and Quartos) to Stevenson.

The Bridgewater House Library was originally founded by Sir Thomas Egerton (for whom see p. 59 below). A great patron of men of letters, Egerton, during his long career, had many works dedicated to him and received many presentation copies from authors who were, or who hoped to be, under obligations to him. Unfortunately, there is no sign that Shakespeare was one of them, but he was represented by four Folios (of which three were retained) and many Quartos, including a *Titus Andronicus* of 1600. There are also rarities of most of the Elizabethan and Jacobean dramatists. Milton's minor works are almost complete. A virtue of the Bridgewater items is that many of them passed straight from their authors or printers into the hands of the Egertons and then, without ever running the hazards of the auction room or bookseller's shop, to Huntington.[3]

The Library has many association copies of famous men. One of the most charming is Ben Jonson's *Seianus His Fall* (London, 1605) which has on its front fly-leaf: "To my perfect Freind, Mr. Francis Crane I erect this Altar of Freindship And leave it as the eternall witnesse of my Love. Ben: Jonson." Then follow four lines of Latin "Hic est Ben Jonson...F[rancis] M[undy]". On the title-page to John Selden's *Jani Anglorum Facies Altera* (London, 1610) appears in Jonson's hand: "*Tanquam explorator Sui Ben Jonsonii Liber ex dono Autoris mihi chariss.*"

Two items testify to the Earl of Bridgewater's interest in music. Thomas Ravenscroft inscribed on the front fly-leaf of his *Brief discourse . . . on measureable music*: "To the honorable knight Sir John Egerton", and added twelve lines praising the recipient for his love of music and his bounty to a "poor brother of mine". Henry Lawes signed a copy of Francis Beaumont's *Poems* (London, 1640) which he presented to the Earl. John Smith, presenting a copy of his *General History of Virginia* (London, 1624) to the company of Cordwainers of London, took the opportunity to insert a full-page inscription soliciting their aid for his colonizing enterprises. William Wycherley gave Swift in 1709[4] a copy of *The Plain Dealer* (London, 1700), bound with three others of his plays, and wrote in it "For my worthy, Learned and most Ingenious Friend, Dr. J. Swift, from his humble servant, W. Wycherley".

The practice of *en bloc* purchases prevented any narrow specialization even had Huntington been so disposed, which he was not. There was a danger that he might be tempted to try to make a corner in some rarities inasmuch as the collectors whose books he bought had often each purchased the same book in the same edition. No sign that he contemplated such a step has ever come to light. Instead, he had his several copies carefully collated and if they proved identical decided which one to retain. The others, with very few exceptions, were disposed of by auction. It is a striking tribute to those responsible for the collating, often in a hurry, that very few books were let go that have since been discovered not to be duplicates. At one time a printed catalogue of the Library was contemplated. Under Cole's supervision, Lodewyk Bendikson, C. K. Edmonds and Herman R. Mead, the last-named still happily a member of the staff, compiled descriptions of many of the early English books on 5×8 in. cards, which are still worth consulting because they contain information not on the official catalogue cards.

When Huntington began to form his library, he was primarily interested in collectors' items, but he became more and more interested in the search for background material. From about 1917 he began to buy on a large scale books and manuscripts which reflected every side of life in his chosen fields. Ecclesiastical, economic, literary, political, scientific, and social history—in fact every subject that contributed to the advancement of civilization—was now included in the scope of his collecting. The very fine collection of Elizabethan music is described in *Catalogue of Music in the Huntington Library Printed Before 1801*, by Edythe N. Backus (1949).

After the Founder's death, there were three main tasks. The first was cataloguing, because hitherto the chief energies of the staff had been absorbed in aiding Huntington to select collections and single books for purchase. The decision was made to replace the 5×8 in. cards by Library of Congress cards when available and, when they were not, to use cards conformable in size, 3×5 in., and in content. The second was to form a reference library. Huntington realized the need for one but left its formation to the future. "Others will do that after I am gone", he said. "My interest is in collecting those things that others might not get." The heavy burden has been mainly borne by Leslie E. Bliss, first associated with Huntington in 1915 and appointed librarian in 1926. Much assistance, however, was given by Max Farrand, the first director, members of the research group and the Library staff, fellows and visiting scholars. The results of this united effort have been most gratifying, if reliance can be placed upon the testimony of scholars who know the Library best. There are still gaps, of course, but these are caused more often by failure to find desiderata than by ignorance of the need for them. That the scholar generally finds ready at hand the reference works he needs is rather surprising and proves that they have been chosen carefully, because they are relatively few in number. On 30 June 1950 there were in the reference library 12,215 works classified as English history and 11,620 as English literature. The total number of volumes in the library a few months ago was 181,140 rare books and 133,140 reference books. Within its boundaries, the Library is exceptionally well equipped with bibliographies, guides and auction and booksellers' catalogues. It has also a fine representation of books that show the development of printing. It has copies of about one-third[5] of the books printed by Caxton, including his first edition of the *Canterbury Tales* (1478), and all but a few of those from the Merrymount Press (and most of the latter's ephemera), and choice examples of the output of very many other famous printers.

The third task was to supplement the source material already in the Library. To the extent of about three hundred titles it has been possible to add first or early editions of books printed before 1641, but many more, nearly two thousand, have been secured by the aid of the camera. So far as English books printed before 1641 are concerned the policy was early adopted of trying to secure in one form or another—original, reprint, photostat, or film—every item that a scholar may be reasonably expected to need. In particular, hundreds of photostats have in many cases completed an author's bibliography to this degree, that at least one version of everything he is known to have written is in the Library. The same method has been applied to selected subjects for which good bibliographies exist. The most striking success is in the drama. The Library is believed to have a copy in some form of every play known to have been printed in England before 1800, and it has, in the Larpent collection, for the eighteenth and early nineteenth century, a number never printed. The rule has been to build to strength first and then to attend to weaknesses. Certain types of literature have rarely become collectors' items, so they sometimes escaped Huntington. Nevertheless, some of them are of the first importance for a study of civilization. Character and conduct books, encyclopaedias, scientific or pseudo-scientific treatises, etc., have all been eagerly sought during the past twenty years. Practically all the astronomical, astrological, and medical works listed in the *Short-Title Catalogue of Books Printed in England, Scotland, & Ireland, 1475–1640*, compiled by A. W. Pollard and G. R. Redgrave, are present in one form or another, but the record is not so good for herbals and other botanical items. Religious treatises and sermons which used to form so high a percentage of the output of presses have been secured in large numbers, particularly those recognized as presenting a social philosophy or supplying biographical and historical data. Sermons preached at Paul's Cross or before the Long Parliament, or commemorating the Gunpowder Plot or the execution of Charles I are especially well represented.

A problem that confronts all research libraries is whether to rest content with one edition of a book or to seek others, especially those published in an author's lifetime and presumably embodying his successive revisions. To adopt the second alternative for all authors would be beyond the resources both in money and space of any institution. Therefore, a selection has to be made. Two books at least choose themselves—the Bible and *Mr. William Shakespeare's Comedies, Histories and Tragedies*. Of the 290 complete Bibles listed in the *Short-Title Catalogue* the Library has eighty-seven, including all the main editions, plus six not in the *Short-Title Catalogue*. The Shakespeare Folios are discussed below. In general, the selection is based on the intrinsic importance to scholars of individual authors and their works. As a rule the Library does not try to secure issues that vary only in minor typographical details, but recognizes that when important works have significant alterations from edition to edition all editions should be secured. An example is *The Mirror for Magistrates* which was completely transformed between 1559 and 1610. When Lily B. Campbell compiled her two volumes—*The Mirror for Magistrates* and *Parts Added to The Mirror for Magistrates* by John Higgins and Thomas Blenerhasset—she found ready at hand all the editions and made her collations without having to look beyond the Library's resources. Other examples are Camden's *Annals* of which the Library has all the editions in the *Short-Title Catalogue* except the issue of 1634 and his *Britannia*, of which only the first (1586) is lacking. To compensate, there are the two editions edited by Edmund Gilson (1695 and 1722) and by Richard Gough (1789 and 1806). As to Sir Richard Baker's *Chronicle of the Kings of England*, originally published in 1643, the continuation by Edward Phillips is so important for the Restoration that an edition after 1660 is essential. Inasmuch as it was continued from time to time, with corrections, all editions down to the last (1733) are being acquired. While all the editions of Defoe's *Tour* are being picked up as opportunity offers, all editions of the novels published before his death have not been sought, inasmuch as the alterations seem to be stylistic only.

A more difficult problem of selection is presented by a voluminous writer like Thomas Dekker. Of the sixty-six items in the *Short-Title Catalogue* the Library lacks a baker's dozen. It has no copy of *Britannia's Honor*, so a photostat is being acquired, but it has at least one edition of all other items, plus *The Black Rod and the White Rod*, which is not in the *Short-Title Catalogue*. The question whether photostats should be obtained of all the rest not in the Library was difficult to answer, so recourse was had to F. P. Wilson, who studied the Library's holdings for his eagerly awaited edition of Dekker's prose works. His advice was that eight only of the missing issues should be acquired in order to have all the Dekker a scholar is likely to need. It has been followed. Other examples of the possibility of including all the editions that might be needed are: Ben Jonson, of which six of thirty-seven entries in the *Short-Title Catalogue* are lacking; Middleton, nine lacking out of thirty-six; and Beaumont and Fletcher, one first edition only missing. Massinger presents no problem because the Library has all fourteen entries.

The following statistics serve to define more exactly than generalizations the present position, although inevitably in a Library that is always growing the figures are slightly out of date. Of the 26,000 numbered items listed in the *Short-Title Catalogue*, the Library has slightly more than 40 per cent.[6] But, if titles only are considered, and if photostats are included, the Library has at least 50 per cent of the 17,000 titles in the *Short-Title Catalogue*. Mary Isabel Fry, Reference Librarian, checked the proof sheets of the *Short-Title Catalogue, 1641–1700*, compiled by Donald Wing for the American Index Society, and found that the Library had 15,686 originals and 931 film or photostat copies of the 72,204 items listed. As the checking was spread over ten years the figures are naturally out of date, and another thousand or more should be added to the Library's holdings.

A test of the dramatic holdings is provided by a check of Sir Walter Greg's *A Bibliography of the English Printed Drama*, Vol. I, to 1616. Of the 349 plays and masques listed, 311 are in the Library in some edition mentioned in the Bibliography, most of the thirty-eight lacking being the very early items. However, these are all available either in photostat or reprint.

The Huntington Library's holdings of the early editions of the separately or collectively printed works of Shakespeare can be ascertained from the *Short-Title Catalogue* or the two volumes of Henrietta C. Bartlett—*A Census of Shakespeare's Plays in Quarto, 1594–1709* (1916, with

A. W. Pollard, and 1939, alone) and *Mr. William Shakespeare* (1922). Therefore, they are not listed here, though a few samples are cited to show how strong the Huntington Library is in Shakespeariana. Of the poems there are the following editions: *Venus and Adonis*, nos. 2, 5 (unique and in the original binding), and 10; *Lucrece*, nos. 1, 4–8 (the last having the engraving); *The Passionate Pilgrime*, no. 2; *Loves Martyr*, no. 1; *Sonnets*, no. 1 (both the Aspley and the Wright imprints); and *Poems*, no. 1. The plays are even better represented. The Library has the first quartos of all the plays published separately with the exception of *Titus Andronicus*. To compensate for this omission it has one of the two known copies of no. 2 and a copy of no. 3. This is a collection unsurpassed even by the British Museum. But the holdings are by no means restricted to firsts. Take the most popular play, *Hamlet*, for which there are all the first nine editions (though only one of the two issues of no. 9) and the 'Bornardo' and 'Barnardo' editions of nos. 10 and 11. *Richard II* lacks no. 3 only, but *Richard III* has all eight. The record is equally good for the plays which appeared separately only late in the seventeenth century. *Julius Caesar* is an example. The Library has all the six editions published from 1684 to 1691. Of the Folios the Library has four firsts, including the Bridgewater copy in a contemporary binding. Two leaves are missing, and seven leaves were added from a small copy. Among the ten seconds (including all the various imprints) is the famous, or infamous, Perkins copy with the forged John Payne Collier manuscript notes. Inasmuch as many of the third Folios perished in the Fire of London, the Library is fortunate to have seven. Of the fourth Folio there are eight.

As to the spurious plays, the Library has most in Miss Bartlett's list, but not first editions of *Faire Em* and *Thomas, Lord Cromwell*, and no edition of *Cupid's Cabinet Unlocked* (if this collection of poems can be classed as a play whether spurious or not). Of the adaptations two editions are missing—the first issue of Davenant's *Macbeth* (1674), though the Library possesses the second issue of the same date, and Garrick's *Florizel and Perdita* (1762), though it has the 1758 edition which evaded Miss Bartlett's vigilance. That learned lady listed eighty-nine source books, of which the Library has nearly eighty, but these are not all first editions. It does have, however, a unique copy of the second edition of Arthur Brooke's *Romeus and Juliet* and of the first edition of *The Taming of a Shrew*, as well as the second and third, and all the editions of *The Troublesome Reign of King John*.

Among the Shakespeariana are two copies of the second edition of *The First Part of the Contention*, 1600. The two copies—Bridgewater and Kemble-Devonshire—differ only in signature B. The outer form (B1^r, B2^v, B3^r and B4^v) in the Bridgewater copy has twenty-one proof corrections, all of which with one exception are to be found in the corrected state in the Kemble-Devonshire copy. Facsimiles of the relevant pages and a note by Tucker Brooke are to be found in the *Huntington Library Bulletin*, no. 2 (1931). Whereas for eighteenth- and nineteenth-century writers the Library usually has the first editions and modern sets, with little in between, for Shakespeare it has most of the various editions from Nicholas Rowe's onward, but a fair sample only of those of the present day. The Library has numerous critical studies of Shakespeare by English and American writers, but relatively few by foreign scholars. The same is true, *mutatis mutandis*, of periodicals devoted to history and literature.

The manuscript source material in the Huntington Library for the pre-Shakespearian period can be conveniently grouped into two categories, archives and codices. The archives are almost wholly to be found in four large collections: the Battle Abbey muniments, and the Ellesmere,

Hastings and Stowe collections. These contain a total of 5,300 deeds, 270 court rolls, 480 account rolls, and 95 rentals for the period. The largest localized groups are for Wotton-Underwood, Buckinghamshire, in the Stowe Collection, 650 deeds of the thirteenth to fifteenth centuries, and twenty-five years of court rolls; and for Battle Abbey, Sussex, 720 deeds, plus 240 in two cartularies, 440 account rolls, 80 court rolls on 362 sheets, and 23 rentals. Attached to these deeds are many examples of royal seals, and a few unique specimens. Comparatively, it is believed that the medieval English archival material in the Huntington Library is more extensive and more important than that held by any other library outside of England.

There are 190 codices from the eleventh to the fifteenth centuries. Among them are twenty-seven Bibles and sixty-three Books of Hours, several of which are notable for their illuminations, including a Jean Bourdichon, a Simon Marmion, the 'Prince of Miniaturists' to his contemporaries, and Gerard David. The outstanding group is the forty-seven manuscript volumes in Middle English, again the largest and most important collection of such manuscripts existing outside of England. Owing to the custom of writing several texts in one volume, there are actually 140 catalogue entries for the Middle English manuscripts. The finest of early English literary manuscripts is the Chaucer *Canterbury Tales* in the Ellesmere Collection, containing the equestrian portrait of the author, and drawings of all the other pilgrims. Three holograph manuscripts are: John Capgrave's still unpublished Life of Saint Norbert, dated 1440, the only known manuscript of this work; and two volumes of verse by Thomas Hoccleve, one of Chaucer's most devoted admirers. Among noteworthy items are the unique manuscript of the Towneley Plays; four manuscripts of Piers Plowman (two B and two C texts);[7] four of the *Prick of Conscience* (from one of which type was set for a printed edition unknown to bibliographers); texts by Lydgate, Hilton, Mandeville, Richard Rolle, Love, Wycliffe, and a manuscript from the fifteenth-century lending library of John Shirley, another ardent admirer of Chaucer.

For the Elizabethan period and up to 1640, the manuscript material is to be found mainly in the four large English collections mentioned above. Letters, accounts, deeds and papers of various kinds relating to land predominate. Shakespeare's county of Warwick, where the Temple family bought land in Burton Dassett about 1555, is well represented in the Stowe collection. In addition to the 150 deeds there are 1,200 documents about law suits in Warwickshire, and much related correspondence. A letter of about 1631 from Sir Thomas Temple to his factor Harry Rose, instructing him to get cuttings from the vines at Shakespeare's house, New Place, in Stratford-on-Avon, then occupied by John Hall, the dramatist's son-in-law, was published in the *Huntington Library Bulletin*, no. 1 (1931).

The correspondence and other papers of the Temples have survived in sufficient quantity to provide ample material for reconstructing the life of an Elizabethan family. The activities of Peter and Sir Thomas Temple, founders of the family fortune, were investigated by the late Edwin F. Gay, and his conclusions published in the *Huntington Library Quarterly*.

A collection of greater literary and political importance came from the Bridgewater House Library. The Library was founded by Sir Thomas Egerton, Attorney-General, 1592, Master of the Rolls, 1594–1603, Lord Keeper, 1596, and Lord Chancellor, 1603. It contains his personal papers along with many of an official nature, the legal material being especially extensive. Over 12,000 documents and letters are in the collection; about 210 volumes; and a group of 2,400 plays (1737–1824), submitted to the examiner, which were in John Larpent's possession at the time of his death in 1824. They are listed in Dougald MacMillan's *Catalogue of the Larpent Plays*. Aside from the Larpent manuscripts, and a group of medieval deeds, the main part of the collection dates from the last quarter of the sixteenth century to about 1700. Large numbers of the volumes are still in their characteristic limp vellum bindings of the Elizabethan and Stuart periods, and their general nature can be seen from a few of the more interesting examples: Robert Ashley's *Of Honour* (ed. by Virgil B. Heltzel, 1947), Ralph Crane's 'Faultie Favorite', John Donne's 'Poems and Problems', Edward Topsell's 'Fowles of Heaven', Giovanni Coprario's 'How to Compose', Sir Arthur Gorges' *Olympian Catastrophe*, John Penry's *Journal* (ed. by Albert Peel for the Royal Historical Society) and Francis Thynne's *Animadversions*.

The papers of the Hastings family for this period are more numerous. Henry Hastings, 3rd Earl of Huntingdon, was Lord President of the North, 1570, and Chief Commissioner of the county of Leicester, 1592. Through his mother, Catherine, great grandniece of Edward IV, he could claim the English throne, and this may have been one reason for Elizabeth's giving him custody of Mary, Queen of Scots. Letters and documents relating to these matters are in the collection along with the usual financial, estate and housekeeping accounts, and other papers customarily found in private family archives. Descriptive reports on this collection were published by the *Historical Manuscripts Commission*, and in the *Huntington Library Bulletin*, no. 5 (1934).

A small group of dramatic manuscripts was acquired from several other sources. A copy of the Chester Plays, written in 1591 by Edward Gregorie, contains all the plays excepting the Banns and Tanners' Play, both of which were on the now lost opening leaves of the volume. It appears to be the earliest manuscript of the whole cycle. John Bale's *Kynge Johan*, about 1540, is partly in Bale's hand, and has his numerous corrections, both in text and punctuation, throughout the remainder. Anthony Munday's *John a Kent and John a Cumber* is also in the author's hand, dated 1596, and signed by him. It is bound in leaves from the same medieval manuscript used for binding Munday's play of *Sir Thomas More* in the British Museum, three pages of which have been stated to be in Shakespeare's hand. Among the dramatic manuscripts of the period before 1640 are Thomas Legge's *Richardus Tertius*, 1579; Ben Jonson's *Gypsies Metamorphosed*, 1621;[8] Middleton's *Game at Chess*; John Marston's *Entertainment*; Marston's (or Thomas Campion's) *First Anti-mask of Mountebanks*, about 1603; William Percy's *Comedies and Pastorals*, about 1610; Thomas Randolph's *Drinking Academy*, about 1620; and Edward Forsett's *Paedantius*, about 1631.

A few 'Commonplace Books' which contain texts, mainly verse of the period, should be mentioned, and a contemporary manuscript of Sir Philip Sidney's *Arcadia*, from the Ashburnham Library. There are also three of the Shakespeare forgeries of Ireland, and six forgeries by Collier of documents and letters relating to Elizabethan drama.

The largest bulk of the English historical manuscripts, numbering several hundred thousand items, falls into a later period, and is found in the Hastings and Stowe collections. In subject-matter they reflect the activities of the families represented: Hastings, Earls of Huntingdon; Campbells, Earls of Loudoun; Rawdons, Earls of Moira; Temples; Grenvilles, Earls of Buckingham and Chandos; Brydges, Dukes of Chandos; and others. The literary material has been gathered into a 'Literary File' in one part of the manuscript stacks, where it fills four sections of shelving, or roughly, a total of about 60,000 items.

Among the auxiliary materials which merit consideration by the Shakespearian scholar are the graphic illustrations available in the Huntington Library's collection of prints, drawings, and photographic reproductions. Most numerous of these are the engraved portraits—over three hundred of Shakespeare, ninety odd of Ben Jonson, and substantial numbers of principal Shakespearian performers, particularly of the eighteenth and early nineteenth centuries. Indicative of scope, too, are the four hundred early seventeenth-century engravings by William Marshall. Most generally interesting to the researcher, however, are prints contained in the extra-illustrated book collection, of which the outstanding examples are George Steevens's *The Dramatic Works of Shakespeare Revived* (1802), extended by Thomas Turner to forty-four large folio volumes, in which there are upwards of 3,000 portraits, scenes, and curious oddments; and Charles Knight's *The Pictorial Edition of the Works of Shakespeare* extended from eight to a hundred volumes by W. C. Prescott, and containing great numbers of inserted illustrations. The great collection of engraved English portraits formed in the eighteenth century by Richard Bull of Ongar, Essex, has just been acquired as a gift from a most generous friend, Mrs Edward L. Doheny. Nineteen of the thirty-six volumes, containing perhaps 21,000 very fine prints, form an extra-illustrated Granger's *Biographical History of England* (1769–74), and the remaining volumes include portraits of notable individuals down to the reign of George III. Among the items is William Shakespeare by Martin Droeshout, in the third state.[9] Nearly all of the major extra-illustrated works have been card-indexed by subject and portrait. Somewhat akin to extra-illustrations are engraved title-pages and the prints to be found in the Kemble-Devonshire collection of plays. Other graphic research aids are included in a file of English topographical material. These consist of engravings and photographic reproductions arranged alphabetically by name of house, county, city, royal houses and by London. Card indexes are maintained for this file, which list wherever possible architects, builders, owners and reference data. Of the Huntington Art Collections, chiefly representing the eighteenth century, mention should be made of Reynolds's famous portrait of Mrs Siddons as the 'Tragic Muse' painted in 1784, and Benjamin West's painting of 1794 entitled 'The Meeting of Lear with Cordelia', the latter presumably intended for Boydell's *Graphic Illustrations of the Dramatic Works of Shakespeare*. There is also a small canvas said to be a portrait of Ben Jonson by an unknown artist and, in the Hogarth print collection, a fine engraving of David Garrick as Richard III. Finally, in the art reference library a repository is maintained of many hundreds of photographs of the works of sixteenth-century and seventeenth-century artists.

In order to facilitate the scholar's task and to give him all possible assistance, many guides and lists have been provided for him. These, whether printed or not, may be found in *Aids to Research*, compiled by Lyle H. Wright, Head of the Reference Department and Reading Room. The two aids most used are two chronological files: the one of the Library's English holdings to 1800 and the other of every item in the *Short-Title Catalogue*. The great value to research of the second file was at once recognized by William A. Jackson, Professor of Bibliography and in charge of the Houghton Library at Harvard, who had it photographed for Harvard. Other libraries have obtained copies from Harvard.

At an early stage of his amazing career as collector Huntington decided to leave the treasures he had gathered, together with his home and gardens, to the people of California. In 1919 he executed a deed of trust to that end and named five trustees, though retaining control in his own hands during his lifetime. The next year he began to transfer his books from New York to the new building near his home in San Marino. In 1925 he approved a statement of policy drawn up by George Ellery Hale after consultation with his fellow trustees and interested scholars. This document ensured that the institution should become a centre of research in the humanities. A comprehensive programme was approved by the Founder just before his death on 23 May 1927, a director of research, Max Farrand, was appointed, and additional funds were added to the endowment to provide for a small permanent research staff and the annual appointment of fellows and recipients of grants-in-aid. To-day the research staff is depleted in numbers, but the intention is to enlarge it. The plan provides for scholars in English history and literature, in the American colonial field, and in modern Southwest history. A historian of art who is also curator of the art gallery, Theodore A. Heinrich, has recently been appointed. More recently still, Frederick B. Tolles has accepted a position in the Research Group in American Colonial History. Whenever a director of the institution is named he is likely to become a member of the permanent research group. For the academic year 1950-1 there were five fellows, two in the English Renaissance, two in the later Stuart period and one in the American colonial period. Recipients of grants-in-aid were rather more numerous and their investigations more diversified. In recommending applicants to the trustees the committee on fellowships is mainly influenced by two considerations—whether the candidate is likely to make a significant contribution to knowledge and whether the Library has material essential for his studies. European scholars are eligible for fellowships and grants.[10]

In order to spread knowledge of its materials and to make some of its choicest available for study, the Library has issued some seventy volumes to date. These comprise lists, sources and monographs mainly relating to the Renaissance, the American colonial period, and California and the Southwest. The first number of the *Huntington Library Bulletin* appeared in May 1931 and the eleventh and last in April 1937, when this occasional publication was replaced by the *Huntington Library Quarterly*. Both, and particularly the former, supply information of the Library's holdings, but their main purpose has been to print articles written by scholars working at the Library. However, outstanding articles on the English Renaissance are accepted even if their writers have never used any Library materials.

Thus the attempt is made, so far as funds permit, to supply three essentials—a rich collection of sources and reference works, subsidies for scholars, and publication of the results of the research undertaken. The many scholars who come to the Library every year bear witness to the achievement of the Founder's ideal to establish an institution comparable in its field with the Mount Wilson Observatory and the California Institute of Technology in the sciences. Another comparison is with the great English libraries founded long ago. The Huntington Library has about the same number of English books printed before 1641 as the Bodleian—more if photostatic copies are included—and about four-sevenths—five-sevenths if photostatic copies are reckoned—of the number in the British Museum.[11]

NOTES

1. For a brief life and an account of how he formed the Henry E. Huntington Library and Art Gallery, see *Henry Edwards Huntington* (1948) by Robert O. Schad, Curator of Rare Books and Administrator of Exhibitions, who first became associated with Huntington in 1918.

2. A prospectus prepared for a sale at Sotheby's is entitled *Chatsworth Library Kemble-Devonshire Collection of English Plays & Play-bills* (190–?) and supplies a summary description of the purchase. *The Catalogue of the Library at Chatsworth* (1879) can also be consulted.

3. John Payne Collier (1789–1883), librarian to the first Earl of Ellesmere, published *A Catalogue...of Early English Literature...at Bridgewater House*, and edited the *Egerton Papers* for the Camden Society.

4. At least the title-page has "J. Swift 1709", which I interpret to mean that the dean received the play in that year.

5. To be precise, thirty of the ninety-six titles listed in E. Gordon Duff, *Fifteenth Century English Books* (1917). The Library also has two of the works Caxton printed at Bruges.

6. The reader should consult C. K. Edmonds's *Supplement* to the *Short-Title Catalogue* issued as the fourth number of the *Huntington Library Bulletin*. It corrects errors, lays ghosts, and includes about a hundred items not recorded in the *Short-Title Catalogue*.

7. See R. W. Chambers in *Huntington Library Bulletin*, no. 8 (1935).

8. In *Ben Jonson* (ed. C. H. Herford and Percy and Evelyn Simpson), vol. VII, p. 541, is the following: "There are five texts of the masque. First and most important is the manuscript, formerly Richard Heber's, now in the Henry E. Huntington Library: any edition of the masque to-day must be based upon it."

9. See the *Catalogue of Fine Engravings and Etchings* issued by Sotheby and Co. for the sale on 10 April 1951.

10. Since this article was written the Research Group has been brought up to strength by two appointments: of John E. Pomfret, formerly President of the College of William and Mary and a specialist in the American colonial period, as Director; and of French R. Fogle, formerly assistant professor of English literature at Barnard College and a specialist in the English Renaissance, as a member of the Research Group.

11. I acknowledge with gratitude the assistance afforded by the following members of the staff of the Library: Leslie E. Bliss, Librarian; Robert O. Schad, Curator of Rare Books, and Carey S. Bliss, Assistant Curator; Herbert C. Schulz, Curator of Manuscripts; Lyle H. Wright, Head of the Reference Department; Mary Isabel Fry, Reference Librarian; William A. Parish, Assistant-in-charge of Prints; and Eleanor MacCracken, Research Secretary. F. P. Wilson, a former Fellow of the Huntington Library, and Allardyce Nicoll, Editor of *Shakespeare Survey*, both supplied constructive criticism of a rough draft of my article.

AN EARLY ELIZABETHAN PLAYHOUSE[1]

BY

CHARLES TYLER PROUTY

Our knowledge of the drama during the early years of Queen Elizabeth is fragmentary. We know the names of a few playwrights; a certain number of plays have been preserved; some actors are known; and we have the names and locations of a few early playhouses such as the Saracen's Head in Islington and the Boar's Head in Aldgate. In spite of this insufficient knowledge we can be reasonably certain that there was a great deal of theatrical activity during the middle years of the century, and the following passage written by John Strype in 1720 well describes the growth and development of the drama during the years in question.

In those former Days, ingenious Tradesmen and Gentlemens Servants would sometimes gather a Company of themselves, and learn Interludes, to expose Vice, or to represent the Noble Actions of our Ancestors in former Times: And there they played at certain Festival Times, and in private Houses at Weddings, or other splendid Entertainments, for their own Profit; acted before such as were minded to divert themselves with them. But in process of Time it became an Occupation; and many there were that followed it for a Livelihood. And which was worse, it became the Occasion of much Sin and Evil; great Multitudes of People, especially Youth, in Q. *Elizabeth's* Reign, resorting to these Plays; and being commonly acted on Sundays and Festivals, the Churches were forsaken, and the Playhouses thronged. And great Disorders and Inconveniences were found to ensue to the City thereby. It occasioned Frays and evil Practices of Incontinency. Great Inns were used for this Purpose, which had secret Chambers and Places, as well as open Stages and Galleries. Here Maids, especially Orphans and good Citizens Children under Age, were inveigled and allured to privy and unmeet Contracts. Here were published unchast, uncomely and unshamefac'd Speeches and Doings. There was an unthrifty Waste of the Money of the Poor; Sundry Robberies by picking and cutting of Purses; uttering of popular and Seditious Matters: Many Corruptions of Youth, and other Enormities; besides sundry Slaughters, and Maimings of the Queen's Subjects, by Ruins of Scaffolds, Frames and Stages, and by Engines, Weapons, and Powder, used in the Plays. And in Time of God's Visitation by the Plague, such Assemblies of the People in Throngs and Presses were very dangerous for spreading the Infection.[2]

The first recorded performances of plays in a known playhouse belong to the year 1557 when *A Sackfull of Newes*, described as a lewd play by the Privy Council, was played at the Boar's Head, Aldgate.[3] Presumably there were performances during this same year at the Saracen's Head in Islington, for certain Protestants, on the pretence of attending a play at that Inn, held a communion service in English, for which they were punished.[4] Neither of these inns is again recorded as being the scene of plays, but later evidence shows other hostelries in use as playhouses. There was a trade dispute about the building of play-scaffolds at the Red Lion in Stepney dated 1567;[5] and the Bull in Bishopsgate was the scene of a fencing 'prize' in 1575 with the first notice of plays following in 1578.[6] Also by 1575, if we are to judge from Gascoigne's reference, there were plays at the Bel Savage on Ludgate Hill.[7] Some kind of dramatic entertainment was performed at the Bell in Gracechurch Street in 1576-7.[8] Finally, in 1576, the Theatre was built in the Liberty of Holywell, outside the jurisdiction of the City, and Farrant established the First Blackfriars Theatre.

In one or two cases we have the names of the plays performed in these early playhouses, but the frequency of performances and the financial details of rentals and the like have vanished along with the buildings themselves. No contemporary pictorial representations of any of the inns, or of the Theatre or Blackfriars exists and our knowledge of their interiors is largely theoretical.

Fortunately, however, certain records and other documents do survive which give us valuable information regarding a London playhouse in use from 1557 on to 1568. The Accounts of the Churchwardens of St Botolph without Aldersgate record receipts from the rental of Trinity Hall to "dyuerse players" or "for playes" in the years 1557–8, 1558–9, 1562–3, 1564–5, 1565–6, 1566–7, 1567–8. The Accounts are missing for the years 1561–2, 1563–4, so that the only years for which we have Accounts and no mention of plays or players are those of 1559–61. It was in 1559, however, that two proclamations established stringent controls over dramatic presentations.[10] These controls may well have been the reason why Lord Robert Dudley's Servants journeyed to the north[11] and probably other players followed their example to avoid prosecution.

Aside from definite prohibitions, the plague was another factor which curtailed or eliminated completely the presentation of plays in London. The only time during the period covered by the above accounts when the plague would have stopped the actors was the summer and autumn of 1563 when the soldiers returning from the unsuccessful defence of Havre brought the infection to England.[12] Therefore, since we have no record of plague or official prohibition except for the years 1559–60 and 1563, it seems reasonable to conclude that plays were regularly performed in Trinity Hall from 1557 to 1568, with the foregoing exceptions.[13] The absence of the Accounts in certain years is to be regretted, but the inference that they would contain a further record of receipts is not unwarranted.

Thus we are able to establish the identity and location of one of the "other places" referred to in the City Precept of 12 May 1569, where we read:

Forasmuch as thoroughe the great resort, accesse and assembles of great multitudes of people vnto diverse and severall Innes and other places of this Citie, and the liberties & suburbes of the same, to thentent to heare and see certayne stage playes, interludes, and other disguisinges....[14]

Aside from one reference to a play in the Carpenters' Hall in the reign of Henry VIII,[15] there is no other record of plays being presented in a hall or enclosed space until the days of the First Blackfriars, except these accounts of Trinity Hall. Furthermore, there are no other records of any playhouse from 1557 (the Bull and the Saracen's Head) until 1567 (the Red Lion) and then there is a hiatus until 1576. Those details which have survived concerning Trinity Hall therefore seem worthy of full examination.

In 1374 there was ordained in the Church of St Botolph without Aldersgate the Fraternity of the Holy Trinity "in honour of Corpus Christi and for the sustentation of thirteen wax lights burning about the sepulchre in the same church during Easter time".[16] Three years later a Hospital for the Poor was, as Stow tells us,[17] founded by a brotherhood of St Fabian and Sebastian, and since a stained glass figure of St Fabian occupied the major portion of the east window of Trinity Hall that building must have been erected before 1446. In that year, the property, which had been seized by Henry V in the suppression of alien foundations, was granted by Henry VI to Dame Joan Astley, his nurse, for a fraternity or perpetual guild of the Holy Trinity.[18] Thus the earlier fraternity was confirmed and received quarters of its own. The buildings were conveniently near St Botolph's, being situated on the west side of Aldersgate Street, slightly beyond Little Britain. The Hall was still standing in 1790 when Capon made a sketch of the interior, but by 1799 it had been destroyed.

The property consisted of a Common hall, which became the Fraternity's chapel, lodgings of the priest, and eight tenements or messuages, all of which remained as a unit until December 1548 when Edward VI by Letters Patent granted the entire property, which had come into Royal hands by suppression, to William Harvey, Somerset Herald at Arms.[19] Shortly thereafter the parish of St Botolph leased Trinity Hall from Harvey and in 1560–1 purchased it and its appurtenances for the sum of £45.[20] In the interim rent was, of course, paid by the parish but the specific amount is nowhere mentioned. Clearly possession of the Hall was a profitable arrangement.

Beginning in 1548–9 the Churchwardens' Accounts for St Botolph's record monies received for the rental of Trinity Hall. The Accounts are divided into the two usual categories of Receipts and Expenditures, under each of which are various subdivisions. The particular division in which we are interested is that known as "Casuall Receptes"; in other words income that varied from year to year. Sometimes there is here recorded such items as the proceeds from the sale of "all tholde peynted clothes (12ˢ)", or at a very early date "4ˢ 4ᵈ [received] of the good wyfe Chilnestre that was left in her hands by certeyn children that made a maye game to these of the Church".[21] Three items recur regularly, but with varied receipts, and these are:

1. "Receyued of diuerse psons for standinge abowte the Churche at Bartilmewe tyde"
2. "Receyued of the warmote Inquest"
3. Rentals for the use of Trinity Hall.

The first refers to tradesmen or vendors who used the Church as a place of business during Bartholomew Fair, which was held in the yard of the nearby priory of St Bartholomew, and it would seem that the fair extended to the general neighbourhood. The income from this source ranged from fourteen to eighteen shillings.

Aldersgate ward was composed of two sections, that lying inside the city walls and that outside. Since St Botolph's was situated in the latter, the delegates to the Wardmote Inquest from that division did not have to pay for the privilege of using Trinity Hall, but "Those dwelling within the gate" were charged varying amounts. Such variation from year to year complicates our problem, since the Churchwardens treat all receipts for the rental of Trinity Hall as one lump sum. Therefore we shall have to disentangle, as best we can, these rental figures to discover just how much was paid by the players.

The first entry mentioning plays or players is in the account for the year 1557–8 which was submitted to the parish in June 1558. This entry will be given in full, but succeeding ones will will be presented in abbreviated form.

Roll 63:

Casuall **Receptes** *And* they [the Churchwardens] are also charged wᵗ xviˢijᵈ for money by them receyved of dyuerse / psons for standinge about the churche at Bartholomewes tyde and of thapplewief / for all the yere And wᵗ vjˢiiijᵈ for money by them receyued of the Warmot / inquest and of dyuerse players for the hyre of Trinitie hall during the tyme of / this accompt And w^t viij^d Receyued of Mr Bellmor for recourse had to the / well in Trynitie hall kitchin during the tyme of this accompt.

Roll 64 (1558–9):

18^s 0^d for wardmote inquest and "of diuerse players".

Roll 65 (1559–60):

7^s 4^d for wardmote inquest and "diuerse other".

Roll 66 (1560–1):

2^s 8^d for wardmote inquest.

Roll 67 (1562–3):

44^s 2^d for wardmote inquest "and sondry others for playes and mariages".

Roll 68 (1564–5):

38^s 8^d for wardmote inquest and "others for the hyer of Trynitie hall for playes & mariages".

Roll 69 (1565–6):

15^s 0^d for "Playes, Mariages and other assemblyes".

Roll 70 (1566–7):

22^s 2^d "for playes, the warmouthe inquest and other assemblyes".

Roll 71 (1567–8):

16^s 0^d "for playes and weddinges".

At the end of roll 70, as is the case with several other rolls, mention is made of money received "after thengrosing of this accompt". One such receipt came from

Edwarde Pereson for three sev^{r}all dayes having playes in Trinitie hall viz xv^{mo} october xvj^d xviij^{mo} octobr xvj^d & xiiij November xij^d as by the said boke of pcelles may Appeare iij^{s}viij^d

Unfortunately "the said boke of pcelles" or account book does not seem to be extant. The only books of this nature which I have been able to find date from 1596 on, but inspection of these indicates that names, dates and the like are given in detail.[22] The rolls which we have are really summaries prepared by a scrivener or parish clerk from the mass of details in the day by day account books.

In the absence of any further information, it becomes our task to estimate how much of the yearly receipts came from the players and how much from the Wardmote Inquest and other sources. The first mention of the Inquest occurs in 1555–6[23] when the payment from this source alone was 20^d. From this date to 1564–5 the Inquest payment is part of the total rental receipts. In 1565–6 there is no mention of the Inquest, but in the following year we find valuable information. At the end of roll 70 (1566–7) there is a report of action taken at the meeting of the parish at which the Churchwardens submitted their account. It was there ordered that henceforth the payment should be at the rate of 12^d for each of the men from within the gate. A year later, probably as the result of a protest, the rate was reduced to 6^d, but with the stringent restriction that the key to the Hall was to be given only to "one of the same Inqueste beinge of this pishe". Evidently there had been some difficulty in collecting the fee, for it is further stated that each must pay or "els not to be suffered in the same hall".

We may, I think, assume that for the period prior to 1567–8, the regular fee was 6^d, but that on occasion not all of the seven men from within paid, which would account for the total of 2^s 8^d received in 1560–1.[24] This, of course, should have been 3^s 6^d, if there were at this time seven men and if the rate was 6^d. At any rate if we deduct 3^s from the totals for the years 1560 to 1566, we shall have an approximate figure. For the years before 1560, it seems reasonable to deduct a smaller sum in view of the 1555–6 payment of 20^d. Perhaps 2^s will be a fair average deduction for these years.

After 1562 another problem arises.[25] Two other items in addition to plays are included in the rental receipts: "mariages and other assemblyes". It is impossible to arrive at any accurate deduction to be made for these items, since we have no means of knowing how many marriages or assemblies were held. Thus only the most general conclusions can be stated.

For 1557–8, after deducting the Inquest, we have 4^s 4^d as the approximate receipts from "dyuerse players". Now the only figures we have on individual performances are those mentioned in connexion with Edwarde Pereson where two performances brought 16^d each and a third, 12^d. Since these figures are for 1567–8, I would incline to an estimate of 1^s or less per performance for the earlier period, as there was throughout Elizabeth's reign a continuing decrease in the real value of money. Therefore we may reasonably conclude that there were between four and six performances in 1557–8. The following year, on the same basis, yields between sixteen and twenty-four performances. The next year in which plays are mentioned is 1562–3 when 41^s 2^d was received for plays and marriages. I would assume that there were quite frequent performances on the basis of the receipts, if we arbitrarily assign two-thirds to the players.[26] The year 1564–5 with rentals at 35^s 8^d for plays and marriages would again indicate as many as thirty or more plays. The next year receipts declined to 15^s for "Playes, Mariages and other assemblyes", and it is evident that the frequency of performances declines as well. 1566–7 saw an increase to 19^s 0^d for "playes and other assemblyes". Eight or ten plays might be a rough guess for these years. And the final year for which plays are mentioned, 1567–8, yields the three performances for which Pereson paid the rental plus a total of 16^s 0^d for plays and weddings. Here again we may estimate eight or ten presentations. Although such estimates are far from accurate, they do reveal that the actors made frequent use of Trinity Hall as a playhouse, performing, as nearly as we can tell, over 100 times during the seven years for which we have documentary evidence.

It may not be amiss to suggest that Trinity Hall was very probably used by the players during the years 1561–2 and 1568–9, even though the relevant accounts are missing.[27] The only years in which there is no mention of plays are 1559–61, when, as we have noted, Royal Proclamations established strict controls over the actors. And it may well be that Trinity Hall was used as a playhouse before 1557–8. The accounts mention rental receipts from 1548 on, but without specifying the source. The Wardmote Inquest is not mentioned until 1555–6, and even if it were meeting in Trinity Hall before that date, the receipts are in excess of the fees paid by that body. Clearly someone was using the Hall and was paying rent for it.

Since we do have specific evidence of rather extensive activity in Trinity Hall and since we know from the Royal Proclamations, City edicts, and other documents that there were frequent performances of plays in London even before 1559, it would seem reasonable to conclude that Trinity Hall was probably used by the players before 1557 and that it was one of several halls which, in addition to various inns, were used for popular dramatic presentations. And it is the more striking to find a parish church willingly letting its hall to the players, since many of the later objections to plays are based on religious grounds. It would seem clear that the opposition by the religious authorities became a strong force only in the 1570's.

Even though we lack direct evidence of what players used the Hall, we know of at least thirty companies in existence before 1567–8.[28] The majority of these companies are thought to have played almost exclusively in the country, because practically all references to them are found in provincial records. Such a conclusion does not seem warranted, particularly in view of the evidence of the use of Trinity Hall. In the country the players had to secure permission of the local authorities before they could perform; hence names will appear in the records. But such was evidently not the case in London, or else the records have disappeared. The only specific references to actors in London before the 1580's are few indeed.[29] If a company appeared at Court, the Revels Accounts, a prologue, or epilogue, or a title-page (if the play came to be printed) might record the fact. But for a company playing before a popular audience in the City of London, there would be no record, unless something happened which brought the players before a court or administrative official. Thus the fact that the only evidence of performances at Trinity Hall is found in the Churchwardens' Accounts takes on added importance. The actors who there performed stayed out of trouble and therefore we have no other record of them. Surely we may conclude that some of the thirty companies known to be in existence during the years in question did visit London, even though our evidence is inferential. Playing in the City would be more profitable than one or two performance stands in small provincial towns.

The name of Edwarde Pereson may at first seem a clue to the group of actors involved in 1566; but thus far the search has been fruitless.[30] Rather the available evidence suggests that Pereson was custodian of the Hall. The performances for which he paid took place in October and November 1566, but Pereson did not pay the Churchwardens until the following June. An actor would be unlikely to pay a debt avoided so long; instead Pereson seems to have followed the example of the Churchwardens themselves who, year after year, were constantly in arrears.

Extant records show a John Pereson as one of the parishioners of St Botolph's who, on 28 April 1549, assented to the lease of certain tenements belonging to the parish.[31] Another reference to a person of the same surname is first found in the Accounts for 1583–4[32] where is recorded the payment of 20s to "Mris Pereson govrninge or ovrseeynge the maydes". In the year 1571–2, there had been erected in the Church "The youngemennes Galleree" and "The Maydens gallerie", and Mistress Pereson's duties were to keep good order among the maidens during divine service. From the foregoing evidence of the existence of a Pereson family in the parish, it would seem likely that Edwarde Pereson belonged to the parish and in some capacity collected money for the rental of Trinity Hall.

Although we lack any knowledge of the players[33] who used Trinity Hall as a playhouse, and of the plays which they performed, we are exceptionally fortunate in having detailed information about the physical characteristics of the Hall. Indeed, we have an architectural drawing[34] of the Hall, and from other evidence we may conclude that this drawing represents the interior as it was in the sixteenth century when used by the actors.

On 12 July 1782 John Carter made several sketches of the interior of Trinity Hall while it was in use as a non-conformist chapel, and the most valuable of these is a floor plan and elevation of the four walls. Particularly valuable are the scale and the notations of details which Carter included. Another of Carter's sketches[35] displays the great east window which contained a stained glass representation of St Fabian, patron of the original foundation which, it will be remembered, was suppressed by Henry V. In this same window there appears a memorial glass in honour of Roger Hillet and his wife, with an inscription. This inscription as shown in the Carter sketch is identical with a transcript of it made on 17 July 1611 by Nicholas Charles, Lancaster Herald.[36] Therefore it seems certain that the window remained unchanged from 1611 until 1782, and further that the only alteration since the original foundation in the fourteenth century was in the nature of additions, because the figure of St Fabian endured until Carter's time. Finally, the architecture of the interior shows no alteration of the original late fourteenth or early fifteenth century design.

While the Churchwardens' Accounts contain many references to Trinity Hall, such as, "xx^d for mending wyndowes in Trynytie Hall";[37] "Mr. Belmore viij^d for recourse to the well in Trynitie hall kytchin";[38] "v^d receved for an old stone that lay in Trinitie Chapell";[39] "To Mason the Joyner of xiiij yardes of Seeling bourde for the styres at trynitye hall";[40] "for playninge the Table in Trinitie hall",[41] and the like, the first full description of the property is not found until 1616. A Terrier or a description of "Landes appertaining to this parish" (St Botolph's) was compiled in this year and survives among the muniments of Westminster Abbey.[42] Among other items is "The Contents of a Lease of Trinity Hall" to the Farriers' Company in 1612 where the following description is found:

All that their messuage, Tenement and howse called the Trinitie hall or the common hall late pcell of the late dissolved ffraternitie or Guild of the hollie Trinitie heretofore sometimes founded in the said parrish of St Bottolph without Aldrichgate of london aforesaid and now dissolved, And the kitchen and Buttrie to the same etc And also free libertie of ingresse etc into the said messuage or Tenement house kitchen et Buttrie by the way now leading from ye streete of Aldrichgate aforesaid unto ye stayres of ye hall of the said Messuage Tene^t or howse by a Gate nowe leadinge to the said Trinitie hall withall ye lightes comodities etc (except and all waies of this present demise reserved free libertie to and for the Aldermen the Aldermens deputie and to and for the parishoners of ye said parish, and the wardmotes enquest of Aldersgate ward from tyme to tyme for ye tyme beinge and at all tymes hereafter to have free ingresse etc at their will and pleasure of and into ye premisses; for the keeping of their or any of their courtes Sessions or Assemblies or any other such issues as heretofore they have usually had and used. And also except and out of this present lease Reserved all such wainscott household stuffe and other implements as are conteyned in a Schedule hereunto annexed....

From the foregoing, we may see that the kitchen and buttery occupied the ground floor underneath the Hall proper, that access to the kitchen was by means of a passageway, at the end of which stairs led up to the Hall. Thus we have the same general plan as that of the First Black-friars; but, in contrast with that playhouse, about whose interior so little is known, we have detailed knowledge of the structure and interior of Trinity Hall.

Situated on the west side of Aldersgate Street, Trinity Hall was a short distance north of the Church of St Botolph. The building was about 19 feet wide and approximately 30 feet high. The Hall itself was 35 feet long, 15 feet wide, and 17½ feet high. At the east end was the stained glass window to which we have referred; on the south wall an ornate fire-place,[43] and at the west end a gallery supported by a central pillar. The doorway leading to the stairs which led to the ground floor and to the gallery was located on the south wall underneath the gallery. I take it that the actors must have used the western end of the Hall, since to have used the eastern would have required considerable preparation of some sort of enclosed space whence entrances and exits could have been made.

The western end was admirably suited for dramatic purposes. Behind the west wall was an enclosed space, some 7 by 10 feet which would have been quite satisfactory as a temporary green room. The entrance to the Hall was right at hand so that the entrance fees could be easily collected by a member of the company, and the performance would not begin until all the audience were inside. Moreover, the gallery provided two playing areas, in essence an upper and a lower stage, both 7 feet 10½ inches deep and 15 feet wide. A curtain hung from the gallery would shut off the lower area, thus providing an inner stage with direct access to the temporary green room.

Since the area under the gallery had a clearance of only 6 feet 5 inches, no platform or scaffolding could have been erected, and there would be little need of any, because we may assume that the spectators were seated on the benches which were part of the furniture of the Hall. Even though the players might use part of the floor in front of the gallery, there would remain ample room for an audience of two hundred. Financially such a number would have been sufficient, because the admission charge would certainly have been greater than that charged for standing in the yard of an inn.[44]

At any rate, the good fortune that we have in possessing Carter's detailed sketch does suggest some interesting ideas as to methods of performance. Unlike the typical collegiate hall where the area under the gallery is occupied by the screens, Trinity Hall provided a natural inner stage, and an upper stage which could be easily reached by means of stairs hidden from the view of the audience. A balcony of an inn yard might be used as an upper stage, but it would be narrow and the actors would be exposed on three sides. Similarly the area underneath the balcony of an inn yard would be much too small for use as an inner stage.

The whole problem of the inner stage is a vexing one,[45] for, as is well known, in the only contemporary sketch of a public theatre which we have, that of the Swan, there is no inner stage at all, merely two pairs of double doors which remind us of the entrances from the screens in a collegiate hall. On the other hand it is clear from certain plays that a rather large inner stage was necessary for the action. And the evidence of Trinity Hall is suggestive, for its interior shows just how such a playing area could have come into being with the space beneath the gallery being 15 feet wide and nearly 8 feet deep. A fairly large number of people or even properties could be concealed herein by drawing the curtains. Whether Trinity Hall was used in the manner suggested is conjectural; but the clearly defined use of the inner stage and upper stage in such early plays[46] as *The Spanish Tragedy* and *The Famous Victories of Henry V* indicates well-established custom which is not completely explained by reference to the inn yard.

If other halls used by the players had the same structure as Trinity Hall, it might be that this arrangement, so satisfactory from a dramatic viewpoint, was imitated in the building of the professional theatres. The proposal of C. Walter Hodges[47] that the tiring house may not have been part of the frame but extended forward into the stage proper, together with his conjectural sketch render such an hypothesis at least possible.

Any consideration of the development of Tudor drama is at best tentative, but the facts that we possess concerning the use of Trinity Hall as a playhouse give certain grounds for inferential conclusions. We may quite rightly say that there was widespread dramatic entertainment available to the London public during the middle years of the century. The City Precept of 12 May 1569,[48] for example, well describes the variety of places of entertainment.

Thes [the authorities] are, in the quenes maiesties name, streightly to charge and commaund, that no mannour of parson or parsons whatsoeuer, dwelling or inhabiting within this citie of London liberties and suburbes of the same, being Inkepers, Tablekepers, Tauernours, hall-kepers, or bruers, Do or shall, from and after the last daye of this moneth of May nowe next ensuinge, vntill the last day of September then next following, take vppon him or them to set fourth, eyther openly or privatly, anny stage play or interludes, or to permit or suffer to be set fourth or played within his or there mansion howse, yarde, court, garden, orchard, or other place or places whatsoeuer, within this Cittye of London, the liberties or suburbes of the same, any mannour of stage play, enterlude, or other disguising whatsoeuer....

As we have seen, the Churchwardens' Accounts give us documentary proof of one such "other place". Certainly there were many others and many companies of players, else the great concern of the City authorities would have been unwarranted. That we possess very few plays for the period in question and practically no mention of specific players except in the Revels Accounts does not deny the foregoing conclusion. As has been pointed out, there is a very good reason why provincial tours are on record, and to conclude that the actors confined their activities to the country, avoiding the largest potential audience in the kingdom, is the height of false logic. Similarly we need only reflect on the low estate of the players to realize that popular plays could not be regarded as having any literary value which would warrant their publication. It was only after the turn of the century that men like Jonson, Marston and Webster thought enough of their plays to oversee the printing. We should remember that Shakespeare associated himself only with the publication of *Venus and Adonis* and *Lucrece*, not with any of his plays.

The Elizabethan drama did not emerge Pallas-like with the appearance of Peele, Greene, Kyd and Marlowe, nor did playhouses suddenly appear in 1576. Nor should we rely exclusively on Court entertainment, simply because we have documentary evidence. Actor playwrights, from the unknown author of *Hickscorner* (1516) to that of *Cambyses* (1569), provided material with which their fellows entertained the popular audience, not with Senecan rhetoric but with violent action. It was this tradition that reached its first known fruition in *The Spanish Tragedy* and it was this tradition which had created a theatre-loving public whose attendance made the erection of the Theatre and Curtain profitable ventures.

We may lament the loss of "the boke of pcelles" with its possible references to players and plays, but enough has survived to give us a glimpse into the theatrical world in the early years of Elizabeth when the players used Trinity Hall as one of their several playhouses in London.

NOTES

1. A grant from the American Philosophical Society materially aided the research of which this article represents a part. I wish, also, to record my sincere appreciation of the kind offices of the Librarian and staff of the Guildhall Library. The Librarian has granted permission to quote from documents and to reproduce the original sketch by

John Carter. Dr A. E. J. Hollaender, Archivist of the Guildhall, aided me in a variety of ways, chiefly through his great knowledge of all records relating to the City of London. Mr J. L. Howgego, Keeper of Prints, was another whose helpfulness I wish to acknowledge. Finally, the other members of the staff, whose courtesy and cheerful assistance made the research conducted by my wife and myself both easy and pleasant, deserve our thanks.

2. John Stow, *A Survey of London*, ed. John Strype (1720), Book I, p. 247. One need only examine Appendix C (Documents of Criticism) and Appendix D (Documents of Control) in the fourth volume of Sir Edmund Chambers's *The Elizabethan Stage* to see factual evidence of this growth and development.

3. J. R. Dasent, *Acts of the Privy Council of England* (1890–1907), VI, 168. Cited by J. Q. Adams, *Shakespearean Playhouses* (1917), p. 10.

4. John Foxe, *Acts and Monuments*, ed. S. R. Cattley and George Townsend (1837–41), VIII, 444. Cited by Sir Edmund Chambers, *The Mediaeval Stage* (1903), II, 190.

5. Bower Marsh, *Records of the Worshipful Company of Carpenters* (1913–16), III, 95. Cited by Sir Edmund Chambers, *The Elizabethan Stage* (1923), II, 379–80.

6. Sloane MS. 2530, f. 11. John Florio, *First Fruites* (1578), A1ʳ. Both cited by Chambers, *Elizabethan Stage*, II, 380.

7. J. W. Cunliffe (ed.), *The Complete Works of George Gascoigne* (1910), II, 6.

8. A. Feuillerat, *Documents Relating to the Revels in the Time of Queen Elizabeth* (1908), p. 277. Cited by Chambers, *Elizabethan Stage*, II, 381.

9. Guildhall MS. 1454, Rolls 63, 64, 67, 68, 69, 70, 71. One item relating to plays, that in Roll 70, the receipt of 22ˢ 2ᵈ "for the hyer of Trynitie Halle for playes the warmouthe inquest and other assemblyes...", was pointed out by G. Fothergill in *Notes and Queries*, 10th series, VI, 287. This was cited by Chambers, *Elizabethan Stage*, II, 356.

10. Proclamation of 7 April 1559. This is not extant but is known from references in *Calendar of State Papers, Venetian* (1890), VII, 65, 71; *Machyn's Diary*, p. 193; and Holinshed's *Chronicle* (1587), III, 1184. All are cited by Chambers, *Elizabethan Stage*, IV, 262. This forbade all plays or interludes until Allhallows.

Proclamations of 16 May 1559 (*S.T.C.* 7896, printed in Chambers, *Elizabethan Stage*, IV, 263). This required the licensing of all plays and forbade any play dealing with national or religious affairs. All noblemen and gentlemen having "seruantes being players" were ordered to obey these regulations.

11. Dudley wrote in behalf of his players in 1559 to the Earl of Shrewsbury requesting a licence to play in Yorkshire (*Elizabethan Stage*, IV, 264). The company was back in London by Christmas 1560, when they played at Court.

12. On 30 September 1563, a Precept from the Lord Mayor to the Alderman prohibited all interludes and plays during the infection (*Elizabethan Stage*, IV, 266).

13. The accounts for 1568–9 are also missing and since there was no plague and no prohibition until 12 May 1569, it may be suggested that the players made use of Trinity Hall during that year as well.

14. *Elizabethan Stage*, IV, 267.

15. John Foxe, *Acts and Monuments*, ed. Cattley and Townsend (1837), V, 446. Cited by Chambers, *Mediaeval Stage* (1903), II, 221. According to Foxe, one Shermans, keeper of the Carpenters' Hall, "was presented for procuring an interlude to be openly played...". The account book of the Wardens of The Worshipful Company of Carpenters (Guildhall MS. 4326/2) does not mention the use of the hall for plays.

16. John Staples, *Notes on St Botolph Without Aldersgate* (1881), p. 17.

17. *Op. cit.* Book III, p. 112.

18. Sir Walter Besant, *Mediaeval London* (1906), II, 384.

19. *Calendar of the Patent Rolls, Edward VI* (1924), I, 271.

20. Guildhall MS. 1454, Roll 66.

21. Roll 50, 26–7 Henry VIII (1535).

22. Westminster Abbey through its control of St Martin-le-Grand, which in turn exercised some control over nearby parishes, came into the possession of several records relating to St Botolph's. Through the great kindness of Mr Lawrence E. Tanner, Keeper of the Muniments and Library, we were able to examine these documents. The Dean and Chapter of Westminster Abbey have graciously given permission to quote from records in the Muniment Room. Among them are books of "pcells" for 1595–6 (W.A.M. 13470), 1596–7 (W.A.M. 13471) and 1628–9 (W.A.M. 13472).

23. Roll 61.

24. Roll 66.

25. Roll 67.

26. In 1569–70 (Roll 72), 3ˢ 4ᵈ was received for the use of the Hall for marriages. In 1570–1 (Roll 73) there were no receipts from this source. In 1571–2 (Roll 74) only 2ˢ was paid for marriages. Thus we may reasonably conclude that the bulk of the receipts came from the players.

27. See note 13.

28. According to the facts adduced by J. T. Murray (*English Dramatic Companies*), we have documentary evidence of the existence of thirty-nine companies between 1556 and 1568. Some of these may well be a realignment of other companies, but the number is indicative of widespread activity.

29. The extant information is, with a few exceptions, available in Appendices B, C, and D of *The Elizabethan Stage*.

30. Thomas Pierson, scrivener of St Pancras, mentions in his will (P.C.C. 23 Sheffeld, 1569) a son Edward, but this son had deceased by the time of the I.P.M. (Chanc. I.P.M. 11 Eliz. no. 75). Another Edward Peerson of "Gilston, co. Hertford, brickmaker" received a pardon for a felony on 8 October 1555 (*Calendar of Patent Rolls... Philip and Mary* (1936), II, 33). Neither of these men can be connected with either the players or the parish of St Botolph's.

31. W.A.M. 13,489.

32. Roll 74.

33. The Revels Accounts show performances at Court during the years in question by the Queen's Interlude Players, the Children of the Chapel, Lord Robert Dudley's Men, the Children of Paul's, the Earl of Warwick's Men, The Children of Westminster, and the Children of Windsor. The earliest known title of a play is *Cambyses* performed at Christmas 1560, but there are many references to performances with no mention of the particular play or the players.

34. The original is preserved in the Guildhall Library, Portfolio 591/TRI.

35. *Ibid.*

36. A tracing of the original is in the same Portfolio, 591/TRI.

37. Roll 62.

38. Roll 61.

39. Roll 53.

40. Roll 67.

41. Roll 71.

42. W.A.M. 13,468.

43. The fireplace is of a different style from the rest of the interior, being clearly a product of Renaissance craftsmanship. There are several references to mending the chimney, but rebuilding the fireplace is not mentioned.

44. Trinity Hall could not, however, be called a 'private house' in the sense of the edict of 1574 which W. J. Lawrence so ably discussed (*Those Nut-Cracking Elizabethans* (1935), pp. 28–43).

45. Cf. the various articles which have appeared in *Shakespeare Survey* beginning with Allardyce Nicoll's 'Studies in the Elizabethan Stage since 1900'.

46. Both of these would seem to have been produced by 1585, if we can place any reliance on the testimony of Heywood and Dekker. The former (*Apology for Actors* (1612), quoted in *Elizabethan Stage*, IV, 252) refers to Knell, Bentley, Mils, Wilson, Crosse, Lanam and others as actors "before my time". He had, however, seen Tarleton who died in 1588. Therefore, if Heywood was born between 1573 and 1575 (A. M. Clark, *Thomas Heywood* (1931), pp. 1–6), the actors referred to must have left the stage by 1585 at the latest. Thus if *Tarleton's Jests* is to be believed, *The Famous Victories* was presented before this date since an anecdote tells of Knell and Tarleton appearing in this play. Similarly Dekker's reference to Bentley, who was dead by August 1585, as being "molded" out of "the pens of Watson, Kyd, and Atchlow" (*A Knight's Conjuring* (1607) quoted in McKerrow's *Nashe*, V, 152) indicates that Kyd had written several plays before that date. Among them may well have been *The Spanish Tragedy*.

47. 'Unworthy Scaffolds', *Shakespeare Survey*, 3 (1950), 88, 89.

48. Quoted in *Elizabethan Stage*, IV, 267.

SHAKESPEARE LEARNS THE VALUE OF MONEY: THE DRAMATIST AT WORK ON *TIMON OF ATHENS*

BY

TERENCE SPENCER

Timon of Athens has for more than a century been the object of a good deal of speculation; and the workmanship of another hand was for long seen in the apparently weaker parts of the play. But several critics during the last two decades have endeavoured to show that there is more unity of theme and treatment in this play than was commonly supposed. Some of this very detailed analysis may be unconvincing, but most of the discussion has in recent years been concerned with deciding whether the play, as we have it, is in a finished or an unfinished state. Sir Edmund Chambers revived an old suggestion that the weakness of parts of the play was due to their being still in rough draft.[1] That the play as printed in the Folio is in an incomplete state was likewise surmised by Sir Walter Greg, drawing particular attention to the stage-directions ("Some read almost more like directions for composition than production");[2] and Professor Una Ellis-Fermor has, on literary grounds, persuasively argued the same opinion.[3]

This may be regarded as one of the most important outstanding problems of Shakespearian scholarship. If we could feel confident that the play is in part still in rough draft, then we should have a unique opportunity of getting close to Shakespeare's method of writing during the years of his greatest creative activity. We should be confirmed in our belief that he was a conscientious artist, prepared to correct and revise his work; and we could draw several interesting conclusions regarding his manner of constructing a play: that he put structure before composition, taking care, even in an early draft, to unify his play by means of ironic preparation and anticipation, symbolic contrast of plot and sub-plot, 'chorus-statements' by disinterested observers, iterative words, etc., but paying little attention, at first, to the characterization of minor personages and to the prose-verse form of the speeches.

It is the purpose of this note to consider a piece of evidence to substantiate the surmise of several modern investigators that parts of our text of *Timon* have never been reasonably completed, polished, or corrected for performance or perusal.

There are many sums of money mentioned in the play. These were listed and analysed by Fleay in a paper of 1874 and used as evidence for his theory that the play was written by Shakespeare and a botcher.[4] A few of these sums are described (by 'anachronism') in "crowns" or in "pieces". But the most important of them are given in "talents", as is appropriate for a play set in Athens. *Timon* is the only play of Shakespeare in which talents are mentioned as a monetary denomination.[5] Sums of money counted in talents Shakespeare found frequently mentioned in North's *Plutarch* (whence he derived the anecdote of Timon the Misanthrope and some information about the career of Alcibiades); he was also familiar with them from the Bible. The talent was a monetary denomination of high value; it was equivalent to 6000 drachmas and was represented by more than half a hundredweight of silver. We used to learn that a talent was worth about £250, but I suppose that nowadays we must at least double that figure in order to get an idea of its equivalent value. When, therefore, Timon finds himself in debt and bids his steward:

> Go you sir to the Senators;
> Of whom, euen to the States best health; I haue
> Deseru'd this Hearing: bid 'em send o' th' instant
> A thousand Talents to me, (II, ii, 205–8)

he is making an immediate request for something like half a million pounds. The sum is absurd. Likewise, his request to his friend Lucullus (III, i) for a loan of fifty talents (about £25,000), which is to be carried away by his servant in a box under his cloak, is quite unsuitable and out of character so far as Lucullus is concerned.

Shakespeare, it must be concluded, when writing these passages did not know, or had forgotten, how much a talent was worth. Of course, this is of not the slightest dramatic significance, and has therefore never deserved much comment.[6] But I think it can be deduced from the text of *Timon* that in the course of writing the play Shakespeare (i) became aware that he did not know the value of a talent, (ii) found out this piece of information from some person or some book, and (iii) then in several places got his figures right.

Perhaps Shakespeare recalled the Parable in Matthew xxv, 14–30 (which he had already so effectively adapted in *Measure for Measure*, I, i, 30 sqq.); there the sums of talents which the man travelling into a far country delivered unto his servants were five, two and one, clearly considerable amounts. At any rate, in parts of *Timon* the author was well aware of the value of the talent and made his figures appropriate. Timon pays five talents to settle Ventidius's debts and thus to release him from prison. This is introduced as an example of his lavish expenditure; Timon is prepared to make the sacrifice for a friend in need. The Old Athenian, who has from his youth been inclined to thrift, intends to give three talents as a dowry for his daughter; Timon promises to bestow an equal sum on his retainer, Lucilius, who loves the maid and who thus will be able to marry her. It is a liberal, indeed a prodigal gift; but the gentleman has served him long, and "to build his fortune" Timon is willing to "strain a little, For 'tis a bond in men". To bestow five talents upon a friend and three talents on a gentleman-servant are the illustrations, in this explanatory first scene, of Timon's squandering his wealth. Clearly the author knew the value of the money he was writing about.

In view of the unsuitable sums mentioned elsewhere in the play, the numbers of talents in this first scene may reasonably be regarded as corrections. If so, the correction had not extended very far in Shakespeare's manuscript. For, in four passages, realizing his ignorance of the value of the sums he was writing about and anxious to get things right, he had left the amounts indefinite in his manuscript. In III, ii Lucius is talking with some "strangers" who discuss rumours of Timon's financial distress. He expresses his indignation at those who have refused money to Timon, and then shortly afterwards hypocritically evades Servilius's request for a loan on his master's behalf.

(*a*) One of the strangers says:

But beleeue you this my Lord, that not long agoe, one of his men was with the Lord *Lucullus*, to borrow so many Talents, nay vrg'd extreamly for't, and shewed what necessity belong'd too't, and yet was deny'de. (ll. 11–15)

(b) Lucius in reply concludes:

...yet had hee mistooke him, and sent to me, I should ne're haue denied his Occasion so many Talents. (ll. 24–6)

(c) Timon's servant, Servilius, asks for the loan:

Has onely sent his present Occasion now my Lord: requesting your Lordship to supply his instant vse with so many Talents. (ll. 39–41)

(d) Lucius replies:

I know his Lordship is but merry with me,
He cannot want fifty fiue hundred Talents. (ll. 42–3)

In (a) and (c) it is necessary for the sense that some definite figure should be mentioned; and *fifty* instead of *so many* was naturally supplied (from III, i) by the early editors—by Theobald in (a) and by Rowe in (c). You cannot go up to a man and say, "Will you please lend me *so many* pounds?" You cannot gossip about a friend by saying, "The other day he tried to borrow *so many* pounds from...". To talk sense you must name a sum. In (b) *so many* might stand, but only if a definite figure is stated in (a); and even then the phrase is a long way from the figure to which it refers; and one can sympathize with improving editors who would like to read "twice so many" or "thrice so many", in order to make the phrase neater.

The author wrote "*so many* talents" in these passages because he had not made up his mind what figure to put and intended to fill it in later.[7] Moreover, in (d), Lucius's reply to (c) is quite unsatisfactory as it stands; "fifty fiue hundred talents" is unsuitable and arithmetically abnormal. This phrase also may be explained as revealing Shakespeare's uncertainty; it represents his manuscript indication for "*either* fifty *or* five hundred, according to whether the loan is for five or fifty talents; this I shall decide when I have found how much a talent was really worth". The transference of *both* the alternatives from the manuscript to the printed text is similar to the inclusion of both of Timon's epitaphs (which are contradictory) in V, iv.

The inadequacy of the statements about sums of money in this scene can hardly be compared with examples of Shakespeare's untidiness of plot, careless anachronism, inconsistency of characterization, and other petty negligences, which very minute analysis sometimes seems to reveal in his plays. A scene which is still in this state of incompleteness can only be regarded as unpolished, uncorrected, unprepared for reader or actor. It has not been worked over and tidied up. It is still an author's draft. If this has been demonstrated regarding one scene, then we have reason to suppose that the curious quality of the text in some other parts of the play can, with great probability, be interpreted in the same way.

NOTES

1. *Shakespeare: A Survey* (1925), p. 273, and *William Shakespeare, A Study of Facts and Problems* (Oxford, 1930), I, 482.

2. *The Editorial Problem in Shakespeare* (2nd edition, Oxford, 1951), p. 149 (cf. p. 187). He continues: "It can hardly be doubted that the play was set up from foul papers that had never been reduced to order."

3. *Review of English Studies*, XVIII (July 1942), 270–83.

4. *Transactions of the New Shakspere Society* (1874), Part I, pp. 144–5. They were skilfully re-examined by J. M. Robertson in his *Shakespeare and Chapman* (1917) (see especially pp. 133–4), where several valuable observations are unfortunately likely to be neglected because Robertson introduced them to support his improbable theories of the multiple authorship of Shakespeare's plays.

5. The phrase "beyond all talents" occurs in *Cymbeline* (I, vi, 80) and, if the text is correct, presumably means "beyond all financial estimation".

6. J. M. Robertson (*op. cit.*), noting the absurdity of the thousand talents, concluded that the lines were not written by Chapman, a good scholar.

7. Fleay was near to this suggestion (though he used his interpretation to support an unjustifiable theory) when he wrote that the vague sums of money in this scene "look like the work of a man who had some misgivings as to his previous amount of 50 talents; but was finally too hurried to remember to alter it" (*op. cit.* p. 145). J. M. Robertson developed the idea as showing that the scholarly Chapman's play was revised and added to by a less well-informed playwright.

SHAKESPEARE'S FRENCH FRUITS

BY

J. W. LEVER

...a book the sprightly raciness of which none can deny...the testament of an age when...a sense of colour and character pervaded all, man-of-action and man-of-letters, so that every gallant is half a poet and every poet half a swasher. On this common ground of courageous merriment they all met; and there it is that Shakespeare and Eliot might have boused together and amused themselves with the chatter and febrile rages of Doll Tearsheet, and by their side some roaring Alsatian bravo....

JACK LINDSAY, Foreword to The Parlement of Prattlers.

John Eliot's picaresque life certainly accords with the most colourful notions of the Elizabethan author. A Warwickshire man, like Shakespeare, who was two years his junior, he spent some time at Brasenose, Oxford, one of the generation of university wits; subsequently, through most of the 1580's, he studied, taught and roamed from place to place in France, Italy and perhaps Spain. A schoolmaster, a hack journalist, a novice for monkhood who was released without taking his vows, he was somehow mixed up in French politics (possibly as a secret agent) and on the assassination of Henri III in 1589 found it expedient to return to his native country. During the next four years Eliot was in London, teaching French in rivalry with the Huguenot refugees and translating political tracts from across the Channel for Wolfe, the book-seller who specialized in French affairs. Through Wolfe he may have met Gabriel Harvey, who, according to Nashe, did not leave the publisher's shop all the time the plague was raging: he already knew Greene, for whose *Perimedes the Blacksmith* he had written a commendatory sonnet in French. An ardent Rabelaisian, in 1593 he—to quote his own words—"retired among the merry Muses" and "dezinkhornifistibulated a fantasticall Rapsody of dialoguisme" under the title *Ortho-epia Gallica*, or *Eliot's Fruits for the French*. Written in lively colloquial French, with an equally vivid English rendering on the opposite page, the book consisted of a series of dialogues on contemporary life and manners, describing walks through London, conversations in shops, a visit to the Exchange, revels in taverns, foreign travel and modern French poetry—all with a wealth of humour and lyricism unmatched in any language manual from Eliot's day to ours. Without doubt *Ortho-epia* promised a remarkable literary career for its author. And then, at the age of thirty-one, Eliot disappeared from the English scene as abruptly as he had arrived. Perhaps with the accession to the throne of Henri of Navarre he returned to the France he so much loved; perhaps he met with some unrecorded accident. At any rate, nothing more is known as to what became of him from 1593 onwards.

Much of Eliot's personal elusiveness pertains also to his literary reputation. *Ortho-epia*, which should long since have been recognized as a minor Elizabethan classic, is still known only to a few. In 1920 Kathleen Lambley gave the book favourable mention in her monograph on Elizabethan teaching of French;[1] the scope of her subject, however, limited her to pedagogical considerations. Not until 1928 was *Ortho-epia* reprinted, under the title—taken from one of its sections—*The Parlement of Prattlers*.[2] This edition, besides omitting a portion of the text and the French side of the dialogues, was restricted to seventy-five copies, and hardly added to the book's accessibility. However, Jack Lindsay, in his enthusiastic preface, for the first time considered Eliot's little manual as an outstanding document of the age, and significantly enough, guessed at an association between Shakespeare and the author. (It will presently be seen how indeed the exercise of fancy quoted at the beginning of this article may not have been far from the truth.) Even after Lindsay's hint, Eliot's work continued to be neglected by the scholars. Eight years later, it is true, Frances A. Yates came forward with the claim that *Ortho-epia* was an important Shakespearian source-book.[3] Unfortunately the one analogue she specified was made the prop for an elaborate edifice of conjecture as to the occasion of *Love's Labour's Lost*, and its intrinsic interest has been generally overlooked. Since then there has been no further investigation. Even that intrepid source-hunter Leslie Hotson seems to have walked past *Ortho-epia* without stopping to notice the treasure at his feet.[4]

After these false starts, an inquiry into the relation between Eliot and Shakespeare is overdue. The results may serve to throw fresh light on familiar passages and long-accepted interpretations; they also afford some interesting evidence as to Shakespeare's methods of composition.

It is pleasant to surmise that Shakespeare and Eliot were personal friends, and while there is no objective proof, the notion is not far-fetched. Literary London in the early 1590's was a small world, and these two brilliant young men, both bred in Warwickshire, with common acquaintances, complementary interests, and no cause for professional rivalry, must at least have heard of one another's work. *Ortho-epia* would certainly provide Shakespeare with both amusement and instruction. The style of the dialogues was close to his own, with its mixture of Petrarchan lyricism, shrewd observation and low tavern humour; while Eliot's types—roisterer and dandy, braggart soldier, brawling highwayman and servile shopkeeper—were of the same wide range as his own comic characters. At the same time, *Ortho-epia* afforded the reader an exceptional opportunity of picking up French idioms, broadening his vocabulary, and gaining some information about contemporary French literature. By all indications Shakespeare's French was, like most of his knowledge, self-acquired, and when it came to writing the language, he was liable to make elementary slips. His French, as Miss Lambley observed, "contains just enough mistakes and anglicisms to make it extremely unlikely that he received help from any Frenchman". In these circumstances Eliot's Elizabethan brand of *French Without Tears* was the sort of book to remain on his shelf for years, to be dipped into again and again in leisure hours. Phrases and turns of speech would imprint themselves on his mind from close perusal and cross-reference between English and French; the little extracts of contemporary verse would be remembered more distinctly than a good deal of poetry in his own tongue. Most of us know from our own experience how ineffaceable are the impressions made by our early foreign language primers.

So much for conjecture. But it happens that Shakespeare has left fairly conclusive proof of the derivation of his French in the shape of two interesting clues, both from *Henry V*. One is the use of the strange word "asture" in Act IV, scene iv. It occurs where Pistol on the battlefield of Agincourt is terrorizing the unfortunate Monsieur le Fer. His boy thus translates the menaces to his victim:

Il me commande a vous dire que vous faite vous prest, car ce soldat icy est disposee tout ASTURE de couppes vostre gorge. (IV, iv, 37–9)*

* Unless otherwise indicated, quotations from Shakespeare are taken from the First Folio or the 1609 Quarto of the *Sonnets*. Line references are to the Globe edition.

Rowe rightly re-wrote "asture" as "à cette heure": but how did the error come about? While the other mistakes in the text may reasonably be attributed to the printers of the First Folio, this must surely have been Shakespeare's own. The answer is that he had picked up one of Eliot's idiosyncracies. In Chapter 14 of *Ortho-epia* is a dialogue presenting a situation that closely recalls that of Pistol and le Fer at Agincourt. The Thief has surprised a traveller on a lonely road: he terrifies him with a pistol and a torrent of threats, demanding the immediate surrender of three hundred and fifty crowns (M. le Fer, it will be remembered, got off with two hundred).

> ...viste, viste, depeschez, rendez vous, descendez, ou ie vous tireray un boulet au ventre.
> Où est ta gibbeciere?
> Vous me deuez trois cens cinquante escus, & m'en paierez ASTEURE.   (*Ortho-epia*, p. 104)

The Traveller is as poor-spirited as Pistol's victim, and complies at once. But the Thief continues his demands, using, by the way, Pistol's favourite gallicism:

> Compagnon baillez moy le licol de ta manche. Ne criez pas villain, car ie vous couperay la gorge.
>   (*Ibid.*)

At last the Traveller is securely bound, and the Thief repeats the word in his comment:

>   Il est bien garrotté ASTEURE.   (*Ibid.*)

The second clue is Pistol's odd (and unrebuked!) use of French while on guard in the English camp. It is, to say the least, unusual for a war-time sentry to make his challenge at night in the language of the enemy.

>   *Pist.* Che vous la?
>   *King.* A friend.   (*Henry V*, IV, i, 35–6)

Here too, the spelling is garbled. The Quartos have it, more recognizably but not more accurately, as "Ke ve la". But if we return to the same dialogue in Eliot's chapter 14, we find the Thief challenging the Traveller in just these words.

>   Kiuala? Stand. Sblood! Swoundes!
>   Yeeld thy purse....   (*Ortho-epia*, p. 105)

In contrast, the phrase is spelled regularly in the French version on the opposite page:

> Qui va la? Demeurez la. Ventre Dieu, sang Dieu, ça la bourse....   (*Ibid.* p. 104)

The misspelling is clearly intentional: it indicates the pronunciation of a stock piece of Elizabethan thieves' argot. Shakespeare, with Eliot's Thief at the back of his mind, is surely doing the same, and trusting that Pistol's pronunciation of the phrase will eliminate the incongruity of a French challenge in its dramatic context.

We shall have more to say soon about Pistol's connexion with *Ortho-epia*. For the present it is enough to note the evidence that Shakespeare had, for better and for worse, consulted the French of Eliot.

A further check may be added. It has been suggested that passages of foreign verse in a language manual are liable to impress themselves acutely on the student's memory. There are few more apt examples than the quatrain of Du Bartas which Eliot quoted, for the first time in England, in his *Ortho-epia*. The ingenious use of onomatopoeia makes this verse almost a mnemonic:

> La gentile Alouëtte auec son tyre-lire
> Tire l'yre à l'iré, & tiri-lyrant vire
> Vers la voute du Ciel, puis son vol vers ce lieu
> Vire, & desire dire, adieu Dieu, adieu Dieu.   (*Ortho-epia*, p. 147)

Beside this we set three familiar Shakespearian allusions to the lark:

> (1)   Ile say yon gray is not the mornings eye,
> 'Tis but the pale reflexe of *Cinthias* brow.
> Nor that is not [the] Larke whose noates do beate
> THE VAULTY HEAUEN so high aboue our heads.
>
> (*Romeo and Juliet*, III, v, 19–22)

> (2)   Haplye I thinke on thee, and then my state,
> (Like to the Larke at breake of daye arising)
> From sullen earth SINGS HIMNS at Heauens gate.   (Sonnet XXIX, 10–12)

> (3)   The Larke, THAT TIRRA LYRA CHAUNTS.   (*Winter's Tale*, IV, iii, 9)

Since Malone's time it has been recognized that the phrase "Heauens gate" in Sonnet XXIX was inspired by the song in Lyly's *Campaspe*:

> Braue prick song! Who is't now we heare?
> None but the Larke so shrill and cleare;
> How at heauens gats she claps her wings
> The Morne not waking till shee sings....   (v, i, 36–9)

But apart from this phrase, in all the above excerpts the images have a close connexion with Du Bartas's lines. "The vaulty heauen" is a direct translation of "la voute du Ciel"; the hymn-singing conceit, of which there is nothing in *Campaspe*, implies the lark's "adieu Dieu" as nearly as English allows; and the "tirra-Lyra" call is of course the French "tyre-lire", "tiri-lyrant", even more obviously with the Folio spelling than in most modern editions, where it stands as a Tennysonian tirra-lirra.[5] Evidently Shakespeare's larks are not, as is generally thought, the offspring of one parent, but have a more complicated family tree in which Lyly shares paternity with Du Bartas. It is to be remarked that this intertwined imagery spans a Pacific-like expanse of some sixteen years of Shakespeare's creative life, from the writing of *Romeo and Juliet* to the late romances.

After quoting the French lines on the lark, Eliot follows them up with an exceptionally lyrical passage of dialogue:

> Harke, harke, tis some other bird that sings now.
> Tis a blacke-bird or a Nightingale.
> The Nightingale sings not but euening and morning.
> Where is she I pray thee?

Tis a Nightingale I heard her record.
Seest thou not her sitting on a sprig?
O how sweetly she sings without any stop,
and ceaseth not! (*Ortho-epia*, p. 149)

Back we turn to the same scene of *Romeo and Juliet* in which Du Bartas's "voute du Ciel" was echoed, and in the same context we find a familiar lover's altercation.

Juliet. Wilt thou be gone? It is not yet neere day:
It was the Nightingale, and not the Larke,
That pier'st the fearefull hollow of thine eare,
Nightly she sings on yond Pomgranet tree,
Beleeue me Loue, it was the Nightingale.
Romeo. It was the Larke the Herauld of the Morne:
No Nightingale.... (III, v, 1–7)

With his keen sense of the ludicrous, however, Eliot was not the man to indulge for long in romantic sentiments. After some desultory talk about the music of birds, relieved by humorous digressions, the dialogue winds into a satire on the Petrarchan lover in which all the stock conceits of the contemporary sonnet craze are lumped together.

O caitiffe boye!
One while you shall see him faine a sea of teares, a lake of miseries, wring his hands and weep, accuse the heauen, curse the earth, make an anatomie of his heart, to freeze, to burne, to adore, TO PLAIE THE IDOLATER, to admire, to faine heauens, to forge hels, to counterfait Sisyphus, to play the Tantalus, to represent Titius Tragedie. And by and by he exalteth in his verses THAT DIANA[6] WHOM HE LOUETH BEST: HER HAIRE IS NOTHING BUT GOLD WIRE, her browes arches and vautes of Ebenus: HER EIES TWINCKLING STARRES LIKE CASTOR AND POLLUX, her lookes lightnings: HER MOUTH CORALL: her necke Orient-Pearle: HER BREATH BAULME, AMBER AND MUSKE: her throate OF SNOW: her necke milke-white: HER DUGS THAT SHE HATH ON HER BREST, MOUNTAINS OR APPLES OF ALABLASTER. All the rest of her body is but a prodigalitie & treasure of heauen & of nature, that she hath reserued to work the perfectiõ of his mistres & dear.
Tis great danger least he fall beside himselfe in the end. (*Ortho-epia*, pp. 159, 161)

While most of these conceits are traceable to the sonnet-sequences of the previous year, we know of no other instance where they are ranged as above in one sarcastic inventory. Shakespeare's Sonnet CXXX might almost be a versified reply to Eliot, taking image after image from his parody.

My Mistres eyes are nothing like the Sunne,[7]
Currall is farre more red, then her lips red,
If snow be white, why then her brests are dun:
If haires be wiers, black wiers grow on her head:
I haue seene Roses damaskt, red and white,
But no such Roses see I in her cheekes,
And in some perfumes is there more delight,

83

6-2

Then in the breath that from my Mistres reekes.
I loue to hear her speake, yet well I know,
That Musicke hath a farre more pleasing sound:
I graunt I never saw a goddesse goe,
My Mistres when shee walkes treads on the ground.
And yet by heaven I thinke my loue as rare,
As any she beli'd with false compare.   (Sonnet CXXX)

King John shows in one passage the continuing influence of *Ortho-epia*. This is the analogy pointed out by Frances A. Yates, who observed that the digression in the Bastard's first soliloquy was reminiscent generally of Eliot's parodies of polite dialogue in other manuals, and in particular of a passage in his dialogue entitled 'The Painter', where a map of the world is the topic of conversation.

                    . . .now your traueller,
Hee and his tooth-picke at my worships messe,
And when my knightly stomacke is suffis'd,
Why then I sucke my teeth, and catechize
My picked man of Countries: my deare sir,
Thus leaning on mine elbow I begin,
I shall beseech you; that is question now,
And then comes answer like an Absey booke:
O sir, sayes answer, at your best command,
At your employment, at your seruice sir:
No sir, saies question, I sweet sir at yours,
And so ere answer knowes what question would,
Sauing in Dialogue of Complement,
And talking of the Alpes and Appenines,
The Perennean and the riuer *Poe*,
It drawes toward supper in conclusion so.   (*King John*, I, i, 189–204)

See Affrick! Here is the mountayn of the Moone! Seest thou the Fennes of Nyle?
Lo here the red Sea. Looke vpon the great Caire! On this side is Europe. This top here, all white, are the Hyperborean mountains. Here are the Alpes, ouer which we go downe into Italie. There are the Appenines: and here are the Pyrenaean hilles, by which you may go directly into Spaine.

                                        (*Ortho-epia*, p. 79)

Miss Yates's comments on "my picked man of Countries" with reference to Eliot, and on the term "Absey booke" as descriptive of such a work as *Ortho-epia*, sufficiently spot-light the analogy.[8]

One suspects that for several years Shakespeare gave only desultory attention to his French studies. But around 1598—perhaps through finding himself in the Gallic environment of Mountjoy's household—there are clear signs of a revival of interest. Patches of French dialogue appear in *Henry V* and *The Merry Wives of Windsor*, and *Ortho-epia* would seem to have come into its own again, providing idioms and a characteristic spelling oddity, as has been remarked.

But one could hardly study Eliot's French without absorbing his English subject-matter at the same time; and the Thief episode which makes up Chapter 14 of *Ortho-epia* became a model for Pistol's encounter with le Fer at Agincourt. This was not the only hint in Eliot that might have shaped the character of the gallant ancient. Six dialogues further on, in the person of The Bragger, the authentic Ur-Pistol may be heard at the top of his form:

Ho Caetzo great Diuel of hell, awake thy sleepie Cyclopes: Thou Vulcan who limpest with thy cosins Asteropes, Brontes, Steropes, Polyphemus and Pyracmon, I will set you a worke. I giue my selfe to an hundred pipes of old Diuels, in case that if you will not fight, I do not make you eat the two egges of Proserpina....

Where is this so furious Hercules? I would fight with him for a litle quarter of an houre....

Where is Hector that Troian Lad? I haue a great desire to breake a Lance against his Cuirace.

Where is Alexander, the great drunkard of Greece? I will make him drinke a carouse. To marciall men we must not spare good wine.

Where is Achilles the Grig, Captaine of the Mirmidons, I would send his soule by and by into hell.

Where is this pettie companion Ulysses? He should do me a message unto Pluto.

Where is this quaking-quiuering coward Julius Caesar?...

I feare death no more then a butterflie, or the tickling of a flea in mine eare: and as for me, I feare not to fight with a whole Army, if it be not of these mescreant Tartarians, Canniballes, Indians and Moscouites....[9]

(*Ortho-epia*, p. 139)

While this has an obvious generic resemblance to the style of Pistol, there is a particular parallel to be adduced if only to right an age-old injustice. It occurs, rather as Lindsay conjectured, in the tavern scene where Pistol and Doll Tearsheet have their tiff: a situation whose real-life counterpart (as Lindsay thought) Shakespeare and Eliot might well have witnessed together.

Pist. Ile see her damn'd first: to *Pluto's* damn'd Lake, to the Infernall Deepe, where *Erebus* and Tortures vilde also. Hold Hooke and Line, say I: Downe: downe Dogges, downe Fates: haue wee not *Hiren* here?

Host. Good Captaine *Peesel* be quiet, it is very late; I beseeke you now, aggrauate your Choler.

Pist. These be good Humors indeede. Shall Pack-Horses, and hollow-pamper'd Iades of Asia, which cannot goe but thirtie miles a day, compare with *Cæsar*, and with Caniballs, and Troian Greekes?

(*II Henry IV*, II, iv, 169–81)

Remembering the Bragger's challenges, Pistol's meaning may at last be expounded. What for him are the triumphs of Tamburlaine that he has heard Alleyn declaiming? Nothing to compare with the fustian boasts of his prototype in *Ortho-epia*. Single combats with all the Trojan Greeks, and the quavering-quivering coward Julius Caesar, are as nothing to him. But for that matter, why draw the line at Tartarians, Cannibals, and the like? He will take on Cannibals too! It is a worthy utterance: yet generation after generation of commentators has attributed to Pistol a certain confusion, to be expected only from such uninformed persons as the Hostess, between cannibals and Hannibal. Let us hope that future editors will put a stop to this calumny —else damn them with King Cerberus; and let the welkin roar.

A final example of Eliot's influence, drawn from *Henry V*, provides incidentally a rare instance of the workings of unconscious association. Here again is a satirical portrait, this time of a flamboyant foreign nobleman:

Enter the Constable of France, the Lord Ramburs, Orleance, Dolphin, with others

Const.　Tut, I haue the best Armour of the World: would it were day.

Orleance.　You haue an excellent Armour: but let my Horse haue his due.

Const.　It is the best Horse of Europe....

Dolph.　What a long Night is this? I will not change my Horse with any that treades but on foure postures: ch'ha: he bounds from the Earth, as if his entrayles were hayres: *le Cheual volante*, the Pegasus, *ches les narines de feu*. When I bestryde him, I soare, I am a Hawke: he trots the ayre: the Earth sings, when he touches it: the basest horne of his hoofe, is more Musicall then the Pipe of *Hermes*.

Orleance.　Hee's of the colour of the Nutmeg.

Dolph.　And of the heat of the Ginger. It is a Beast for *Perseus*: hee is pure Ayre and Fire; and the dull Elements of Earth and Water neuer appeare in him, but only in patient stillnesse while his Rider mounts him: hee is indeede a Horse, and all other Iades you may call Beasts....

　　　　...my Horse is my Mistresse.

Orleance.　Your Mistresse beares well.

Dolph.　Me well, which is the prescript prayse and perfection of a good and particular Mistresse.

Const.　Nay, for me thought yesterday your Mistresse shrewdly shooke your back.

Dolph.　So perhaps did yours.

Const.　Mine was not bridled.

Dolph.　O then belike she was old and gentle, and you rode like a Kerne of Ireland....

(*Henry V*, III, vii, 1–5, 11–26, 47–56)

The model for this passage may be found in Chapter 8 of *Ortho-epia*, entitled 'The Horseman'. It is a dialogue in Eliot's characteristic medley of burlesque and lyricism concerning a crack foreign equestrian.

See you that fine horesman there? He is a Prauncer of Ferrara.

He is an Italian gentleman, and rideth better a girle then a gelding.

He is mounted for all that on a braue nag, on a gennet, on a barded horse.

How like you his horse, is he not a fine courser.

...He trotteth maruellous well. See, see he falleth to his amble againe. He is of a most fierce courage and proud.

...He hath great and faire eyes, and plaieth without cease with his bit froathing and foming.

He sheweth that the bit is not his maister.

Ah! what a mincing pace he hath? He is quicke in managing. See you him go one while ouerthwart, now on the left side, then on the right, and toucheth the ground but a verie litle, with the tip of his hoofe onely?

O that this light horse fetcheth fine friskes, he is as light as a feather, and runneth verie swift.

O that he raineth well, how he frounceth his necke, carrying his head aloft and his eare vpright.

See how he moueth with fiercenesse and heate his browes, and trampleth with all his members brauely. Behold how the sitter makes him fluce in the aire, leape the ditch, skip ouer the pales, turne round in a circle as well to the right hand as to the left.

Here is an Irish Hobby.

Thou hast hit the naile on the head. Tis an English Hackny. But view a litle the slouen who rides him.

He is like an Ape on a Beares backe.

He starteth and stumbleth at euerie foote... The poore Iade is verie leane, he hath nothing but bones, he is blind of an eye: he is lame of a legge: he hath all the hoofes of his feete spoyled.

(Ortho-epia, pp. 87, 89)

The transition, aided by the spirit of the French side of the dialogue, from "prauncer of Ferrara" to the Dauphin, is smooth enough. The undercurrent of burlesque which accompanies the lyrical description of the horse's volatility is the same in Shakespeare as in Eliot; so too is the indecent innuendo, which Shakespeare links up with the comic contrast of the "Irish Hobby", while (led by the Irish allusion to the thought of topical issues) he turns the rider of the "poore Iade"—like an ape on a bear's back—into an Irish kern. But the most interesting example of unconscious influence yet remains. While reading the above passage in *Ortho-epia* our eye caught the tail-end of Eliot's previous dialogue, printed in English and French on the same pages as the beginning of the Horseman dialogue in the 1593 edition. The relevant passage is from the description of a visit to an apothecary's shop:

Whats that within that box there?

Tis pepper or GINGER.

What haue you within this great sacke?

They are cloues, NUTMEGS, saffron, cynnamon and almonds.

What fine drogues are within these boxes there bepainted with shapes of Harpies, of HARES, of FLYING HORSES and flying harts?
(Ortho-epia, p. 87)

The last passage appears in the French version as

Quelles fines drogues sont dedancs ces boites-la peintes des figurez d'Harpies, liebvres, CHEUAUX & CERFS VOLANTS?
(Ibid. p. 88)

What happened was that the above details on the same page—the ginger, nutmeg, hares and flying horses (with the French for this last phrase, too)—coalesced unconsciously in Shakespeare's imagination with the description of the horse and rider that had consciously caught his attention. Accordingly the Dauphin's steed, patterned on that of the "prauncer of Ferrara", developed into a Pegasus, like the flying horse on the apothecary's painted box—*le Cheval volante*, as the Dauphin called him—with the colour of the nutmeg and the heat of the ginger that were part of the apothecary's store. One is reminded of the account of Coleridge's mental processes with which J. Livingston Lowes has familiarized us in *The Road to Xanadu*.

One point more remains to be cleared up: the Dauphin's description of his horse bounding from the earth "as if his entrayles were hayres". Modern editions of the play invariably spell the last word "hairs"—as if the Dauphin sat on a rocking-horse—and gloss it with an irrelevant parallel which suggests that this magnificent spirited steed is to be thought of as stuffed like a tennis-ball. Thanks to Eliot and his apothecary we may now confidently emend the description to an image far more worthy of Shakespeare:[10]

Ça, ha! he bounds from the earth as if his entrails were HARES: *le cheval volant*, the Pegasus, *qui a les narines de feu*.

In general, Shakespeare's readers have more to thank Eliot for than has hitherto been suspected. Nevertheless, it would be a pity if *Ortho-epia* should henceforth come to assume only the reflected glory of a source-book. It generates its own light, and deserves to be read for its intrinsic merits —as Shakespeare himself knew well.[11]

NOTES

1. Kathleen Lambley, *The Teaching and Cultivation of the French Language in England during Tudor and Stuart Times* (1920).

2. *The Parlement of Prattlers*, edited by Jack Lindsay (1928).

3. Frances A. Yates, *A Study of 'Love's Labour's Lost'* (1936). An article by Miss Yates on the relations between Eliot and Florio, as well as other language teachers of the time, had previously appeared in *The Review of English Studies*, VII (1931), 419–30.

4. Leslie Hotson, *Shakespeare's Sonnets Dated* (1949). Hotson refers on p. 23 to Eliot's use of the word 'Pyramides' in relation to Shakespeare's Sonnet CXXIII, but passes on hurriedly. *Et pour cause*: too much stress on it would weaken his case for dating the sonnet back to 1588.

5. This, according to the *Oxford Dictionary*, is the first appearance of the word in English, with the exception of an obscure work entitled *The Silk Worms and their Flies* (1599) which has the line "let Tyry-tyry-leerers upward flie". Eliot's translation of Du Bartas's verse renders "Tyre-lire" as "Tee-ree-lee-ree", from which it may have been taken. Shakespeare's spelling alone preserves the sense of the original French as given by Eliot.

6. Eliot would seem to have in mind Henry Constable's *Diana* sonnet-sequence, first published in 1592. Shakespeare, in Sonnet CXXX, takes the name Diana literally for the Moon-Goddess walking the sky, and plays delightedly with the idea. He "never saw a Goddesse goe", *his* mistress "treads on the ground", yet "by heaven" his love is as rare as any she.

7. Shakespeare used the sun conceit for his mistress's eyes instead of Eliot's "twinckling starres like Castor and Pollux", presumably because he thought the former more typical of the convention he was satirizing. But Eliot's image was too pretty to be forgotten: it reappeared, with an extra coat of polish, in *Romeo and Juliet*, where Castor and Pollux travel *incogniti*.

> Two of the fairest Starres in all the Heauen,
> Hauing some businesse do entreate her eyes,
> To twinckle in their spheres till they returne. (II, ii, 15–17)

8. See *A Study of Love's Labour's Lost*, pp. 51–6.

9. When it comes to hard realities, of course, the Bragger's reactions are much the same as Pistol's.

> The Infanterie is almost all ouerthrowne.
> The cornets of light horse retire.
> They fetch their carrier towards me.
> O what raine of lead! What a smoke of lightening
> and fire! By God I will runne away.

10. The *Oxford Dictionary* gives "hayre" as a legitimate Elizabethan spelling variant for hare. Cp. Porter's *Two Angry Women of Abington* (1599): "Hee is gone to seek a hayre in a hennes nest" (Percy Society, l. 103).

11. It is the occupational disease of source-hunters to see a bear in every bush; but in so happy a hunting-ground as *Ortho-epia*, a case or two of mistaken identity may be forgiven. If we are right, the following parallel will be of special interest to the patriotic anthologist.

On the last page of *Ortho-epia*, Eliot reproduces a second specimen of French verse, also from Du Bartas (Deuxième Semaine), together with his own rendering in English. This translation had previously appeared in the preface to Eliot's *Survey or Topographical Description of France* (1592) and evidently the passage was one of his favourites. We quote from it in part:

> *The Praise of France, translated out of the workes of William Salustius, Lord of Bartas*
>
> O Fruitfull France! most happie Land, happie and happie thrice!
> O pearle of rich *European* bounds! O earthly Paradise!
> All haile sweet soile! O France the mother of many conquering knights,
> Who planted once their glorious standards like triumphing wights
> Upon the banks of *Euphrates* where *Titan* day-torch bright
> Riseth, and bloodie swords unsheathed where Phoebus drounds his light,
> The mother of many Artist-hands whose workmanship most rare
> Dimmes Natures workes, and with her fairest flowers doth compare.
> The nurse of many learned wits who fetch their skill diuine
> From *Rome* from *Greece*, from Aegypt farre, and ore the learnedst shine,
> As doth the glymmering-Crimsin-dye over the darkest gray:
> Titan ore starres, or Phoebus flowers ore marigolds in May.
> Thy flouds are Ocean Seas, thy Townes to Provinces arise,
> Whose ciuill gouernment their walls hath raised to loftie skies;
> Thy soile is fertill-temperate-sweete, no plague thine aire doth trouble,
> Bastillyons fower borne in thy bounds: two Seas and mountaines double....
>
> (*Ortho-epia*, last page)

The above lines at least had sincerity and topical appeal: what killed them was the deadly jog-trot of the archaic poulter's measure. But tightened up into blank verse and given a firm declamatory beat, they had the makings of a fine passage of stage rhetoric. What then if Shakespeare turned to them for one of his most celebrated purple patches? All that Du Bartas said in praise of France might be applied with advantage to England. Her geographical position made her an even more secure fortress against war and infectious disease. She was immune, so far, to the civil wars whose evils formed the peroration to the French poem—though the cycle of history plays Shakespeare was engaged upon was largely concerned with precisely this theme. English knights—and kings too—had also won glory in the Crusades, while the ordinary Englishman of Shakespeare's age was undoubtedly happier than his French counterpart. As for the "pearl of rich European bounds"—how much more aptly could a jewel metaphor be applied to one's own island country! And so, in our view, the France of Du Bartas became Shakespeare's This England.

> This royall Throne of Kings, this sceptred Isle,
> This earth of Maiesty, this seate of Mars,
> This other Eden, DEMY PARADISE,
> This FORTRESSE built by Nature for her selfe,
> AGAINST INFECTION, AND THE HAND OF WARRE:
> This happy breed of men, this little world,
> This PRECIOUS STONE, SET IN THE SILUER SEA,
> Which serues it in the office of a wall,
> Or as a MOATE DEFENSIUE to a house,
> Against the enuy of LESSE HAPPIER LANDS,
> This blessed plot, this earth, this Realme, this England,
> This NURSE, this TEEMING WOMBE of Royall Kings,
> Fear'd by their breed, and famous for their birth,

Renowned for their deeds, as farre from home,
For Christian seruice, and true Chiualrie,
As is the sepulcher in stubborne *Iury*
Of the Worlds ransome, blessed *Maries* Sonne. (*Richard II*, II, i, 40–56)

This is not the only echo of the passage. In Act I, iii of *Richard II*, where Bolingbroke takes leave of his father to go into exile, the thought of France leads Shakespeare to recur to Du Bartas's theme despite its inconsistency with the transference of the fortress-against-plague idea to England.

> ...Suppose,
> Deuouring pestilence hangs in our aire,
> And thou art flying to a fresher clime. (I, iii, 284–5)

And at the end of the scene Bolingbroke deliberately inverts Du Bartas's salute to France—or rather, Eliot's, in translation, for the phrase is his:

> All haile sweet soile!

so that it becomes a farewell to England:

> sweet soil adieu,
> My Mother, and my Nurse, which beares me yet.... (I, iii, 306–7)

It is indeed, in a sense hitherto unperceived, the speech of a true-born Englishman.

AN ELIZABETHAN EYEWITNESS OF
ANTONY AND CLEOPATRA?

BY

JOAN REES

Discussion of the relationship between Shakespeare's *Antony and Cleopatra* and the 1607 version of Daniel's *Cleopatra* has up to the present turned on claims for verbal similarities and an examination of the changes made in the structure of Daniel's play between 1594 and 1607. There is, however, one curious passage in Daniel's 1607 play to which attention has not hitherto been drawn and which may possibly provide a more intimate link with Shakespeare's play than has before been suspected: it may, in fact, be a reminiscence by Daniel of an actual production of *Antony and Cleopatra*.

The passage in question occurs in Dircetus's account of Antony's last visit to Cleopatra, a part of Plutarch's story which Daniel had not used in the earlier, 1594, version of his play. Dircetus recounts what happens after Antony has given himself the fatal wound:

> . . . Which when his love,
> His royall *Cleopatra* understood,
> Shee sends with speed his body to remoove,
> The body of her love imbru'd with blood.
> Which brought unto her tombe, (lest that the prease
> Which came with him, might violate her vow)
> She drawes him up in rowles of taffaty
> T'a window at the top, which did allow
> A little light unto her monument.
>   There Charmion, and poore Eras, two weake maids
> Foretir'd with watching, and their mistresse care,
> Tug'd at the pulley, having n'other aydes,
> And up they hoise the swounding body there
> Of pale *Antonius*, showring out his blood
> On th'under lookers, which there gazing stood.
>   And when they had now wrought him up halfe way
> (Their feeble powers unable more to doe)
> The frame stood still, the body at a stay,
> When *Cleopatra* all her strength thereto
> Puts, with what vigor love, and care could use,
> So that it mooves againe, and then againe
> It comes to stay. When she afresh renewes
> Her hold, and with reinforced power doth straine,
> And all the weight of her weake bodie laies,

> Whose surcharg'd heart more then her body wayes.
> At length she wrought him up, and takes him in,
> Laies his yet breathing body on her bed....[1]

At this point Shakespeare is content to leave details to the actors and the stage manager. "Come, come, Antony", says Cleopatra:

> Help me, my women—we must draw thee up:
> Assist, good friends.
> *Antony.* O, quick, or I am gone.
> *Cleopatra.* Here's sport indeed! How heavy weighs my lord!
> Our strength is all gone into heaviness,
> That makes the weight: had I great Juno's power,
> The strong-wing'd Mercury should fetch thee up,
> And set thee by Jove's side. Yet come a little—
> Wishers were ever fools—O, come, come, come. (IV, xv, 30–7)

The corresponding passage in Plutarch reads:

Cleopatra would not open the gates, but came to the high windowes, and cast out certaine chains and ropes, in the which Antonius was trussed: and Cleopatra her owne selfe, with two women only, which she had suffered to come with her into these monumentes, trised Antonius up. They that were present to behold it, said they never saw so pitiefull a sight. For, they plucked up poore Antonius all bloody as he was, and drawing on with pangs of death, who holding up his hands to Cleopatra, raised up him selfe as well as he could. It was a hard thing for these women to do, to lift him up: but Cleopatra stowping downe with her head, putting to all her strength to her uttermost power, did lift him up with much a doe, and never let goe her hold, with the helpe of the women beneath her that bad her be of good corage, and were as sorie to see her labor so, as she her selfe. So when she had gotten him in after that sorte, and layed him on a bed....[2]

From a comparison of these passages several points of interest emerge.

(i) "She drawes him up in rowles of taffaty." This detail is not in Plutarch or in Shakespeare. It seems most naturally to mean that lengths of taffeta (presumably thrown from Cleopatra's window) were wrapped round Antony and that he was actually drawn up by means of them. It is a curious detail. In the situation where the "chains and ropes" of Plutarch's account would appear appropriate and obvious, Daniel's taffeta seems to call for some explanation.[3]

(ii) Charmion and Eras "tug'd at the pulley" but in spite of their efforts "the frame stood still, the body at a stay". These remarks suggest that Daniel had imagined in some detail the apparatus used in the hoisting of Antony, and in doing so he had received no help from Plutarch or from Shakespeare's text. Daniel, evidently, like recent students of *Antony and Cleopatra* (see the 'New Cambridge' edition, 1950, p. 230, and the references there given) was aware of the physical problems involved in hauling Antony up. He emphasizes the difficulty of the undertaking by the recurrent stops in the progress of "the frame" upwards and draws our attention to the position of Antony's body swinging in mid-air all the time, the blood from his wound "showring out", meanwhile, "on th'under lookers".

(iii) This last detail stands out from the narrative with startling effect. It is the kind of detail that might be expected to stick in the mind of someone who had recently watched such a scene and it gives a touch of immediacy to the whole report. It suggests in Daniel's mind a vivid visual picture of the whole episode.

These points, curious as they are, may, of course, all be explained as the result of a working over of Plutarch by Daniel with the intention of adding "corroborative detail" to the narrative. If this is the proper explanation, then we must claim for Daniel a sense of scene and drama not often acknowledged as his. In support of the view that it is to Plutarch and not to Shakespeare that we must look for the basis of this speech, there may be urged the small piece of evidence that Daniel thinks of Cleopatra as joining her efforts to those of her women when they are near exhaustion; it is possible to get this impression from Plutarch, but Shakespeare makes it clear that Cleopatra is involved in the hauling process from the beginning. The intervention of Cleopatra at a later stage in the operation adds to the tension and drama of the scene as Dircetus describes it.

But can the possibility that Daniel had seen a performance of *Antony and Cleopatra* be discounted? "Rowles of taffaty" would not be at all unlikely in a theatre wardrobe;[4] in a stage performance, Daniel's attention would inevitably be directed to the mechanics of hauling Antony up far more insistently than it would be in a reading of a description of the scene, and Daniel's concern with the mechanics of the action in the Dircetus speech is surely surprising in a "closet dramatist" writing for his *nuntius*. The dramatic pauses and the picture of the suspended body which give vividness and reality to Dircetus's story might be a reminiscence of the way the *Antony and Cleopatra* scene was actually managed by an imaginative company—or perhaps when he saw it such hitches occurred rather by accident than design but impressed Daniel as life-like and effective. This would account for the impression Dircetus's speech makes, that these events are recounted by one lately present at them and still full of what he has seen. I do not think that, out of his own imaginative resources, Daniel was necessarily incapable of visualizing a scene with this degree of clarity, but it is true that he writes to fill more usually the mind with thought than the eye with telling detail, and where he elaborates a scene it is with sympathetic touches, and not as a rule with sensational events.

If this suggestion can be accepted, that Daniel in the Dircetus speech is recalling a performance of *Antony and Cleopatra*, the details that Daniel gives provide useful hints for the solving of a production problem that has exercised students of the Elizabethan theatre. That an eyewitness account may be embedded in a play originally designed as a companion-piece to the Countess of Pembroke's *Antonie* is a possibility of some piquancy.

NOTES

1. *The Tragedie of Cleopatra nach dem Drucke von 1611*, ed. M. Lederer (Louvain, 1911), I, ii, 238–64.

2. *North's Plutarch* (1896), VI, 80.

3. If Daniel had looked at Dio Cassius (a detail from whose account of Cleopatra's interview with Caesar he shares with Jodelle), he would have learnt that the monument was unfinished and the ropes with which Cleopatra draws Antony up were there to lift the stone blocks needed to finish the roof (Dio Cassius, *Roman History*, trans. E. Cary (1917), VI, 31).

4. M. Channing Linthicum, *Costume in the Drama of Shakespeare and his Contemporaries* (Oxford, 1936), pp. 113, 123–5.

OTHELLO'S "IT IS THE CAUSE..."
AN ANALYSIS

BY

JOHN MONEY

It is always dangerous to treat a great Shakespearian speech as an isolated piece of verse, since the greatest speech will be the most deeply rooted in the total context of the play. On the other hand, there are some speeches which are, as it were, focal, gathering up the main themes and concentrating the "extended metaphor" of the whole play. Detailed analysis of such passages, far from constituting a risky 'academic exercise', is in fact imperative. And it goes without saying that the speech which I have chosen (Othello's "It is the cause, it is the cause, my soul"), seems to me eminently suitable for such an analysis; for without analysis at this point there is the danger of a simple, emotional surrender, and, consequently, of a fatal misinterpretation.

I have undertaken this study as an actor, but it would be false to imagine that I am deliberately aiming to represent the 'actor's point of view', or to suggest a method of 'characterization', or to offer any opposed alternative to the academic approach. Instead, I hope to indicate not an opposition, but a fundamental uniformity. Shakespearian actor and Shakespearian critic meet in the study of the words, but the actor's 'characterization' and the critic's analysis are alike valueless, unless they are related to the play in its wholeness. There *are* two approaches, but there is only one end.

> "*Enter* Othello *with a light*[1]
>
> It is the cause, it is the cause, my soul."

The first three lines of the speech make it clear that Othello thinks himself about to execute an act of justice. It is important to note at once that "the cause" is deceptive in more ways than one. Othello's words recall the words of Emilia to Desdemona.

> *Desdemona.* Alas the day! I never gave him cause.
> *Emilia.* But jealous souls will not be answer'd so;
> They are not ever jealous for the cause,
> But jealous for they are jealous. (III, iv, 158–61)

And Cassio faintly echoes Othello at the end, "Dear general, I never gave you cause" (V, ii, 299). In this sense, the word means simply 'reason' or 'occasion'. But two connotations may be noted. The word may be used in the specifically legal sense of 'a matter requiring action', or the word may be used in the more general and implied sense of 'a good cause', as in Macbeth's "for mine own good, All causes shall give way" (III, iv, 135), or Brutus's "hear me for my cause" (*Julius Caesar*, III, ii, 13). A modern analogy for this usage can be found in such phrases as 'the cause of freedom'. These last two senses frequently overlap. The idea of the cause is inseparable from the idea of justice, although not necessarily one with it. We remember Othello's comment on Iago's suggestion that he should "strangle" Desdemona "in the bed she hath contaminated": "Good, good: the justice of it pleases: very good" (IV, i, 222). And when Othello is indeed about to strangle his wife he charges her with making him call his act "a murder, which I thought a sacrifice" (V, ii, 65). In the fullest sense the scene is set for an act of justice. But the audience knows that "the cause" is no cause, that this is indeed a murder and not a sacrifice. So there is terrible irony in the solemn beat of these opening lines, in which "the cause" is invested with an almost mystical significance. This solemn preparation for the murder of Desdemona is also in ironical contrast with the swift and calculated killing of Roderigo in the preceding scene, and with Iago's comment upon that scene: "This is the fruit of whoring" (V, i, 116).

The tone of the opening is slow, deliberate, half-prayer, half-incantation. This incantatory effect is supported by the use of repetition and by the monosyllabic movement of the lines, with the long-drawn vowels, "cause", "soul", "you chaste stars". This first line is ambiguous as well as ironical. The weighty repetition mocks itself. But there is ambiguity, too, in Othello's appeal to his own soul to justify "the cause". For there is a sense in which his soul *is* "the cause", and this sense is pointed by the final placing of the words in the line. ("It is the cause, it is the cause, my soul.") In his second appeal—to the stars—Othello, in expressing his inability to name the cause, names it indirectly. There is a parallel here with Desdemona's words:

> I cannot say 'whore':
> It does abhor me now I speak the word.   (IV, ii, 161–2)

> "Let me not name it to you, you chaste stars."

The alliteration and repetition of the first line are carried on into the second, another monosyllabic line. The language is intensely deliberate. This echoing repetition and the effect of slowly increasing tension secured by the accumulating monosyllables prepare the way for a decisive emphasis on the word "chaste". This emphasis is likewise demanded by the sense. "Chaste" is the first adjective, the first precisely descriptive word in the speech, and its precision is sharpened by the lofty vagueness which precedes it. Moreover, as we have noted, Othello through this word indirectly names "the cause". But the word "chaste" is itself a means of evading "the truth" which Othello cannot name. It is forced from him. So the sense demands that the word be isolated, singled out, and, in speaking, the conjunction of 'st' in "cha*ste st*ars", enhances this isolation still further.

Othello's appeal to the stars is characteristic. At the end of the great 'temptation scene' (III, iii) Othello and Iago kneel, pledged to revenge.

> *Othello.*   Now, by yond marble heaven,
> In the due reverence of a sacred vow
> I here engage my words.
> *Iago.*   Do not rise yet.
> Witness, you ever-burning lights above,
> You elements that clip us round about....   (III, iii, 460–4)

Later, in the 'brothel scene' (IV, ii), Desdemona also kneels, to swear her loyalty.

> *Othello.*   Come, swear it, damn thyself;
> Lest, being like one of heaven, the devils themselves

Should fear to seize thee: therefore be double damn'd:
Swear thou art honest.

Desdemona. Heaven doth truly know it.

Othello. Heaven truly knows that thou art false as hell. (IV, ii, 35–9)

It is to be noted that Othello swears by "yond marble heaven" and Iago addresses the "ever-burning lights" and the "elements". The heaven to which each kneels to make his "sacred vow" is conceived in these generalized, impersonal terms. It is the fixed ("marble") heaven of Fate. The heaven to which Desdemona appeals is not presented in terms of Fate. Moreover, Desdemona is appealing with justice on her side, whereas Othello and Iago are playing a solemn and terrible charade. The fixed heaven which they are invoking, the fate to which they kneel, is the fixity of their own wills. The irony of the moment is again patently stressed by the solemnity of the words. Othello's appeal to Fate, to "the stars", is, therefore, double-edged. The stars may be invoked to justify a human action; in this case the human will identifies itself with the divine will, Othello is the appointed instrument of divine justice. Or the stars may be invoked to excuse a human action; in this case the human will denies its own power of choice, Othello is the victim of Fate. The first invocation is an assumption of responsibility, the second invocation is a denial of responsibility. In the temptation scene, in the opening of the murder scene, Othello calls heaven to witness his "sacred vow", to sanction his action. Here he sees himself as the instrument of heaven's justice. But, even here, his heaven is pre-eminently fatalistic and non-Christian. Justice and revenge are synonymous; there is no room for mercy. So, when the murder is done, Othello is ready to see himself (and Desdemona) as victims of Fate. The essential references are to be found in his long speech to Gratiano (V, ii, 264–5).

O vain boast!
Who can control his fate?

And later in the speech he echoes himself, with the same sublime incomprehension, in his cry to the murdered Desdemona, "O ill-starr'd wench!" Othello dies, still uncomprehending, fatally true to himself to the end.

The ambiguity of the first line is now becoming pointed. Othello is concerned to justify an act of justice and, at the same time, to disclaim his personal responsibility for the act.

"It is the cause. Yet I'll not shed her blood."

Shakespeare in *Othello* made free use of the rhetorical device of repetition, and he used it with psychological exactness. The second, delayed, repetition of "It is the cause" has its own peculiarity. It is as if Othello were speaking under the influence of a drug. This effect is achieved partly by the delay in repetition, so that the words return with an almost monotonous insistence. Othello is drugging himself with words in order to convince himself. But he cannot be finally convinced. He had said, "to be once in doubt Is once to be resolved" (III, iii, 179) and again,

I'll see before I doubt; when I doubt, prove;
And, on the proof, there is no more but this—
Away at once with love or jealousy! (III, iii, 190–2)

But he has found that things do not work out like this, that "the proof" is never final. He has, in fact, failed to find the satisfaction he had demanded; so he can escape neither from his love nor his jealousy.

Within the third line a very subtle transition is taking place. Othello, continuing the process of self-justification, begins to persuade himself that, by refusing to shed Desdemona's blood, he can preserve her beauty and so, indirectly, exonerate himself from blame. The lines recall his original pleasure at the "justice" of strangling Desdemona, as opposed to poisoning her. The contrast is significant. For now Othello sees himself as just, not because he is strangling Desdemona in "the bed she hath contaminated", but because by strangling her (and so not shedding her blood), he may still (or so he implies) preserve her beauty. When we come to the ghastly afterthought,

> I that am cruel am yet merciful;
> I would not have thee linger in thy pain (v, ii, 86–7)

the course of justice is almost complete.

It is now possible to see the transition of the third line more specifically in terms of a confusion. Othello turns from the contemplation of "the cause" to the contemplation of Desdemona. At once justice begins to lose its reasoned finality, and becomes confounded in the awareness of Desdemona's beauty. ("It is the cause. Yet I'll not shed her blood.") It is literally a confusion that is taking place. So there is no violent shift of emotion, no sudden movement from "the cause" to Desdemona, from jealousy to love. The first five lines, the first 'movement' of the speech, have an unmistakable unity of tone. The movement is gradual and continuous, best described in terms of an increasing slowness, culminating in the unbearable protracted "monumental alabaster". The sibilants, the alliteration, the long vocalic stresses, which reinforce the ponderous invocation of justice in the opening lines, are maintained to the end of the movement, where they serve to intensify the anguished contemplation of Desdemona's beauty. The unity of tone thus achieved reflects a complex fusion (or confusion) of emotion. We may compare

> O thou weed,
> Who art so lovely fair and smell'st so sweet
> That the sense aches at thee, would thou hadst ne'er been born!
>
> (IV, ii, 67–9)

The agony of this contradiction is here revived, with a difference.

Desdemona's beauty is still conceived in purely sensuous terms. Othello's insistence on her whiteness carries undertones suggestive of his own blackness and of Desdemona's chastity. These undertones are all the more forceful in that they are not explicitly stated. Othello is not fully conscious of his own meaning.

"Nor scar that whiter skin of hers than snow."

"Snow" is placed at the end of an elaborate inversion, and the effect is of an almost incongruous gravity. But more is involved than simply the sensuous appreciation of Desdemona's beauty.

The word "snow", here placed in connexion with whiteness, suggests by connotation both chastity and coldness. To Coriolanus, Valeria was

> chaste as the icicle
> That's curdied by the frost from purest snow
> And hangs on Dian's temple.
>
> (v, iii, 65–7)

Posthumus thought Imogen "as chaste as unsunn'd snow" (II, v, 13). And Lear cries out in his madness

> Behold yond simpering dame,
> Whose face between her forks presages snow;
> That minces virtue, and does shake the head
> To hear of pleasure's name.
>
> (IV, vi, 120–3)

The suggestion of coldness is reinforced by the "monumental alabaster" of the next line, where the implication of the coldness of death becomes explicit. The sliding sibilants and labials and the long-drawn stresses build to an ecstatic climax. But the words are all the time undermining the rapture which they serve to express.

> "Nor scar that whiter skin of hers than snow,
> And smooth as monumental alabaster."

In the final ecstasy physical touch is felt as at once infinitely desirable and infinitely unbearable. Desdemona is desired warm and alive. The words seem to cry out for this. But Othello can conceive of her only as cold and dead. Desdemona's whiteness ironically suggests her chastity. But the particular application of her chastity and of her beauty is in terms of coldness—("Nor scar that whiter skin of hers than snow", and we may compare "Cold, cold, my girl! Even like thy chastity")—and, finally, in terms of coldness and death ("And smooth as monumental alabaster"). Desdemona can live only, to use a phrase from another play, "in monumental mockery" (*Troilus and Cressida*, III, iii, 153). So the "monumental alabaster" serves at one and the same time to complete Othello's rapture and to destroy it. Desdemona's beauty is inseparable from her death. It cannot be a living beauty. And since Othello is unable to face the inherent contradiction (the logic of lust), he must make a pretence of being practical. Ecstasy is abruptly cancelled by the flat, prosaic line "Yet she must die, else she'll betray more men". It is worth noting that the use of "yet" is an indication that Othello had indeed desired Desdemona alive. In the second act of *Measure for Measure*, Isabella pleads with Angelo for her brother's life. She prepares to take her leave:

> *Isabella.* Heaven keep your honour safe!
> *Angelo.*   Amen:
>   For I am that way going to temptation,
>   Where prayers cross.
>
> (II, ii, 157–9)

Angelo's charged phrase might almost be read as a footnote to the first movement of Othello's speech.

OTHELLO'S "IT IS THE CAUSE…": AN ANALYSIS

"Put out the light, and then put out the light."

The movement of the line recalls the opening "It is the cause, it is the cause, my soul". The need to act and the impossibility of action are balanced against each other. The first "light" Othello can "restore", the second light (the life of Desdemona) he is powerless to restore. The sense of this impotence is conveyed with great subtlety.

> I can again thy former light restore,
> Should I repent me.

As applied to the light, the word "repent" seems superfluous. But, implicitly, the application is to Desdemona. In psychological terms, Othello is making a subconscious association. Consciously he uses the word "repent" only in speaking of the light; its association with the murder of Desdemona he cannot consciously admit. But the word is there.

"Thou cunning'st pattern of excelling nature."

Here is a different ambiguity, centred in the word "cunning'st". The word means literally 'most knowing' and is so far derogatory. Othello had previously used the word to Desdemona in this unambiguous sense:

> I cry you mercy, then:
> I took you for that cunning whore of Venice
> That married with Othello. (IV, ii, 87–9)

But, for a fairer comparison with the present passage, we may take Antony's words on Cleopatra: "She is cunning past man's thought" (I, ii, 150). The derogatory sense of the word is tempered typically by a kind of baffled admiration, an unwilling approval. So, in the present instance, "cunning'st pattern" is not simply set against "excelling nature". Typically, in terms of Othello's character and in terms of Shakespeare's use of words, the two phrases are confused, that is, brought together. It is not simply that Desdemona is "cunning" and nature "excelling". The "pattern" is part of nature's "cunning" and nature's excellence is inseparable from the "pattern". So the words "cunning'st" and "excelling" refer at once to Desdemona and to nature.

"I know not where is that Promethean heat."

It may be noted in passing that Shakespeare has only one reference to 'Prometheus', a cursory one, whilst 'Promethean' occurs only twice (in the long speech of Berowne in *Love's Labour's Lost*). "Relume" appears to be a Shakespearian coinage, is not used by him elsewhere, and has had a very uneventful history ever since. It is peculiarly apt for *Othello*. The classical reference ("Promethean heat"), like the original reference to the "stars", is typical of what is sometimes vaguely called Othello's "lofty and poetic imagery". Shakespeare solved the problem of Othello's inarticulacy with consummate skill.

> Rude am I in my speech,
> And little bless'd with the soft phrase of peace. (I, iii, 81–2)

These are Othello's own words, and we are prepared to accept them to the end. For the language Shakespeare gave to Othello, variously described as "lofty" or "exotic" or "eastern", has a constant air of strangeness. Admittedly this air of strangeness is not confined to Othello.

Cassio's words "of very expert and approved allowance" are as integral a part of the "Othello music" as Othello's

> Most potent, grave, and reverend signiors,
> My very noble and approved good masters. (I, iii, 76–7)

But "Promethean heat" is felt inevitably to be Othello's phrase. For the simplicity, the rudeness, of his speech is equated with a certain foreign extravagance. This extravagance of Othello's speech (which Cassio, another romantic, at times shares with him), is sharply opposed to the native, 'English' extravagance of Iago's way of talking.

When these mutualities so marshal the way, hard at hand comes the master and main exercise, the incorporate conclusion. (II, i, 267–9)

Moreover, Iago speaks naturally in prose, or in a verse deliberately flattened and drained of colour.

To speak of Shakespeare 'solving the problem' of Othello's inarticulacy is, in any case, to beg the question; for Shakespeare created this problem for himself before he solved it. Othello's inarticulacy, as a foreigner and a soldier, is closely linked with his inarticulacy as a man, with the impotence which we are examining in the present context. And it is this inarticulacy, or impotence, of the man that is really significant. "Promethean heat" is as typical of Othello himself as it is of his way of talking. A final point must be made with regard to the extravagance of Othello's language. It is always in danger of parodying itself. The solemnity of "It is the cause" is ironical, because "the cause" does not exist. But the language justifies itself *poetically*. On the other hand, when Othello, overcome with grief, turns to the murdered Desdemona, the language becomes strained and inflated.

> O cursed slave!
> Whip me, ye devils,
> From the possession of this heavenly sight!
> Blow me about in winds! roast me in sulphur!
> Wash me in steep-down gulfs of liquid fire!
> O Desdemona! Desdemona! dead! (v, ii, 276–81)

This is almost "Ercles' vein", and the reason for this poetic inferiority is that the language is psychologically accurate. It is typical of Othello. Shakespeare allowed Othello to poeticize his emotions, because that is just what the inarticulate Othellos of the world so often do. And from this poeticizing the poetry sometimes suffered.

The kind of confusion represented in the word "repent" is continued through the reference to "Promethean heat". For Prometheus stole fire from heaven in order to set men free and, for his fault, was bound to a rock. Othello implies that the "heat" that could bring Desdemona back to life must come from heaven. He himself does not know where to find it. The desire to find this "Promethean heat", the prohibition against finding it, and the impossibility of finding it, are co-present. Othello does not openly compare himself with Prometheus. His inability to do as Prometheus had done is at odds with the desire, negatively stated, to emulate him.

> "I know not where is that Promethean heat
> That can thy light relume."

"Light" occurs five times in the six lines that conclude with these words. There is, in addition, the typical elaboration of "thou flaming minister". This playing with light is also a playing with life.

In the first movement Othello sees Desdemona alive and finds that he can only conceive of her as dead. In the second movement Othello sees Desdemona as already dead and finds that he cannot bring her back to life. The reference to "Promethean heat" implies the contrasting element of cold, as the light itself insists upon the contrasting element of darkness. Again the end finds Desdemona dead and cold.

Othello's terrible struggle is now to be compressed into a single phrase of extraordinary power.

> "When I have pluck'd the rose,
> I cannot give it vital growth again,
> It must needs wither."

At first reading the phrase appears simply as a concentration of the elaborate conceit which precedes it. In this simple sense plucking the rose is exactly synonymous with killing Desdemona. But "pluck'd the rose" is not a chance metaphor. As a symbol of love the rose has had an enduring history. Its illustrative convenience, as the fairest of flowers, is easy to understand. But more is involved than this. As C. S. Lewis has shown, in the *Roman de la Rose* the Rose itself symbolizes the Lady's love. The lover would pluck the rose, that is, directly consummate his love. This was not a denial of chastity, but an acceptance of it. In the symbol of the Rose this duality of love and chastity is perfectly expressed.

Shakespeare provides examples of a generalized use of the symbol. But here, in *Othello*, the symbol has a particular and concentrated force. The rose *is* Desdemona.

> When I have pluck'd the rose,
> I cannot give it vital growth again.

The final consummation of love in death is here stated in terms of negation. For Antony and Cleopatra this was the supreme achievement.

> I will be
> A bridegroom in my death, and run into't
> As to a lover's bed. (IV, xiv, 99–101)

> The stroke of death is as a lover's pinch,
> Which hurts, and is desired. (V, ii, 298–9)

The impact of these images is physical, vital. For to Antony and Cleopatra death was the 'crown' of life, and only in death was their love fulfilled. But Desdemona's death and Othello's love for her exist independently. Each must be completed, but there can be no consummation. In so far as love and death are mutually related they are mutually destructive. Further, Othello's love carries within itself the seeds of its own destruction.

From another aspect the words can be taken as the romantic statement of Iago's cynical philosophy of love: "It is merely a lust of the blood and a permission of the will" (I, iii, 340). Othello is confessing his failure to love Desdemona. And this is the true nature of Iago's victory.

There is a symbolic appropriateness in the fact that Iago is not killed, but remains with Othello to the end: "I bleed, sir; but not kill'd." And Othello answers

> I am not sorry neither; I'ld have thee live;
> For, in my sense, 'tis happiness to die. (v, ii, 289–90)

His words take us back to the meeting at Cyprus, when he greets Desdemona.

> *Othello.*   O my soul's joy!
> If after every tempest come such calms,
> May the winds blow till they have waken'd death!
> And let the labouring bark climb hills of seas,
> Olympus-high and duck again as low
> As hell's from heaven! *If it were now to die,*
> *'Twere now to be most happy*; for, I fear,
> My soul hath her content so absolute
> That not another comfort like to this
> Succeeds in unknown fate. (II, i, 186–95)

It is not an accident that, in his words to Iago at the end of the play, Othello should take us back to the meeting at Cyprus. Othello is not merely 'unlucky'. His love for Desdemona is subtly presented from the start as inadequate. The nature of this inadequacy, the material upon which Iago goes to work, becomes gradually apparent as the play progresses. In the Cyprus meeting Shakespeare plays upon the theme of death. This is something more than a premeditated irony.

> I cannot speak enough of this content;
> It stops me here; it is too much of joy. (II, i, 198–9)

The romantic excess and the romantic inarticulacy are already present together in Othello's love. They combine to produce a curiously static effect. For a moment Othello and Desdemona are isolated in the scene and the moment is felt to be portentous. Othello is wrongfully inarticulate in his love. Iago makes him kill Desdemona. He also makes him incapable of loving her; and for Iago it is this which constitutes victory, the setting down of the precarious harmony, into which Othello himself had first introduced the theme of death. Iago brought Othello down to his own level, and in the victory he was assisted not only by Fate, but also by the weakness of Othello's nature, the initial inadequacy of Othello's love.

> When I have pluck'd the rose,
> I cannot give it vital growth again,
> It must needs wither.

The words have, to use a phrase of Virginia Woolf's, the "weight of the whole play behind them". Under this crushing necessity, "vital growth" cannot subsist. "It must needs wither." Othello's impotence is complete.

The third, and concluding, movement of the speech begins. With the words "I'll smell it on the tree" Othello kisses Desdemona, in fact he begins to make love to her.

> "Ah, balmy breath, that dost almost persuade
> Justice to break her sword!"

We may recall Iachimo's words over the sleeping Imogen:

> 'Tis her breathing that
> Perfumes the chamber thus.   (*Cymbeline*, II, ii, 18–19)

Desdemona's breath is, of course, also the visible sign of her life. Othello confesses later to Gratiano

> There lies your niece,
> Whose breath, indeed, these hands have newly stopp'd.   (v, ii, 201–2)

Lear, entering with Cordelia dead in his arms, cries

> She's gone for ever!
> I know when one is dead, and when one lives;
> She's dead as earth. Lend me a looking-glass;
> If that her breath will mist or stain the stone,
> Why, then she lives.   (v, iii, 259–63)

Again, Isabella, pleading with Angelo, reminds him that God could judge him as he is, and cries

> O, think on that;
> And mercy then will breathe within your lips,
> Like man new made.   (*Measure for Measure*, II, ii, 77–9)

These words of Isabella have a clear affinity with the words of Othello:

> Ah, balmy breath, that dost almost persuade
> Justice to break her sword!

Justice is here presented as a personification, a female figure carrying a sword. The figure, the idea, of justice is remote, lacking the original urgency of "the cause". The whole phrase hints at a possibility of mercy ("dost almost persuade"), a possibility which Othello cannot accept. For Othello is making love to the woman he must kill. His love and her death are each necessities, and they cannot be reconciled with one another. This, of course, is the sense of the whole speech, but here, in these closing lines, it is treated with a peculiar, almost mathematical, precision.

> "One more, one more.
> Be thus when thou art dead, and I will kill thee,
> And love thee after. One more, and this the last:
> So sweet was ne'er so fatal. I must weep,
> But they are cruel tears: this sorrow's heavenly;
> It strikes where it doth love. She wakes."

One kiss begets another, yet each kiss must be the last. The repetition of "one more", delayed and then taken up again with "one more, and this the last", echoes the original repetition of "It is the cause". The sharpness of the contrast, the conflict, is emphasized by the opposition of "sweet" and "fatal", "sorrow" and "heavenly". This is a love-making interspersed with pithy paradox and sententious phrase. The phrases are finely wrought, but it seems that there is a slight slackening of pressure and compulsion behind the words. One might hazard another objection. Partly because the essential contrasts are so artfully drawn, Othello's love-making carries a suggestion of the bizarre. It is almost comic, the righteous murderer unable to stop kissing the victim with whom he is hopelessly in love. Here, at least, is a highly self-conscious frustration.

> Be thus when thou art dead, and I will kill thee,
> And love thee after.

It is a ghastly joke. And Johnson's strictures upon the last two lines deserve attention: "I wish these two lines could be honestly ejected. It is a fault of Shakespeare to counteract his own pathos."

Othello begins to weep and at this moment Desdemona awakes. To Othello she has come back from the dead. To Iago he had said: "I'll not expostulate with her, lest her body and beauty unprovide my mind again" (IV, i, 217–18). And Desdemona cries out to him now "That death's unnatural that kills for loving". But the conflict within him is still unresolved. So Othello, at once resuming his role of high-priest at the sacrifice, must murder his wife:

> *Othello.*   Thou art to die.
> *Desdemona.* Then Lord have mercy on me!
> *Othello.*   I say, amen.
> *Desdemona.* And have you mercy too!   (v, ii, 56–8)

In reading the last movement of the speech, we have already located a sense of uneasiness, which Johnson formulated into a critical objection. The air of contrivance which marks the phrasing of Othello's comments is hard to justify on naturalistic grounds. These phrases seem too intellectually tidy for a literal acceptance of them as Othello's self-conscious observations upon his own feelings. The lines, perhaps, are rather to be taken as Shakespeare's comment upon Othello's state of mind. But, even if this reading is accepted, the objection remains that, by now, this comment is unnecessary, a superfluous simplification. Certainly the poetry of this final movement is less fine than the poetry of the rest of the speech. The regular rhythm of the speech is broken down, to admit of a dual operation within the words. In crude paraphrase, there is Othello's action ("one more, one more"), and there are his comments upon his action ("so sweet was ne'er so fatal"). But this breaking-down of the rhythm is not, in itself, harmful, nor can it explain that falling-off, which we sense in the epigrammatic neatness of "so sweet was ne'er so fatal". May it not, after all, be possible to justify these final lines in terms of character?

Othello and Macbeth die with rhyming couplets on their lips. Macbeth's final couplet is effective on the surface and, at the moment, we expect no more. Othello's last words invite comment at a deeper level.

> I kiss'd thee ere I kill'd thee: no way but this;
> Killing myself, to die upon a kiss.   (v, ii, 358–9)

The self-regarding attitude is tragically conclusive. The formal balancing of the words—their terrible emphasis—recalls the final movement of the present speech.

T. S. Eliot, writing of Othello's last speech ("Soft you; a word or two before you go") has this comment:

What Othello seems to me to be doing in making this speech is *cheering himself up*. He is endeavouring to escape reality, he has ceased to think about Desdemona, and is thinking about himself....Othello succeeds in turning himself into a pathetic figure, by adopting an *aesthetic* rather than a moral attitude, dramatizing himself against his environment. He takes in the spectator, but the human motive is primarily to take in himself. I do not believe that any writer has ever exposed this 'bovarysme', the human will to see things as they are not, more clearly than Shakespeare.

"It is the cause" is also an exposure of "the human will to see things as they are not". Johnson's comment that Shakespeare, here as elsewhere, is counteracting his own pathos, suggests that, in the sense of Eliot's words, he is 'taken in' by Othello. Johnson is clearly embarrassed by the verbal dexterity of

> This sorrow's heavenly;
> It strikes where it doth love.

The phrase seems to require a modification of that unreserved sympathy with the hero, which, at this moment (so Johnson feels) Shakespeare himself is demanding. With his usual integrity Johnson admits to his embarrassment. But to see Othello here as he wishes himself to be seen is to distort the tragedy. For it is Othello's self-deception, and not his bad luck, that is essential to that tragedy.

NOTE

1. This stage direction from the First Quarto has a simple but highly effective symbolic appropriateness. It is omitted from the First Folio. The various lines of the speech discussed in succeeding paragraphs are enclosed in quotation marks.

ON TRANSLATING *HAMLET*

BY

SALVADOR DE MADARIAGA

Every translator is familiar with the difficulties, anxieties, problems and snares of his craft. To begin with, corresponding words in two different languages hardly ever cover the same *area of meaning*. That is why so-called literal translation is so often unsatisfactory. *Plaisir* does not mean *pleasure*; the two words are like two blots of different outline *partly* covering the same spot on the paper but, for the rest, spreading over different areas. Then again, some things cannot be translated at all because the people who speak the second language, unlike those who speak the first, simply do not say them. An English servant will answer an inquiry at the door: "I am afraid Madam is not in." That "I am afraid" is utterly incomprehensible in any other language. The French word *d'ailleurs* is better dropped when translating French into Spanish. The Spaniard simply does not *think* that way. There is no word for *subir* in English; one has to say *to go up*; but there is no word for *up* in Spanish.

These are problems of a general nature which beset the translator of any text from one language into another. But over and above them, the task of translating Shakespeare into Spanish verse bristles with problems of its own. The first is that of the language itself. *Hamlet* is written in the English spoken in London by the wealthy and influential set during the reign of Queen Elizabeth and King James I. A modern translation must appeal to the educated classes of twentieth-century Spain and Spanish America. The translation has therefore to be two-fold: in space, from England to Spain; in time, from 1600 to 1950. A language has to be chosen, in fact, invented, which should not be out of place in either epoch. What is wanted is not precisely that the translation should contain no verbal anachronisms, no words unknown to the Spaniards of 1600; good in itself as a general rule, this practice can in fact be brushed aside in not too glaring cases, without much harm. Rather than philological history or science, taste and art are required, a feeling for style, manner, mood.

Next to language, verse. There are some competent Spanish versions of *Hamlet* in prose. But they cannot be counted as real translations, for *Hamlet* is a poem, perhaps, in the deepest sense of the word, the most poetical of Shakespeare's plays. Verse is indispensable. But what verse? Our classics have now and then used the hendecasyllabic line, a most noble measure in Spanish; but most of their plays are written in lines of eight syllables. This type of verse can be most graceful and flexible in Lope, truly monumental in Calderón. There is a magnificent power in the *décimas* which Calderón often used:

> Apurar, cielos, pretendo,
> ya que me tratáis así,
> qué delito cometí
> contra vosotros naciendo;
> aunque si nací, ya entiendo
> qué delito he cometido:

bastante causa ha tenido
vuestra justicia y rigor,
pues el delito mayor
del hombre es haber nacido.

Nevertheless, this kind of verse, with its equal measure and hammer-like regularity of rhyme, will not suit Shakespeare, and in Shakespeare, least of all *Hamlet*. Something freer and more fluid is needed; a form which may give more scope to the haunting moodiness, to the changes in soul-weather which give its character to the play. The obvious solution—blank verse. This was the course taken by one of my predecessors, the Andalusian ex-priest José María Blanco Crespo (1775–1841), better known as Blanco-White. There are some good examples of Spanish blank verse, but it is a form which does not suit the Spanish language. An explanation of this fact would be out of place here.

So, on the one hand, it is necessary to avoid the rigid rhyme-pattern of the classics; and on the other, blank-verse, which in Spanish is really too 'blank'. My choice had been worked out before I began to translate *Hamlet*. My model had been Goethe's *Faust*; a free and undulating verse, adapting itself easily to the many moods and movements of a play, to the dreamy soliloquies as well as to the give and take of conversation and even to the cut and thrust of action. Rhymes in this kind of verse come and go as the mood or situation may suggest. I had tried it in my play *Don Carlos*. I shall now append the soliloquy "To be or not to be", first in Blanco-White's blank verse, then in my translation.

Blanco-White's Translation

Ser o no ser: He aquí la grande duda.
¿Cuál es más noble? ¿Presentar el pecho
De la airada fortuna a las saetas,
O tomar arma contra un mar de azares
Y acabar de una vez?... Morir... Dormirse...
Nada más, y escapar en sólo un sueño
A este dolor del alma, al choque eterno
Que es la herencia del alma en esta vida.
¿Hay más que apetecer?... Morir... Dormirse...
¡Dormir!... Tal vez soñar... Ahi está el daño,
Porque, ¿quién sabe los horribles sueños
Que pueden azorar en el sepulcro
Al infelice que se abrió camino
De entre el tumulto y confusión del mundo?
A este recelo sólo, a este ¿quién sabe?
Debe su larga vida la desgracia
Si no ¿quién tolerara los reveses
Y las burlas del tiempo? ¿La injusticia
Del opresor y el ceño del soberbio?
¿Las ansias de un amor menospreciado?
¿La dilación de la justicia?... ¿El tono

E insolente desdén de los validos?
¿Los desaires que el mérito paciente
Tiene que devorar...cuando una daga,
Siempre a su alcance, libertarle puede
Y sacarlo de afán?... ¿Quién sufriría
Sobre su cuello el peso que le agobia,
Gimiendo y jadeando hora tras hora,
Sin ver el fin, a no ser que el recelo
De hallar que no concluye en el sepulcro
La penosa jornada...que aún se extiende
A limites incógnitos, de donde
Nadie volvió jamás...confunde al alma
Y hace que sufra conocidos males,
Por no arrojarse a los que no conoce?
Esa voz interior, esa conciencia
Nos hace ser cobardes: ella roba
A la resolución el sonrosado
Color nativo, haciéndola que cobre
La enferma palidez del miramiento,
Y las empresas de más gloria y lustre,
Al encontrarla, tuercen la corriente
Y se evaporan en proyectos vanos.

My Translation

Ser o no ser. De eso se trata, en suma.
¿Que és lo más noble: soportar callando
Hondas y flechas de áspera fortuna,
O tomar armas contra un mar de males
Y darles fin luchando?
Morir. Dormir. No más; y con el sueño
Decir que damos término a la pena
Y a los mil infortunios naturales,
Herencia de la carne—es un empeño
Para devotamente deseado.
Morir. Dormir. ¿Dormir? ¡Soñar acaso!
Ahí está el punto fuerte.
Pues al pensar qué sueños soñariamos
Dormidos en el seno de la muerte,
Se nos suspende el ánimo. Respeto
Es este sin el cual no dejaríamos
Hacer calamidad de larga vida;
Pues ¿quién soportaría
El látigo y la coz de cada día,

Los yerros del mandón, el trato recio
Del soberbio, el dolor vivo y secreto
De un amor desdeñado, la justicia
Con sus constantes plazos,
La insolencia del grande, y los rechazos
Que, con paciencia, el mérito tolera
Del hombre sin pericia,
Cuando su propia paz hallar pudiera
Con un mero estilete? ¿Quién quisiera
Jadear y gemir con tanta carga
Una vida tan larga,
Si no fuera
Que el temor de lo que hay tras de la muerte,
Comarca indescubierta,
Y de cuya frontera no hay viajero
Que a retornar acierte,
La voluntad del hombre desconcierta
Y le hace que prefiera
Los males que ya tiene a los que ignora?
Asi nos acobarda el buen consejo,
Y al ánimo naciente
Que al primer pronto con su albor colora
Lo marchita este pálido reflejo
Del pensamiento. Con lo cual, empresas
De gran momento y fuste
Pierden punto y ajuste
Y hasta el nombre de acción.

May I suggest two other points? The first is that rhyming can at times be used to produce a definite effect. Thus, when in Act I, scene ii Hamlet objects to the word "seems" his mother has used

Seems! Madam! nay it is; I know not "seems",

I have tried to render the pressing grief of Hamlet's protest by repeating the rhyme regularly for the whole first part of the speech:

¿Parece? No, Señora. No parece.
Es. Porque nada de esto, nada madre,
Ni esta mi capa negra y atavío
Con que el luto las ropas ennochece,
Ni del dolor el generoso río,
Ni aliento que en suspiro se enternece,
Ni el rostro aderezado a lo sombrío,
Ni gesto o forma al uso en quien padece,
Aunque en mí, nada es mío. Es un "parece"

Que cualquiera reviste a su albedrío.
Dentro va en mí lo que no sale a escena.
Esto es tan sólo el traje de mi pena.

Similarly, when in the scene with the Actor and later in the induction, Shakespeare goes back to rhymed couplets, an outmoded form in his time, I have tried to convey a similar effect by writing these passages in Royal Octaves, a similarly outmoded form (for the theatre) in Spain in Shakespeare's days.

One word about doubtful passages. They are the pest of the translator, since translating requires understanding. The meaning must be made clear before the new words that must express it are found. In some cases, this task implied a choice, and in one particular case a departure from the accepted text. The meeting of Hamlet with the Norwegian Captain is usually printed thus:

> *Captain.* Yes, it is already garrison'd.
> *Hamlet.* Two thousand souls and twenty thousand ducats
> Will not debate the question of this straw:
> This is the imposthume of much wealth and peace,
> That inward breaks, and shows no cause without
> Why the man dies. I humbly thank you, sir.
> *Captain.* God be wi' you, sir.   (*Exit*)   (IV, iv, 24–30)

This passage raises a number of problems, notably the meaning of lines 25–6 and the attribution of the several sentences. Readers of the Furness Variorum edition may recollect that a suggestion was made in the *Gentleman's Magazine* that lines 25–6 should be said by the Captain, Hamlet taking up the dialogue at line 27; and that "Tschischwitz goes still farther, and gives the whole speech down to 'dies' to the Captain, on the ground that this speech does not accord with what Hamlet says afterwards, where honour is the cause that compels him to struggle, not an 'imposthume of much wealth and peace'."

Finally there is line 60 in which Hamlet speaks of

> The imminent death of twenty thousand men,

which hardly tallies with line 25; while Walker (*vide* Furness) suggests Ten instead of Two for the first word of line 25. In my translation I have made the following assumptions:

(1) That lines 25 and 26 are said by the Captain. He supplies facts. Hamlet could not produce such figures.

(2) That in line 26 the word "not" is a misprint for "now"; for this makes excellent sense while the present text does not. Hamlet has expressed doubts that Poland would fight for "such a straw", and the Captain retorts: "on the contrary; the men are already there; and *now* so many souls and so many ducats will contest this trifle."

(3) That in line 25 "Ten" should be read instead of "Two". This would tally better with an "army of such mass and charge" (line 47); and would explain Hamlet's reference to twenty thousand men in line 60 as a rough doubling of the side he knows.

(4) That Tschischwitz is wrong, for in point of thought lines 27–9 are by no means irreconcilable with lines 54–6, "Rightly to be great...""; and, even if they were, Hamlet is quite capable of emitting thoughts in every direction of the compass.

In conclusion, the above suggestions amount to reading the passage as follows:

Hamlet. Why, then the Polack never will defend it.
Captain. Yes, it is already garrison'd.
Ten thousand souls and twenty thousand ducats
Will now debate the question of this straw.
Hamlet. This is the imposthume of much wealth and peace,
That inward breaks, and shows no cause without
Why the man dies. I humbly thank you, sir.
Captain. God be wi' you, sir.　　*(Exit)*

Finally, I should like to record that this translation has but confirmed an opinion I formed over thirty years ago: that Spanish is a language singularly well adapted to express the English genius—and vice versa.

SHAKESPEARE IN CHINA

BY

CHANG CHEN-HSIEN

[These notes on the difficulties confronting the Chinese translator of Shakespeare relate to the period before 1950. Recent changes in social life create conditions of an entirely different kind.]

I. THE PROBLEMS OF TRANSLATION

Of all the difficulties of producing Shakespeare in China, the greatest are the differences in social etiquette, the language barrier, and the method of translation.

According to old Chinese etiquette, a man cannot touch the hand of a woman. If he should give anything to her, he must put it upon a table instead of handing it to her directly. In spite of many changes during the present century, the same basic principle still holds. Even husband and wife cannot walk hand in hand, or embrace, or kiss in public. Things like that are reserved only for the chamber. Otherwise they are considered as not only vulgar but indecent. That is why on the traditional Chinese stage Duncan cannot say to Lady Macbeth "Give me your hand". That is not courtesy, but seduction.

A compliment, especially a compliment to a lady, is better implied than expressed. We seldom say things like "You are beautiful", even when we are in love. A mere silent admiration is enough. If we should say to a girl things like "You are as beautiful as Helen", we might incur a double charge of hinting that her behaviour is as light as that of Helen and that her only virtue is her beauty. To say the least, she would wonder whether that is a suggestion of an elopement. The chief charm of a young lady is her virtue and not her beauty. Duncan's "Fair and noble hostess, We are your guest to-night" when literally translated would certainly mislead the audience.

When Lady Macbeth says "Had he not resembled my father", she thinks only of Duncan's resemblance to her father. But when we say "Mr A looks like Mr B's father", we may imply that Mr A. not only looks like Mr B.'s father but, at the same time, that Mr A. is having an improper relationship with Mr B.'s mother. A Chinese regards his parents as gods on earth. Filial piety is considered as the greatest of the virtues. That is why nobody, except a very vulgar clown, says, "He looks like my father". Should that line, "Had he not resembled my father", be translated literally, the audience would surely take it, not as a human touch, but as a very coarse joke at the expense of Lady Macbeth's mother.

No violation of filial piety can ever be tolerated on the Chinese stage. No one short of a villain could possibly have behaved like Hamlet to his mother in the Chamber Scene. Let us compare *Hamlet* with the famous story of *Chao's Bridge*. In the story, Mrs Chao, a widow, has been intimate with a monk. Her son bears this family disgrace with silent patience. One day, the mother even goes so far as to hint that it is too cold for the monk to wade across the ford every night on his way to her house. The son goes ahead building a bridge. While it is under construction, he saves the monk from wading by carrying him on his back across the ford. But

112

immediately after the mother's death, he kills the monk and puts the head in front of his father's tomb as a sacrifice. Then he gives himself up to the law.

The Chinese language is a formidable barrier as far as translating Shakespeare is concerned. Its most important difference from English lies in the fact that it has no alphabet and is not based on the phonetic principles of spelling and pronunciation. Most of the characters are pictures or symbols or combinations of both. As Chinese differs fundamentally from English in the method by which it is written, so the thoughts expressed in the language differ from those expressed in English. Therefore, it is often impossible to translate Chinese directly into English or vice versa. The most one can expect to achieve is a rough equivalent that may suggest a similar impression and association.

Even in the case of a good translation, the Chinese equivalent may give rise to associations quite alien to the original. For example, it is not possible to translate the comedian's 'mother-in-law' without misunderstanding. This word written in Chinese gives rise to the picture of a most beloved and respected old lady, the highest authority of a house. The word 'river' in Chinese suggests a very wide and long stream of water. That is why, at my first arrival at Stratford-upon-Avon, I asked for the way to the river, while I was actually standing in front of the Memorial Theatre. The word 'pen' in Chinese suggests a little piece of bamboo with a little soft brush at the end. Consequently, the imagery suggested by this kind of pen and that suggested by an English pen are bound to be different. When the word 'theatre' is written in Chinese, one tends to think of the platform stage, the incidental music, the fancy costumes, the high-keyed chanting and singing, the symbolic dancing, the eager audience, the warm cosy atmosphere. "These hangman's hands" in Chinese certainly does not give the audience the picture of an Elizabethan executioner with hands streaming with blood.

As Shakespeare wrote for the popular stage, the translator must aim at the general public rather than a small group of readers. As some of the audience are illiterate, the work must therefore not only aim at those who do not know a word of English but also at those who do not read a word of Chinese. The common audience rather than the intellectual *élite* should be the chief concern. The technique is of course infinitely more difficult. To translate Shakespeare is difficult enough. To do it for those who do not read English is still more so. To do it for the common crowd who form the necessary majority of the audience is the most difficult of all. On the stage, the dialogue can be spoken only once. If the audience does not understand it, it is lost. Nothing can retrieve the loss. A reader may read the text over and over again, but the audience has no second chance. Therefore, only those words and expressions that are used daily in actual conversation can be used in the dialogue.

Through experience, we see that it is not possible to translate Shakespeare in verse and yet make it comprehensible to the common audience. Therefore, it must be done in prose. No matter whether the original characters talk in blank verse or prose, we must translate the whole thing into prose, though we may vary the style to suit the characters.

II. THE EXISTING VERSIONS

The earliest Chinese translation of Shakespeare seems to have appeared about 1910. Its author, Teng I-che, saw Gounod's opera *Romeo and Juliet* in New York performed by Amelita Galli-Curci. He was so thrilled with the balcony scene that he took out the original play immediately afterwards and translated the scene into what he called a 'rhymed ballad'. A rhymed ballad is a very popular form of entertainment, sung to the accompaniment of a very simple stringed instrument and of wooden sound boards which keep the beats of the rhythm, and Teng's idea of translating the scene into this rhymed ballad is a very happy one in itself. But he becomes so hopelessly lost in the mazes of the English language and of Chinese literary style that his lines are suitable neither for singing nor for reading. Here is an example picked out at random from the first few words of the Chinese text:

> Cover the blood and hide the wound.
> Ah! Look, a light shoots forth from that window!
> That is the east.
> Junee [Juliet]! You are the sun!
> Good sun! Hurry up, in order to knock down this envious moon!
> You just look at that pale long face of hers....
> If you were her maid or girl-slave, I should break my intestines with anger.
>
> (Romeo and Juliet, II, ii, 1–6)

This is neither verse nor prose. Its sentence structure is entirely foreign. One who cannot read the original text can never understand what Teng says. One who can, will discover, after taking all the trouble to trace a line by line comparison, that much of the translation does not make any sense at all. The Chinese and the English languages are so far apart that any attempt at a line by line rendering without digesting and remoulding the whole thing will make the work unreadable and incomprehensible.

The Tempest, by N. C. Yu and his wife, is again a noble attempt and a worthy failure. These authors were among the first who attempted the translation of a whole play. They tried to render blank verse into a very rigid form of five-word lines of Chinese verse. The idea of translating Shakespeare into verse was common among the early writers. But it did not work. The verse form here is very bad: it is indeed not verse at all. Though there are five words in a line, and though the five-word line is one of the most popular verse forms in China, yet not all five-word lines can be considered as verse. Rhythm, tones, euphony, rhymes, beauty of expression, etc. are all necessary qualities. Yet what is happening here is that the translators merely put five words in a line and hope for the best. No one would call any ten syllables put together at random a blank verse line.

> Dear father
> If by your magic
> You make the seas roar with anger,
> Please stop them!
> It seems:

Dirty torrents are pouring down from the sky;
And the sea waters rush up
To God's cheek,
And strike forth the sparkling flame. (*Tempest*, I, ii, 1–5)

The rhythm of Chinese verse is based primarily on tone quality while that of English is based on stress. To translate blank verse into five-word Chinese verse, in fact, is ridiculous. The whole text becomes cramped and twisted out of shape. That is why it is absolutely unreadable.

The balcony scene of *Romeo and Juliet* translated, in 1920, by Hsu Chih-mo is one of the best of the early works. Hsu was one of the best known of the modern poets in his time. He translated the scene word by word into a very beautiful modern free verse form. By modern free verse form, I mean verse with no rules for variety of tones, no limit to the number of words in each line, and no need for a rigid rhyming scheme. The diction is more colloquial. The only necessary qualification is poetic beauty.

But for all its merits, this version is far from an ideal work. A translation is primarily for those readers who have no knowledge at all of the foreign language upon which the text is based. Hsu's version of the scene can be appreciated only by himself and by a small number of readers. No Chinese scholar who cannot read English can really understand and appreciate it. It is English written in Chinese words. In fact, the Chinese is more foreign to me than Shakespeare's English itself. In many points, it is so confused that a word by word comparison with the original text is necessary for understanding. There are still errors, though the rendering is far more accurate than the earlier ones by Teng and Yu.

Ah, soft! What light shines bright from yonder window?
That is the east, Julieh [Juliet] is the eastern sun.
Arise, beautiful sun, and outshine quickly
That envious moon. Since you, being her maid,
Are far more beautiful than she, she is already completely pale with grief.
(*Romeo and Juliet*, II, ii, 2–6)

Tien Han's *Hamlet* (1922) is translated in prose. The simple fact that it is done in prose marks in itself great progress. Tien is one of the most famous modern playwrights in China. One would naturally expect him to translate his *Hamlet* with an eye upon the stage. But unfortunately, though it is relatively more readable, it is still unactable. He is still thinking of his small group of readers rather than of anything else. It may be of some help to a Chinese college student, but as an actable version, it is far from adequate. Had he translated *Hamlet* solely for the stage, he might have scored a much greater success. As a translator of *Hamlet* will certainly pay particular attention to the famous "To be or not to be" soliloquy, I pick out the following few lines from that passage as an example:

Is it better to live or not to live...this is a question: Should the so-called heroes suffer the slings and arrows of tyrannical Fate, or should they resist the tempestuous waves till death?
(*Hamlet*, III, i, 56–60)

After this rather dismal picture (made more dismal by the astonishingly bad *Hamlet* of Shao Ting, 1930), there seems to be some hope when we come to Liang Shih-chui's translations.

Liang is by far the most voluminous worker in this field. His renderings are very faithful, though still not without errors. His *As You Like It, Twelfth Night, Merchant of Venice, Hamlet,* and *Macbeth* published in 1936 are all as readable as Tien's *Hamlet,* though, to a certain extent, still less actable. His style is less beautiful than Hsu's. These translations may help a Chinese student to read Shakespeare, but for those readers who know no English at all or for use on the stage, they are of little service. Here is an example again from the famous soliloquy:

> To live or not to live, this is a question; whether to suffer the slings and arrows of this tyrannical Fate, or to draw for a life-and-death struggle against this towering hate... which way is deemed more heroic?
>
> (*Hamlet,* III, i, 56–60)

Owing to the wide divergence of the Chinese and English languages and the misconception that Shakespeare is only for the Chinese students of English literature, none of the existing translations, so far as I am aware, is suitable either for the stage or for the general reading public.

INTERNATIONAL NOTES

A selection has here been made from the reports received from our correspondents, those which present material of a particularly interesting kind being printed wholly or largely in their entirety. It should be emphasized that the choice of countries to be thus represented has depended on the nature of the information presented in the reports, not upon either the importance of the countries concerned or upon the character of the reports themselves.

Australia

The Old Vic visited Australia in 1948 presenting *Richard III* (along with two other non-Shakespearian plays). In 1949–50 the Shakespeare Memorial Theatre Company brought productions of *Macbeth* and *Much Ado about Nothing*. These were the last professional companies to play Shakespeare in Australia until the John Alden Shakespearian Company, an amateur Australian group, became professional in December 1951. This company started with a production of *King Lear* which ran for six months in Sydney. The repertoire now includes *A Midsummer Night's Dream*, *The Merchant of Venice* and *The Merry Wives of Windsor*. *Othello* and *The Tempest* will soon be added.

The National Theatre Movement of Australia in Melbourne, an organization which receives financial support from the State of Victoria, has produced three Shakespearian plays during the year. They started with a semi-professional production of *The Taming of the Shrew* with Petruchio and Katherina portrayed by professional English actors while the rest of the cast were local amateurs. Later in the season *Two Gentlemen of Verona* and *The Merchant of Venice* were presented.

An interesting development is the annual Shakespeare Festival held in Swan Hill, a small town (5,000 inhabitants) in the northern part of Victoria. Here, under the guidance of Mrs Marjorie McLeod, the whole town produces and supports a week-long festival in honour of Shakespeare. Since the first festival in 1947 the idea has become firmly established. The major event is the production of a play (*As You Like It* 1950, *Romeo and Juliet* 1951, *Merchant of Venice* 1952) but other events include a pageant, lectures, madrigal singing and folk dancing.

Any article which attempts to summarize Shake-spearian productions in Australia must mention Doris Fitton who has sponsored productions of Shakespeare for the past 22 years at the Independent Theatre in Sydney.　　　　WAYNE HAYWARD

Austria

The Salzburg Festival of the summer 1951 surprised its audience by an exquisite performance of *As You Like It* under the management of Gustav Gründgens of Düsseldorf; the actors were chosen among the best of the Vienna Burgtheater. At the same time Frau Reinhardt-Thimig (the widow of Max Reinhardt) gave open-air performances of *A Midsummer Night's Dream* at Strobl on the Wolfgangsee with the pupils of her Seminar of Dramatic Art.

Just before Christmas the Vienna Burgtheater brought out a new staging of *Othello*, with its best actors in the main parts. It has remained since then in the regular repertory of this leading Austrian theatre. Werner Kraus interpreted Iago as a villain led on by admiration of his own cleverness. Desdemona, performed by Hilde Mikulicz, was pure loveliness and purity. Erich Auer as Cassio, a foil both to Iago and to Ewald Balsen as Othello, stressed soldier-like uprightness and gallantry. The performance made a deep impression on the audience.　　　　KARL BRUNNER

Belgium

The company of the Old Vic scored a great success in Belgium with *King Lear*, which was given in the Théâtre Royal du Parc in Brussels. It was the first time that the play was performed in Belgium in its English text. The Company 'le Rideau de Bruxelles' (Manager, Claude Etienne) had produced Romain Sanvic's French translation of *Lear* at the Palais des Beaux Arts in January 1950.

This was, to my knowledge, the first French *Lear* to appear before the Belgian public. André Berger (who had already played Hamlet, Macbeth and Iago) interpreted the title-role and acted also as producer.

The 'Théâtre National de Belgique' (Manager, Jacques Huisman) had successfully ended its season by performances (in French) of *Richard III*, in André Obey's version. René Hainaux played the title-role and Michael Langham came from England to produce the play.

The Flemish 'Nationaal Toneel' opened its season 1951–2 with *Measure for Measure* in a Dutch translation. At the same time the Flemish 'Koninklijke Toneel' in Ghent played *Romeo and Juliet*. The same play in a French adaptation specially written by a member of the company, Raymond Gérome, has been chosen by the 'Théâtre National de Belgique' for the end of its present season. Pierre Michaël and Jacqueline Huisman will be the lovers of Verona.

The Company of Marie Bell, sociétaire of la Comédie Française, paid a spring visit to Brussels and played in the Théâtre de l'Alhambra André Gide's French version of *Antony and Cleopatra*. ROBERT DE SMET

Canada

As far as cross-country reports reveal, Canada has had to rely on its own talent for the production of Shakespeare during the last twelve months. There were no visits from outside companies, British or American. This self-dependence is recorded with no sense of belittlement or regret. Canada, with its fifteen millions, should in the theatre be able to provide for itself, and in a measure it does so very competently. If it has no professional companies, there is no lack of eager and able amateurs or of 'little theatres' run by dramatic societies, sometimes with expert professional participation or guidance. Naturally the quality of the productions varies, but the general standard, judged by amateur acting elsewhere, is remarkably high. The production of *Richard II*, given recently in Hart House Theatre at the University of Toronto, might be instanced. In one respect at least, in the artistry of the single setting, the undergraduate production compared very favourably with the performance given some six months ago at Stratford. There was not, of course, the same finish to the acting, but, on the other hand, the mistake was not made of playing York as a half-buffoon.

Other productions reported—and they are merely a few of many—are *Macbeth* and *The Tempest* given in the Studio Theatre at the University of Alberta, *Macbeth* by the undergraduates of Queen's University, and *Twelfth Night* and *The Merry Wives of Windsor* at the Little Theatre, Peterborough, under the direction of Robertson Davies, Canada's most successful playwright. The Peterborough plays are said to have been exceptionally good. These are examples of amateur productions. The Earle Grey Players, a semi-professional company, had their usual brief but pleasant summer season of Shakespeare out-of-doors. Fittingly for the warmth of a Canadian summer evening, they chose three comedies: *The Merchant of Venice*, *The Tempest* and *Much Ado about Nothing*.

This may not seem an extensive or exciting Shakespeare chronicle, but again it should be understood that the productions mentioned are only a representative few. If full reports were available, the number might well be five times multiplied. R. S. KNOX

Czechoslovakia

During the last year the capital, Prague, saw only three plays by Shakespeare: *The Taming of the Shrew*, *Othello* (both at the National Theatre in new translations by E. A. Saudek) and *Much Ado about Nothing* (on a suburban stage). All productions were warmly received by the Prague public. *The Taming* and *Othello* were played by two alternating casts. Of special interest was the second cast of *Othello*, whose members took considerable trouble over their parts. Stanislavski's 'Producer's Plan of *Othello*' was conscientiously studied and many hints from his book were used in the creation of the Moor. Iago's part was played unconventionally: Jan Pivec acted him as a warm, hearty, robust fellow, so that his villainy appeared the more astounding and terrifying. Shakespeare's comedies have proved still more popular than his tragedies. *A Midsummer Night's Dream* was produced in four theatres (Carlsbad, Hradec Králové, Kladno, Opava), *The Taming* in three (Prague, Liberec, Benešov), *Much Ado* in three (Prague, Budějovice, Opava), *As You Like It* in three (Budějovice, Teplice, Ostrava), *Twelfth Night* in three (Plzeň, Ostrava, Pardubice), *The Merry Wives of Windsor* in two (Jihlava, Nový Jičín), and *The Merchant of Venice* in one (Nový Jičín). The tragedies were played less: *Romeo and Juliet* was produced in Nový Jičín, Hradec Králové and Brno, *Othello* (Saudek's most recent translation) in Prague, Olomouc and Carlsbad, and *Hamlet* in Bratislava.

A selection from Shakespeare's Sonnets in Jan Vladislav's translation was published by the Vyšehrad publishers with a note on the problem of the *Sonnets* by the present writer. This new translation was used for two successful matinees in Gramoton (gramophone record theatre in Prague), for which another matinee of three famous Shakespearean scenes (from *Romeo and Juliet*, *Macbeth* and *Henry V*) is in active preparation at the time of writing. Saudek's translation of *Hamlet* was the subject of a stimulating discussion in the Translators' Circle of the Writers' Club in March 1952. At the March meeting of the Czech Academy, O. Vočadlo read a paper on 'Channels of Shakespeare's Influence in Bohemia and Slovakia'. After drawing attention to the contribution of various Czech institutions to the public appreciation of the poet's art he proposed the establishment of a Shakespeare association under the aegis of the Academy.   BŘETISLAV HODEK

Denmark

Denmark is a small country with few theatres that are equal to performances of plays from the classical repertoire and only one theatre that actually stages these plays—so small, in fact, that she has few scholars able to do original research on the Elizabethan drama, and only one who publishes the results of his Shakespeare studies.

Paul V. Rubow, the literary historian, has added a few essays, mainly on *Hamlet*, to his studies of Shakespeare (printed in *En Studiebog*, 1950), and has published a book called *Shakespeare's Hamlet* in 1951 (Year Book of the University of Copenhagen).

The only performances of Shakespeare were staged at The Royal Theatre in Copenhagen: *As You Like It* in May 1951 and *Richard III* in November 1951. Characteristic of both productions was a desire to get away from nineteenth-century traditions, and a genuine Shakespearian tone was attempted, although the producers were at pains to avoid anything suggestive of the museum. There was a rush to both plays—as is always the case when Shakespeare is performed in Denmark.

The need of the theatre-going public for Shakespeare performances was also met by a series of guest visits. At the Festival Plays at Kronborg Castle in June 1950 The Old Vic performed *Hamlet*, and in June 1951 a Swedish company (The Norrköping-Linköping Municipal Theatre) staged their interpretation of the Danish tragedy.   ALF HENRIQUES

Eire

Undoubtedly the production of primal importance during the period under review was the *Richard II* staged at the Gaiety Theatre, Dublin, by Hilton Edwards and Micheál MacLiammóir. Anew McMaster, home from Australia, failed to find a suitable theatre for his *King Lear* and so retired to the provinces with *Hamlet*, *Othello*, *The Taming of the Shrew* and *The Merchant of Venice*. Thanks to McMaster, Irish provincial audiences

are better versed in Shakespeare and are generally more appreciative than audiences in the capital.

In *Richard II* Hilton Edwards very wisely decided to make a straight, forthright, approach to the production; there were neither tricks nor frills. He contented himself with having some magnificent settings designed in an Harleian Manuscript manner by a brilliant young artist, Micheal O'Herlihy. MacLiammóir forecast his Richard in a letter to the producer: "... You need have no fears, however, that I share the popular view of him as a saintly hero. This myth came entirely from his own conception of himself after his tragedy began: like so many people who are fundamentally vain, supersensitive, luxury-loving, gay, capricious and egocentric, he inevitably pictured himself in misfortune as the supreme sufferer and did not hesitate to compare himself in his anguish to Christ, as he had compared himself in his triumph to the Sun. A transplanted Frenchman lost in the moralising gloom of the island fogs; an artist, a wit and a sybarite caught in an iron trap; this is how I hope to play him."

In MacLiammóir's speaking (and the same held true for almost all the players) the play became an almost purely lyrical drama, swift and simple. Over against MacLiammóir's handsome, weak and poetic Richard stood a handsome, strong and poetic Bolingbroke in the person of Michael Laurence. This proved to be a major casting weakness. It is in the nature of our materialistic age to dismiss Richard as incompetent and as one "merely dazzled by phenomena instead of perceiving things as they are". With Michael Laurence in the part of Bolingbroke our modern Irish audiences lacked no excuse for turning their backs on what was possibly the finest Richard since Benson. A magnificently rugged Gaunt played by Christopher Casson (whose voice possesses a ruggedness all its own), a nobly spoken Norfolk (played by Dennis Brennan) and a York all fuss and kindness (played by Robert Hennessy) were the other outstanding male performances. Noelle Middleton (whose voice may now be heard from the B.B.C.) played a sad and gentle Queen.

As if to crown their very fine work, Edwards and MacLiammóir have been invited by the Danish Government to present *Hamlet* at Elsinore.   GABRIEL FALLON

Germany

1951 has again been rich in Shakespeare productions in Germany. About twenty of his plays have been performed on the bigger as well as on the smaller stages. Since, however, there has been a growing tendency among provincial theatres to put a play in their repertory once it has been successfully staged by a famous producer, a certain uniformity of repertories has resulted. Only slight changes have to be made to last year's list of Shakespeare performances. Of the tragedies *Hamlet*, though still most frequently performed, was not put on in as many new productions as in previous years. But there was a revived interest in *King Lear*. Of this play a number of theatres put on new productions, the most noteworthy being those in Hamburg (where the play had not been staged for seventeen years), Darmstadt, Freiburg and Halberstadt. *Othello* has had as wide an appeal as in former years; *Macbeth* has been produced only by smaller theatres. As regards the Histories and the Roman plays the situation remains much the same as in 1950. A rather striking production of *Julius Caesar* was put on in Essen. There was no performance of *Timon of Athens* this year, but in its place *Troilus and Cressida* was successfully staged—for the first time after the war—in Krefeld and Stuttgart. The comedies have been as popular with the public as in previous years. *Twelfth Night* ranks foremost with 250 performances in thirteen new productions. *The Taming of the Shrew*, *A Midsummer Night's Dream* and *Much Ado about Nothing* were also frequently presented. Most remarkable were the productions of *Much Ado about Nothing* by Hilpert at Göttingen and by Schalla at Düsseldorf. Of Shakespeare's later plays only *The Winter's Tale* and *The Tempest* have been performed. In the case of *The Winter's Tale*, of which at least one hundred performances were given, we may, however, truly speak of a 'renaissance' of this play. Here again Hilpert's and Schalla's productions were the most outstanding. A Shakespeare week was held at Dresden where among other new productions *Romeo and Juliet* attracted special attention.

As regards the various ways of presenting Shakespeare's plays at German theatres there have been two distinct tendencies apart from the great number of conventional productions. While some producers tried to adapt Shakespeare performances to the style of representation on the Elizabethan stage, others tended to modernize his plays in spirit and costume. The tendency to return to the Elizabethan style of staging was evident in a production of *The Taming of the Shrew* at Oberhausen, where the stage had been modelled after the interior of the Globe Theatre. In Gelsenkirchen the same play was put on in a baroque setting.

Modern staging has ranged from an unconventional simplicity of décor to bold and striking costume and scenic effects, the emphasis in both instances being mainly on modern characterization and symbolic interpretation. The tendency towards economy of setting became apparent in the productions of *King Lear* at Hamburg, Freiburg and Darmstadt. The already mentioned performance of *Much Ado about Nothing* at Düsseldorf was also characterized by an unpretentious décor and absence of musical setting. The theatre at Darmstadt designed a single set for its performance of *Twelfth Night*, the change of scenes being indicated by different lighting effects. The more revolutionary style of modern Shakespeare production was illustrated in a performance of *Julius Caesar* at Essen, where the leading characters wore black uniforms and riding-boots. A rather provocative attempt at modernization was made by Wildhagen of the Flensburg theatre whose symbolic interpretation of *A Midsummer Night's Dream* was hyper-modern in concept. The setting was in the style of Kokoschka and the actors appeared in Bikini shirts, Samba socks and sun glasses.

In addition to the traditional Shakespeare operas two modern compositions caught the attention of the public. *Troilus and Cressida* by Winfried Zillich and *Puck* (based on *A Midsummer Night's Dream*) by Marcel Delannoy were both performed at Berlin.

The German Shakespeare Society with more than 1,000 members still holds a prominent position among Germany's cultural societies. Its new president Rudolf Alexander Schröder has recently added to his translations of Shakespeare's plays a version of *The Tempest* which will be acted next year. The society's annual meeting in 1952, combined with a Shakespeare festival, attracted many visitors from all over Germany. Among the lecturers were Richard Flatter from the U.S.A. and Robert Birley from Eton; the Archbishop of Cologne, Cardinal Frings, spoke on *Shakespeare and Music*. Two successful productions of *Hamlet* and *Twelfth Night* shed new light on many passages and scenes, partly due to the use of the eighteenth-century prose translation by Eschenburg.

WOLFGANG CLEMEN

Greece

Othello, translated by Constantine Theotokis, has been produced by the Kotopouli Company at the Royal Theatre of Salonica, in August 1951, and *As You Like It*, translated by M. Skouloudis, was revived by the National Theatre at the Royal Theatre of Salonica in October 1951. The same performance was revived in Athens in November 1951. *A Midsummer Night's Dream*, translated by J. Economidis, is to be produced by the National Theatre in March 1952. A new translation of *Othello* by K. Karthaios was published by the Tcaros Publishing Company.

GEORGE THEOTOKAS

Israel

For the sixth time a Shakespearian play appears in the long list of Habimah's repertoire. *Twelfth Night, The Merchant of Venice, Hamlet, A Midsummer Night's Dream* and *Othello* came before; and now, again, the long-awaited opening night of *The Taming of the Shrew* was a real festive occasion. Both audiences and critics have welcomed the performance most cordially not only because the comedy itself is "a gay flight on the wings of Italianate farce", but because the performance is given in just such a vein.

This is the third Shakespearian play which the guest producer, Julius Gellner, has done for Habimah (*A Midsummer Night's Dream* of three years ago was followed by *Othello* in 1950), and his work is indeed very highly appreciated. In an Elizabethan setting, designed by Joseph Karl, Gellner has succeeded in putting on a really charming and amusing production. It was a jovial, easy-going and easy-flowing performance, not only because the setting was so helpful, but because the Habimah players, old and young, worked in a team under the guiding hand of Gellner. The serious-minded tragedian, Simon Finkel, played a light-moving, almost dashing, Petruchio, with much vigour and virility, most charming in his love-making and admirable even in his taming. The part of Kate was entrusted to two of the younger generation, Ada Tal and Rachel Timor, who alternate in the role, each successfully giving a slightly different interpretation. Raphael Klatzkin, another old-timer, gives an excellent performance of a clownish Grumio, and there is Shlomo Bar-Shavit, of the younger set, who gives a most admirable Tranio. And last but not least: the great Aharon Meskin fills his small part of Christopher Sly, the tinker, with much simplicity and naivety, with much human warmth.   REUBEN AVINOAM

Italy

The actor Renzo Ricci has continued his impersonation of Shakespearian characters with his production of *Antony and Cleopatra* at the Teatro Eliseo (Rome). Ricci had carefully studied Olivier's London production both of that play and of Shaw's *Caesar and Cleopatra*, and he has tried to give an Italian counterpart of both. The reactions of the public have been widely divergent, but on the whole Ricci's *Antony and Cleopatra*, with the mature, but sprightly, Eva Magni as Cleopatra, was a creditable production even in the eyes of those who had witnessed the London performance (not so much in their ears, though, because the poetry of the drama seemed to have vanished in the translation, and only the bare skeleton

of a chronicle play appeared to be left). Ricci has produced a less satisfactory *Hamlet* on the same stage, using a garbled text and a rather inadequate cast. With the aim of providing the Italian stage with crisp acting versions, C. V. Ludovici has brought out this year a very remarkable rendering of *Macbeth*, without being afraid of pushing concision to the point of hardness, as in the original, whereas Salvatore Quasimodo, in his translation of the same play for a Milan production this year, has not avoided occasional dilution and flabbiness. Giorgio Strehler, the indefatigable director of the Piccolo Teatro of Milan, has produced a mediocre *Twelfth Night* at the new theatre of Palazzo Grassi in Venice, on the occasion of the 'Mostra del Costume nel tempo' which took place in that palace in the summer of 1951, and an exceptionally good *Henry IV* (again a Ludovici translation) in the enchanting setting of the Villa Floridiana at Naples, with Gianni Santuccio as Hotspur, Giorgio De Lullo as the Prince of Wales, and Camillo Pilotto as Falstaff. Guido Salvini's production of *A Midsummer Night's Dream* at the Teatro Valle, Rome, with setting and costumes by the celebrated designer Giulio Coltellacci, has come very close to re-creating the fairy atmosphere of the original. Shakespeare's popularity on the Italian stage is indeed so great, that Cesco Baseggio has dared to produce in Milan a *Merchant of Venice* in Venetian dialect, and the Associazione Friulana della Stampa has organized at the Teatro Puccini of Udine a performance, by the Piccolo Teatro Città di Udine, of a curious play based on Shakespeare's life and times, *Shakespeare* by Luigi Candoni.

MARIO PRAZ

The Netherlands

The Netherlands have continued the tradition of Shakespeare-reverence in more ways than one. In the first place, there are the visits of English players which have delighted critical audiences throughout the country as effectively, comparatively speaking, as three-and-a-half centuries ago. These are accompanied by various productions put on by Dutch professional companies. *Julius Caesar* opened at Amsterdam in June 1951, *Measure for Measure*, also at Amsterdam, in July. Deventer saw *A Midsummer Night's Dream* in August. And Rotterdam treated its first-nighters to *Othello*. These productions have been on tour with generally satisfactory results.

We cannot here record the numerous performances of Shakespeare plays by amateur dramatic societies and semi-professional groups. Mostly the play chosen by such companies is the *Dream*, though in July *Love's*

Labour's Lost was produced at Oisterwyk. An exception should be made for Diever, however. This small village in the East of the country has of late years succeeded in creating a Shakespeare-tradition of its own. For, here, it is not merely the Bottoms and the Quinces who turn actors once in a while to divert the gentry and acquire a reputation among their own degree, but also the Town Clerk, the Burgomaster's wife, the hotel-keeper's daughter, the Minister, and 'de Dokter', who—under the latter's infectiously enthusiastic direction—have been 'caught' by Shakespeare to such an extent that, from a curiosity, the annual open-air performances at Diever have become almost an institution.

In this connexion it may be remarked that the translations used are no longer more or less arbitrarily modernized versions of the Dutch standard Shakespeare by that great nineteenth-century scholar, Burgersdijk, but translations for which young and preferably somewhat revolutionary poets have been specially commissioned.

ALFRED BACHRACH

New Zealand

The production of Shakespeare in the Dominion which is furthest from the great centres of dramatic activity raises many problems, some of which have not yet found a solution. The greatest problem is simply stated: there is no professional theatre. This is not to say that the two million people in the country are not interested in seeing plays. On the contrary. But (apart from the few exceptions that will be mentioned later) the staple fare is one of two things. Professional groups from Australia and occasional second-string teams from the United Kingdom tour the country with *Worm's Eye View* or *George and Margaret* or *Annie Get Your Gun*.

The alternative dramatic fare is provided by a group of Repertory Societies, of which the four in the four larger cities are the most important. The name is probably misleading to an English reader. Unlike the Birmingham Repertory, the Wellington Repertory (which may be taken as a sample of the rest) is made up of a group of somewhat over two thousand subscribers, who receive for their subscriptions entry to at least half a dozen plays in the course of the annual season. The players are all amateurs, drawn from all ranks of society. Until a few years ago the producers were also amateurs, and most of them still are. A few years ago a few of the larger societies have tried the experiment of employing an actor-producer with professional experience. The choice of plays produced is determined largely by the tastes of the subscribers, who on the whole prefer

elaborate scene-painting (a good backcloth receives a round of applause on its first appearance) and the production of a current West-End success. But Shakespeare in moderation is safe, and it would be an unusual season in each of the four main centres if one of the Repertories did not put on a Shakespeare play. On the whole the results are usually mediocre.

If this were the whole story, the outlook for Shakespearian production in New Zealand would be a gloomy one, not relieved even by the undoubted interest in play-going. Fortunately in the last few years the cycle of unrelieved amateurism has been broken and some interesting performances of Shakespeare have been seen. Two professional producers, Kenneth Firth and Frederick Farley, were brought in from England by the Repertory Societies. Firth's *Othello* was an exotic but satisfying performance. The Community Arts Service, an offshoot of the Adult Education movement, some years ago appointed a full-time drama tutor. They secured the services of Harold Baigent, a New Zealander who after graduating in English did a postgraduate course at the Yale School of Drama. The Community Arts Service specializes in performances (on a semi-professional basis) in smaller country centres, often ill-equipped for stage-plays. The actors travel by truck, carrying with them their wardrobe, scenery, properties and a self-contained lighting unit, and stage their plays in school-halls, woolsheds—anywhere big enough to hold the audience. Their success in a variety of plays has been considerable. They have to their credit the best performance of Shakespeare that has been seen for some years, a beautifully though economically staged *Twelfth Night* (produced by Baigent and Farley, who played a nicely balanced Feste and Malvolio). It was costumed in the period of James I, and played on a single set, which had the unusual advantage of looking permanent and solid and yet with skilful lighting never monotonous—and all able to be packed up at the end of a night on to a motor-truck for the next day's move.

New Zealand is divided into two islands. An all-night journey by steamer joins the two. As a result dramatic activity tends to develop separately in each half of the Dominion. So far I have dealt with the North Island. In the South Island some years ago Shakespearian production strode forward with the emergence as a producer of Ngaio Marsh, who, before she sprang into prominence as one of the most popular of detective-story writers, had gained some years of stage experience in England. She took over a group of enthusiastic students in Christchurch, where the University college had a small theatre, and within the space of three or four years trained a company, several of whom have since become professional actors. She concentrated entirely on Shakespeare. *Hamlet, Othello, A Midsummer Night's Dream, Henry V* and *Macbeth* followed each other in rapid succession. Miss Marsh's emphasis was on speed and continuous action, getting rid of "cobwebs, ink-pots and the annotated and expurgated edition". Though some purists might complain that her *Hamlet* had almost the pace and atmosphere of a who-done-it at Elsinore, it was a lively and stimulating performance. Three of her plays had a successful tour of the major cities of New Zealand. As with the Community Arts Centre she solved the problem of transportable sets, on this occasion with the aid of a stage crew largely recruited from students in the Engineering Faculty. More recently Miss Marsh took several of her best student actors over to England where they formed the nucleus of her British Commonwealth Company, which performed in London before they set out on an adventurous tour of Australia and New Zealand, bringing (among other plays) a polished and sweetly moving *Twelfth Night*.

The event of recent years that brought the full potentialities of Shakespearian production to New Zealand was the tour of the Old Vic Company with Sir Laurence Olivier and Vivien Leigh. Apart from the fact that for the first time in this generation New Zealand audiences had the opportunity of seeing two great actors and a fine company in an unforgettable performance, this visit itself left results even more tangible. Owing to the generosity of Sir Laurence Olivier, part of the proceeds of the tour was vested in a fund (which the Government has supplemented) to enable young men and women of promise to spend a year in the United Kingdom studying acting or producing. A group of young actors and producers have already been trained. Several of them are now back once again in New Zealand. It is too early yet to know what the effect will be. There is still no theatre in New Zealand which puts on a full season of drama. There is still no full-time professional company, though planners are conceiving everything from a National Theatre downwards. But the next few years should be interesting.   IAN A. GORDON

Norway

Of the two performances I have noted in 1951, one was only partly Shakespearian: an opera written by a Norwegian composer, Arne Eggen, and based on *Cymbeline*. Naturally, the libretto represented a drastic abridgement of the Shakespearian text: Cloten and the Queen had been cut out—as the composer said to me,

because one villain in a play would suffice—an argument it is hardly proper to discuss in this brief note.

The new opera may be termed a *succes d'estime*. Arne Eggen lacks the faculty of acute characterization that fascinates in Benjamin Britten, but his music, always honest, natural and genuine, charms by a fine lyrical quality. The performance was very uneven; Arviragus was a hero who seemed scared to death; but the general effect was saved by an attractive Posthumus, a cunning Iachimo and above all by a brilliant Imogen created by Miss Aase Nordmo Lövberg.

I regret I was not able to see the *Romeo and Juliet* staged in May at 'Den nationale scene' in Bergen. The reviews suggest that it was a fascinating performance, thanks to impressive acting in the two principal parts.
                                        LORENTZ ECKHOFF

South Africa

Two events of importance marked the Shakespearian year in Johannesburg. The first was the formation of a Shakespeare Society, with nearly one hundred and fifty members; the second, the official opening of the new Repertory Theatre, with a performance of *Much Ado about Nothing*, produced by Gwen Ffrangcon-Davies. There are now at least three Shakespeare Societies in the country, and at Durban a first-rate Shakespeare library collection. All the Societies aim chiefly at theatrical production, which is desirable in a country possessing no permanent professional theatre; but lectures and recitals are also organized. In Johannesburg, where the new Repertory Theatre provides an up-to-date and attractive home for amateur drama, at least one full-scale Shakespeare production will be attempted every year. When *Much Ado* had its première, the blows of hammers in the auditorium had died away barely an hour before the patrons began to arrive.
                                        A. C. PARTRIDGE

Sweden

During 1951 the Norrköping-Linköping troupe has been acting *Hamlet* on the public open-air stages in the countryside and has met with considerable success. The same troupe, with Ingemar Pallin as Hamlet, was chosen as Sweden's contribution to the castle plays at Elsinore that year. If the attempt was not wholly a successful one, it still showed an endeavour to come to grips with the mighty play. The well-known fact that it is not an easy thing to act in the Kronborg courtyard was again confirmed.

If 1951 was on the whole a poor year, a high wave of interest came with the next. February was the month of Shakespeare, with *A Midsummer Night's Dream* in Gothenburg, *Othello* in Malmö, *Antony and Cleopatra* in Stockholm. At the same time the Old Vic's *King Lear* met with liveliest interest from crammed audiences— a truly popular achievement. To many modern critics the scenery may have been to a certain degree unexpected, accustomed as we have been to another style in decorative art, but all agree that the actors brought Shakespeare nearer to us than perhaps ever before.

NILS MOLIN

Switzerland

1951 must be reckoned a lean, if not an altogether barren, year as regards Shakespearian activities in Switzerland. Performances of the plays were few, and limited to two places, Bâle and Zurich. At Bâle a "farcical adaptation to a very small stage" of *Twelfth Night*, to use Professor Lüdeke's own words, was given in German at the Comedy theatre. In the late autumn— 28, 29 November, 1 December—*Much Ado* was performed three times at the Municipal Theatre in German, the translation adopted being von Baudissin's; Leonard Steckel was responsible for that production and boldly cut the text, turning the play into what Lüdeke calls a cheap burlesque, and making it highly successful with the groundlings. The same production of *Much Ado* had been given at the end of the previous season, in March 1951, at the Zurich Schauspielhaus, where it had also proved a popular success. Zurich besides had the opportunity to see *The Two Gentlemen of Verona* at the same theatre, in H. Rothe's German translation, the producer being Steckel again.　　GEORGES BONNARD

U.S.A.

The notes from Broadway for the season of 1951–2 will be brief indeed. The New York theatre itself has ventured only one Shakespeare production since those reviewed last season. This single offering was a production of *The Taming of the Shrew* under Margaret Webster's experienced baton, which was given during the spring repertory season at the City Center in April 1951.

Off Broadway the picture is very different. Shakespeare's flag flies high over half a hundred college and community theatres, over thousands of high schools and summer festivals. The *Shakespeare Quarterly*, published by the Shakespeare Association of America, lists fifty-seven productions during the calendar year of 1951. This includes productions of such resident companies as The Brattle Theatre, Cambridge, Massachusetts, which produced *Henry IV, Part 2* and *Love's Labour's Lost* (the latter with Ian Keith and Hurd

Hatfield under Albert Marre's direction) and plans *King Lear* and *Macbeth*, with William Devlin as star, for this season. It also includes the Barter Theatre production of *The Comedy of Errors* which toured twelve southern and south-western states in true barnstorming style, and Margo Jones's production of *The Merchant of Venice* given 'in the round' in her Dallas Theatre 1951. She schedules *A Midsummer Night's Dream* for Theatre 1952. *Much Ado about Nothing* was something of a favourite last year. It was produced by B. Iden Payne both at the University of Texas and by the same distinguished director at the San Diego Community Theatre; Gilmore Brown mounted it at the Pasadena Playhouse. It was one of the plays given at the Shakespeare Festival, Camden Hills, Maine (Herschel L. Bricker, director-manager) and by the Players Inc., a touring group of Catholic University. According to the *Shakespeare Quarterly* list it even topped the perennial favourite *Hamlet* in number of productions during 1951. However, as the *Quarterly* points out, this list is not all inclusive, but it does show the extent and variety of productions in the college and community theatres.

As this note goes to Stratford, the Third International Theatre Month is being celebrated in the United States with 600 theatres, literally from Maine to California, taking part in this demonstration that the "theatre serves international understanding". In connexion with this nation-wide celebration at least twenty are giving Shakespeare's plays, among them Sawyer Falk's production of *Richard III* at Syracuse University, *Hamlet* directed by Henry Boettcher at Carnegie Institute of Technology, *The Merchant of Venice* directed by Althea Hunt at the College of William and Mary, Williamsburg, Virginia.

If the Bard has become temporarily too expensive for Broadway, he is very much in his element in the vigorous young theatres of the colleges and schools, the communities and universities that are keeping the classics alive throughout the United States.

ROSAMOND GILDER

U.S.S.R.

Shakespeare's extensive popularity in our country was demonstrated once again in 1951. His plays continue to be staged by many Soviet Theatres. In number of performances the list is led by *Othello*, *Romeo and Juliet*, and the comedies *Twelfth Night* and *Much Ado about Nothing*.

Among the productions of *Romeo and Juliet* in 1951 I should like to point to the one in the Uzbek language in the city of Tashkent. Here Juliet is played by Uzbekistan's leading actress, Sara Ishanturayeva, who previously delighted audiences as Desdemona and Ophelia. Then there is the production by the Moscow Regional Theatre of Drama, a travelling company which plays in the clubhouses of factories and collective farms. A glowing production full of genuine lyricism, it is enjoying notable success among workers and collective farmers. I should also like to say a word about the lively interest which children's theatres are showing in this play: *Romeo and Juliet* is highly popular with the Soviet youth. To sum up, *Romeo and Juliet* has won a prominent place in the repertory of our theatres, beginning with the Bolshoi Theatre of Moscow, which for eight years in succession now has been presenting Sergei Prokofieff's ballet based on this play.

Latterly, Soviet theatres have been paying special attention to *The Two Gentlemen of Verona*. This is a play which many consider extremely useful for young actors, since it contains sketches, as it were, of roles subsequently given fuller development by Shakespeare. And so we find that in 1951 young members of the Vakhtangov Theatre, Moscow, one of the country's best, began work on *The Two Gentlemen of Verona*. Soon Moscovites will see this play, acted by young players under the guidance of a young stage director and with the collaboration of a young artist and a young composer. Outstanding masters of the Soviet stage supervised their work.

The basic Shakespeare repertory of Soviet theatres is made up of the following: *Othello, Hamlet, King Lear, Romeo and Juliet, Twelfth Night, Much Ado about Nothing, The Taming of the Shrew, The Two Gentlemen of Verona, The Merry Wives of Windsor, As You Like It, The Comedy of Errors, A Midsummer Night's Dream, The Winter's Tale* and *Cymbeline*.

Parallel with this theatrical activity, our poets continued their work on Shakespeare translations. In 1951 the Children's Publishing House put out a one-volume collection (718 pages) of Shakespeare's tragedies translated by Boris Pasternak; for this edition Pasternak reworked and polished his former translations. The volume contains *Romeo and Juliet, Hamlet, Othello, King Lear* and *Macbeth*. Incidentally, this is the first publication of Pasternak's translation of *Macbeth*. (I will mention in passing that this tragedy, which is so highly appreciated by our readers for its literary qualities— "the creator of Macbeth" is what Pushkin called Shakespeare—has not found much favour on the Soviet stage, no doubt because of its intense melancholy, which is in general alien to the Soviet theatre.) In the foreword on Shakespeare's life and work which I wrote for this volume the reader will in places find a somewhat individual chronology of the plays, several of which are dated earlier than is usually accepted. In this we concur with a number of the latest English investigators of this complicated problem. The foreword also notes the supposition that Shakespeare's contacts with university circles of his day were closer than has hitherto been generally believed. The volume has come out in an edition of 50,000 copies and is intended for pupils in the secondary schools.

The Arts Publishing House last year put out in a separate little volume a translation of *The Merry Wives of Windsor* done by Samuel Marshak, the poet, in collaboration with myself. In 1951 Marshak worked on a translation of *Venus and Adonis* and went over his translation of Shakespeare's *Sonnets* preparatory to their third edition. The doyenne of our translators, T. L. Shchepkina-Kupernik, also revised and polished her translations. I had the great pleasure of editing her translation of *King Lear* for a production of this play by the Maly Theatre of Moscow.

Such are a few highlights of Shakespearian activity in the Soviet Union during 1951.

MIKHAIL M. MOROZOV

SHAKESPEARE PRODUCTIONS IN THE UNITED KINGDOM: 1951

A LIST COMPILED FROM ITS RECORDS BY THE
SHAKESPEARE MEMORIAL LIBRARY, BIRMINGHAM

JANUARY

22   *Hamlet:* The Playhouse, Nottingham. *Producer:* ANDRÉ VAN GYSEGHEM.

22   *Hamlet:* The Playhouse, Sheffield. *Producer:* GEOFFREY OST.

30   *Henry the Fifth:* The Old Vic Company, at The Old Vic Theatre, London. *Producer:* GLEN BYAM SHAW.

FEBRUARY

2–3   *Twelfth Night:* Middle Temple Hall, London. *Producer:* DONALD WOLFIT.

12   *Hamlet:* Guildford Theatre Company. *Producers:* KAY GARDNER and ROGER WINTON.

MARCH

5   *Coriolanus:* Cambridge University Marlowe Society and A.D.C., at the Arts Theatre, Cambridge. Producer and actors are anonymous.

6   *Hamlet:* New Bolton's Theatre Club, London. *Producer:* JOHN HARRISON.

12   *Hamlet:* Cambridge University Undergraduates, at the A.D.C. *Producer:* GEOFFREY DARBY.

12   *Twelfth Night:* Richard Stephenson's Saxon Players, at His Majesty's Theatre, Barrow-in-Furness.

13   *All's well that ends well:* Liverpool Repertory Company, at The Playhouse, Liverpool. *Producer:* GERALD CROSS.

24   *Richard the Second:* Shakespeare Memorial Theatre, Stratford-upon-Avon. *Producer:* ANTHONY QUAYLE.

APRIL

2   *The Merchant of Venice:* The County Players, at The Theatre Royal, Lincoln. *Producer:* DOUGLAS QUAYLE.

3   *King Henry VI, Part 2:* The Repertory Theatre, Birmingham. *Producer:* DOUGLAS SEALE.

3   *King Henry IV, Part 1:* Shakespeare Memorial Theatre, Stratford-upon-Avon. *Producers:* JOHN KIDD and ANTHONY QUAYLE.

9   *As you like it:* The Citizens' Theatre, Glasgow. *Producer:* JOHN CASSON.

MAY

8   *King Henry IV, Part 2:* Shakespeare Memorial Theatre, Stratford-upon-Avon. *Producer:* MICHAEL REDGRAVE.

11   *Antony and Cleopatra:* St James's Theatre, London. *Producer:* MICHAEL BENTHALL.

14   *Macbeth:* The Shakespeare Stage Society, at Crosby Hall, London. *Producer:* C. B. PURDOM.

17   *Hamlet:* New Theatre, London. *Producers:* FRANK HAUSER and ALEC GUINNESS.

17   *Twelfth Night:* 'Poetry and Plays in Pubs.' The Taverners (on tour). *Producer:* HENRY MCCARTHY.

21   *A Midsummer Night's Dream:* Regent's Park Open Air Theatre, London. *Producer:* ROBERT ATKINS.

MAY

21 *The Taming of the Shrew:* The Bristol Old Vic Company, at the Theatre Royal, Bristol. *Producer:* DENIS CAREY.

21 *As you like it:* The Overture Players, at The New Theatre, Bromley. *Producer:* GUY VERNEY.

26 *Macbeth:* Pitlochry Festival Theatre. *Producer:* ANDREW LEIGH.

29 *Twelfth Night:* Perth Theatre Company, Perth. *Producer:* EDMUND BAILEY.

31 *The Merry Wives of Windsor:* The Old Vic Company at The Old Vic Theatre, London. *Producer:* HUGH HUNT.

JUNE

5 *King Lear:* Leeds University Dramatic Society and Union Theatre Group. *Producer:* JOHN BOORMAN.

18 *The Taming of the Shrew,* and *Pericles:* The Norwich Players, at The Maddermarket Theatre. *Producers:* CECILY SMYTH and NUGENT MONCK.

25 *Macbeth:* The County Players, at The Theatre Royal, Lincoln. *Producer:* DOUGLAS QUAYLE.

26 *The Tempest:* Shakespeare Memorial Theatre, Stratford-upon-Avon. *Producer:* MICHAEL BENTHALL.

26 *As you like it:* Pittville Gardens Open-Air Theatre, Cheltenham. *Producer:* IRENE MAWER.

27 *The Winter's Tale:* Phoenix Theatre, London. *Producer:* PETER BROOK.

JULY

2 *A Midsummer Night's Dream:* First Folio Theatre Co., at Walpole Park, Ealing. *Producer:* KENNETH McCLELLAN.

3 *As you like it:* First Folio Theatre Co., at Walpole Park, Ealing. *Producer:* KENNETH McCLELLAN.

3 *Cymbeline:* Oxford Festival of Great Britain Committee Production, in All Souls' Quadrangle. *Producer:* JOHN HALE.

6 *The Taming of the Shrew:* Bristol University Dramatic Society. *Producer:* AUDREY STANLEY.

16 *Othello:* Marlowe Theatre Repertory Co., Canterbury. *Producer:* JOHN LINDSAY.

31 *King Henry V:* Shakespeare Memorial Theatre, Stratford-upon-Avon. *Producer:* ANTHONY QUAYLE.

AUGUST

6 *Two Gentlemen of Verona:* Cambridge University Marlowe Society. *Producer:* JOHN BARTON.

11 *As you like it:* First Folio Theatre Company, at the George Inn, Southwark. *Producer:* KENNETH McCLELLAN.

13 *The Tempest* (Dryden and Davenant's version): Cambridge University Marlowe Society. *Producer:* DONALD BEVES.

23 *The Comedy of Errors:* Cambridge University A.D.C., at the Watergate Theatre, London. *Producer:* JOHN BARTON.

SEPTEMBER

17 *The Tempest:* The Mermaid Theatre, London. *Producer:* JULIUS GELLNER.

17 *Twelfth Night:* Arts Council Plays (on tour). *Producer:* KAY GARDNER.

24 *A Midsummer Night's Dream:* The Playhouse, Nottingham. *Producer:* GUY VERNEY.

OCTOBER

15   *Romeo and Juliet:* The Kings Players, at The Gateway Theatre, Edinburgh. *Producer:* RICHARD MATHEWS.

18   *Othello:* St James's Theatre, London. *Producer:* ORSON WELLES.

30   *King Lear:* The Citizens' Theatre, Glasgow. *Producer:* PETER POTTER.

31   *Othello:* The Old Vic Company, at The Old Vic Theatre, London. *Producer:* MICHAEL LANGHAM.

NOVEMBER

6   *Love's Labour's Lost:* The Bristol Old Vic Company, at The Theatre Royal, Bristol. *Producer:* HUGH HUNT.

10   *The Two Gentlemen of Verona:* The Questors Theatre, London. *Producer:* PETER CURTIS.

12   *Macbeth:* Perth Theatre Company, Perth (on tour). *Producer:* EDMUND BAILEY.

20   *Romeo and Juliet:* Bristol University Dramatic Society. *Producer:* EVAN ROBERTS.

DECEMBER

10   *Love's Labour's Lost:* The Norwich Players, at The Maddermarket Theatre, Norwich. *Producer:* NUGENT MONCK.

26   *A Midsummer Night's Dream:* The Old Vic Company, at The Old Vic Theatre, London. *Producer:* TYRONE GUTHRIE.

SHAKESPEARE'S HISTORY PLAYS
EPIC OR DRAMA?

['*Richard II*', *the two parts of '*Henry IV*' and '*Henry V*', at the Shakespeare Memorial Theatre, Stratford-upon-Avon, summer 1951*]

BY

RICHARD DAVID

Shakespeare's Histories are not popular. They are generally regarded as inferior works, neither flesh nor fowl, lacking alike the Tragedies' direct assault on the emotions and the poetry and fancy of the Comedies. Recent commentators have not made appreciation easier by claiming that the Lancastrian Histories, at least, are not eight plays but one, a continuous argument on the duties of kingship and the dangers of disorder progressively developed through eight linked sections. The man in the street goes to the theatre for a play, not for a political treatise. He is hardly prepared to stomach a trilogy, much less an 'octology' and, if he were, few theatres to-day could stage such entertainments as a matter of routine. The greater honour, then, to the Stratford Governors for devoting almost the whole of their Festival season to a sequence of Shakespeare's four plays on the rise of the House of Lancaster. They thereby provided a unique opportunity of studying Shakespeare's Histories in the most highly recommended perspective, and so of judging what were his purpose and plan in writing them.

The Director, having undertaken to present the plays in accordance with modern theory, very properly committed himself to it wholeheartedly. The programme note to *Richard II* stated unequivocally: "It is generally agreed that the four plays of this season's historical cycle form a tetralogy and were planned by Shakespeare as one great play." Everything in Anthony Quayle's production was focused on continuity, on the connexions and the likenesses between the plays, and their differences were studiously toned down. The set, designed by Tanya Moiseiwitsch, remained the same throughout. Modelled—at one or two removes—on the Elizabethan public stage, it comprised a bulky scaffolding with a canopied balcony above and stairs curving down on either side (Plate V A). To left a throne, to right a penthouse flanked the stage, and the whole was framed in draperies of smoky blue. The space beneath the balcony could be closed by heavy stable doors; when these were open it afforded not so much an inner stage as an ante-chamber to the stage, a halfway house between off-stage and on-stage. This was effectively used for such things as the inn-entry at Rochester, the Jerusalem chamber to which the dying Henry retires, and the gateway of Harfleur massively framing a governor whose submissiveness became by contrast all the more telling. It also provided a dark tunnel-like entry from which surprises might pounce upon the stage. The arrival of Exton and his men, a black thunderclap, with the coffined Richard, was a magnificent use of this resource. The court-scenes, too, usually began with the bursting open of the great doors at the back by a bustle of attendants and men-at-arms who set the stage; when all was in order the King would make his ceremonial entry, often across the balcony and down the winding stair.

A balcony or upper level is essential in the first and last of these plays for the walls of Flint and of Harfleur and hardly less so for the royal stand at the Coventry lists. In addition it was here used—a genuine Elizabethan device—to isolate, to make more ethereal, certain quieter scenes of lyrical relief, such as that of the Queen's forebodings after Richard's departure for Ireland. By an extension of this use it provided in the *Henry IV* plays (which are without battlements and largely without lyrical interludes) a setting, somewhat removed from the main stage, for what were almost introductions in dumb-show to certain key scenes. Thus the laboured entrance of the dying Henry, supported by attendants, across the upper stage, prepared the context in which the audience was to view his clash with Prince Hal. Hal's first entrance was accompanied by even more elaborate business. In a half-light the prince appeared on the upper stage, yawning, stretching, dragging his accoutrements after him, while Falstaff's snores resounded from behind the closed doors of the 'study' below. In his slatternly progress Hal's sword—that symbol of chivalry that should be his most cherished possession—slips from his fingers and clatters down on to the main stage. Still yawning and careless he follows it down the stairway, shuffles it up, and sits to pull on his boots. Halfway through this process Falstaff's snoring gets beyond bearing, and Hal turns to fling a boot against the double doors stage centre. At the crash the audience sits up; the snores cease; a moment's pause and the doors are pushed aside, a red face peers through, and with "Now, Hal, what time of day is it, lad?" we are off. All this may sound in relation a pretentious piece of producer's meddling, but in fact it was entirely effective and even necessary; for if the four plays are taken as one, the hero is this same Prince Hal, and on his first appearance we need time to size him up before being swept off in his company through three long plays.

These are special instances, but in general the scaffolding stage was used with great resourcefulness. No two entrances or exits were the same, yet every one seemed right. Each scene was instantly localized, often by a single significant property—a high settle for Cheapside, a wattle fence for the Gloucestershire orchard, a monkish chair for the Archbishop's palace at York. The set became less a formal framework for action than a space of apparently infinite extension and possibility into which any action fitted naturally. True, in *Richard II*, where there is least scope for diversity, the sombre and unchanging background became monotonous and its one piece of decoration, the trellis and netting on the proscenium arch, distracting (What were they for? Would they represent the "dangling apricocks"? They did not). But in the later plays this stage became protean, everything and nothing, a delight to the eye and invisible, exploding into hundreds of gold streamers for the coronation (Plate VA), sprouting neat foliage for the French court, throwing out shrouds and tackle for King Harry's embarkation (Plate VB). The vast marquee that, swooping from the flies, engulfed the whole scaffold for the final scene was, for all its discordant reminiscence of tree-borders and transformations, merely an extreme example of this gaiety and fluency of staging.

The dresses, by the same designer, were equally helpful to continuity and smoothness of presentation. They did not lack magnificence or expressiveness: the clear blues and greys of the French courtiers contrasting with the serried maroon of the English embassy will long remain in the mind's eye, and the swirling furs of Henry IV suggested not only the pomp and circumstance of power but something of the man's essential ruthlessness. Their greatest virtue, however, was that they sat on their wearers with an every-day comfortableness and seemed inevitable—

a powerful strengthening of the illusion of historicity so essential if the four plays are to be presented as one history.

There are of course enormous and obvious advantages in such a presentation. The ironies and the reminiscences become supercharged. How telling is Richard's warning against Northumberland when we are certain that within a few hours we shall ourselves see it fulfilled; how real the agony of the prayer before Agincourt when we have witnessed the crime that Henry V must expiate! A host of minor correspondences comes to light. What normal reader or spectator of the individual plays will identify the York who at Agincourt dies gallantly for the England of King Harry with the Aumerle who in *Richard II* had plotted against this same King Harry's father, or when enjoying the Hotspur of *1 Henry IV* will remember the lively part that Hotspur plays in *Richard II*? (Oddly enough Stratford, for all the insistence on connexion, missed both these points. The two Hotspurs were played by different actors; and, though Aumerle and York were doubled, Aumerle's plot which, wretched skimble-skamble though it is, gives poignancy to York's death, was cut *in toto*. With it, a much more serious loss, went the first reference to Prince Hal and his unprincely behaviour, an indisputable link between *Richard II* and its 'sequel'.) Such incidental recognitions and cross-references are, however, no more than symptoms of our growing adaptation to the historical environment as the tetralogy proceeds. By the time the fourth play ends we are beginning to know our way about a story that the Elizabethans had by heart before the first play began. Our knowledge of the whole is like a magnetic field, and as we subject each play to it in turn the characters and incidents align themselves and click into place in the total meaning. No longer do we yawn while an undifferentiated crowd of blustering barons keeps us from Falstaff, for the barons are now an element in the design, of equal weight to Falstaff. Indeed, the whole emphasis of the plays has shifted. Henry IV from a rather wearisome character in a subplot becomes a great tragic figure, and Hal is seen as the hero and climax of the whole cycle. Falstaff recedes from his central position and his rejection is recognized as inevitable —and of no importance.

But for the Elizabethans it did not need the performance of the four plays as a continuous cycle to provide this perspective. They were born with it—with, indeed, a longer view, which the single tetralogy cannot offer and actually obscures. The Elizabethans were conscious not only of the rise of the House of Lancaster, but of its fall. They saw not Henry Monmouth but Henry Richmond as the redeeming figure towards which history moved. They believed that Bolingbroke's guilt was the more heinous in that it required not only Northumberland's retributive rebellion but all the blood spilt in the Wars of the Roses to expiate it. To us, concentrating on the mature tetralogy to the exclusion of its immature sequel, Bolingbroke appears an unhappy Fortinbras; to the Elizabethans he was a penitent Macbeth. To us, whose horizon is Henry V and whose utmost premonition is of Shrewsbury and Agincourt, the words of Richard,

> my master, God omnipotent,
> Is mustering in his clouds on our behalf
> Armies of pestilence; and they shall strike
> Your children yet unborn and unbegot,   (III, iii, 85–8)

are but further proof of his fatuity, in that, Canute-like, he can muster only empty threats to withstand the flood of history. To the Elizabethans, who looked beyond to the carnage at

Towton and Tewkesbury, the words held a literal and terrible truth. The Stratford production, so far from encouraging in us this longer vision, cut off the menacing future by a discreet adaptation of the one explicit reference to it (the epilogue to *Henry V*) which turned the cycle back upon itself and made of it a simple success story.

We can hardly claim, then, that the communication of an Elizabethan sense of history is necessarily, or peculiarly, a property of the four plays when united. Can we say nevertheless that their effect in the theatre when presented in this form is so enriched and so indivisible that they are not four plays but one play? For me, the moral to be drawn from the Stratford productions was the opposite. Though every effort was bent on making the four plays coalesce, the effect of each is so distinct, so complete in itself, their styles are so divergent, their loose ends so uncompromisingly resist all attempts to marry them, that no single, comprehensive impression emerges. Not only do *Richard II* and *Henry V* insist on standing out from the main block, but even the two parts of *Henry IV* seem to spring asunder and proclaim their independence of each other.

Richard II is naturally the most irreconcilable of the four, composed, as it was, so much earlier and almost in a different medium. It is a play conceived in verse, a play whose peculiar effect could only be made in verse. Whether the Stratford players could have given it the performance it demands is doubtful. One indeed there was, Barbara Jefford, who made Lady Percy's lament for her husband the most moving single episode in the whole series and gave a compelling beauty even to the few lines with which, in the final scene of *Henry V*, the Queen of France soothes her distracted husband. Such effects are not produced by what is commonly called 'a musical voice'; Miss Jefford has indeed a quality of intonation or of timbre that occasionally jars. She possesses, however, in high degree what musicians would call the power of 'phrasing', the art that marries vitality and coherence, control and spontaneity, balancing the various elements of tempo, rhythm, dynamics and the rest so that each supports the others without distortion of itself. But Miss Jefford had no part in *Richard II*. Michael Redgrave knows the art, but seems to be passing through a stage of experiment, seeking after new subtleties of expression not yet perfected, and with the old certainty lost. In musical terms, his *rubato* is now excessive, and his speeches tend to fall apart into single phrases, losing alike their coherence and their drive. Harry Andrews, not a Chrysostom by nature, has by intelligence and sheer technique so shaped his speaking of verse that it has measure, coordination, and at the same time variety; yet lacking the vital element of spontaneity it often appears manufactured and arbitrary. Of the rest of the cast, few avoided one of the two equal and opposite errors, either straining their lines upon a high-pitched and painful monotone or so carefully denuding them of all measure that not only the musical sense but often the plain meaning was utterly disrupted.

With a company of Jeffords how tremendous *Richard II* might be! But even they could hardly have withstood at Stratford the bias towards prose and naturalism imposed by the need to assimilate the play to its 'sequels'. The scene in which the dying Gaunt bodes the doom of the realm and of its ruler was the most powerful in the play, for Hugh Griffith brought to his "prophet new inspired" a force and a conviction that gave him something of the Old Testament sublimity of Elijah denouncing Ahab; yet it was thought necessary in the cause of realism to portray the dying man's struggle for breath with such exactness that the spectators were sometimes distracted from admiration of his words by embarrassed anxiety lest he should fail altogether to get them out. Elsewhere not only were pauses and business injected into verse speeches for the express purpose of breaking their flow, but on occasion the interruptions actually became vocal. At three climaxes, when Green is sentenced to death, when news is brought of York's defection, when Exton enters with Richard's coffin, the character most affected was made to interject an hysterical "Oh no!" Even in a less formal play the words would have rung false, for there is something peculiarly modern about them; it was not with such lady terms that the Elizabethans received bad news. Here the interruption clashed like a garish botch of the wrong colour. Indeed the hysteria of characters under stress was generally overdone. The Green who so practically reminds the King of his duty as a soldier cannot be accepted a scene or two later as grovelling and screaming at the news of Bolingbroke's landing. Such would-be realism, like the exaggerated ingenuity with which Hotspur's corpse was given the torn and sodden appearance of an actual battle casualty, fails in its purpose, for it immediately precipitates the spectators' disbelief, upon the suspension of which the whole illusion depends. Moreover Green's hysteria made too stark a contrast with the quiet of the earlier part of the scene. Even this was not allowed its full effect at Stratford. Shakespeare wanted a lull here, after the excitement of Bolingbroke's banishment and Gaunt's denunciation, a quiet interlude to cover the passage of time while Richard is away in Ireland and Bolingbroke maturing his revenge. To provide this he wrote a purely lyrical duet between the Queen and Bushy, in which the conceits, like music in King's chapel, dwell "lingering and wandering on as loth to die". A national epic, however, requires more active effects, and Bushy here contrived by "strange oeillades and most speaking looks" to convey that beneath the innocent word-music lurked a sinister meaning, presumably the favourites' plot to unsettle the Queen, later referred to in their condemnation—one of Shakespeare's loose ends that are best left to dangle.

As with realism so with humour; if the tetralogy is to be all of a piece there must be some limbering up of the austerities of *Richard II*. No one would deny that York, tottering out to muster the King's forces and call the rebels to order, is in some sense a comic figure. His fussy lines, disjointed in rhythm as in sense, cannot be otherwise interpreted. But to play the scene solely for laughs, as at Stratford, is to destroy both the pathos of York's position, considered in itself, and its importance as a clue to the real drift of the play. Individually he is to be pitied for being called, a just and well-meaning man, to take sides in a quarrel where both parties are equally right and equally in the wrong:

> Both are my kinsmen:
> The one is my sovereign, whom both my oath
> And duty bids defend; the other again
> Is my kinsman, whom the King hath wrong'd,
> Whom conscience and my kindred bids to right. (II, ii, 111–15)

What matters, however, is that his indecision crystallizes in this very speech the audience's own dilemma: between two rights, two wrongs, where should the moralist take his stand? The serious consideration of such scruples would, however, be treason in a tetralogy celebrating the rise of the House of Lancaster; accordingly York's speech was quavered away into insignificance and Shakespeare's problem was never posed.

Only by such distortions of balance, more serious than any travestying of style, can *Richard II* be fashioned into a prologue to *Henry IV*—proof enough that it is no such thing. The ill-effects of such a misconception were most glaring in the treatment at Stratford of what should be the central figure of the play. Michael Redgrave's performance as Richard was technically brilliant. His make-up followed the traditional portraits, but with every outline softened and blurred. The fine golden fur of beard dissolved the line of the chin; the hollows and shadows of cheek and brow were toned down into dimples and colourless uniformity. This was a face of putty, a watery face over which the fleeting expressions chased each other—the most constant being an uncertain smile, half self-approving half placatory, that appeared whenever smiles were least in season. The indecision of the face was reflected in the nervous gestures, the handkerchief picked at and flaunted, the self-conscious jauntiness of gait intended as a sign of assurance but revealing an acute lack of confidence. As a portrait of a wayward weakling, painfully cockering himself up to exhibitions of arbitrary power, it was superb; but it lacked a quality essential to Shakespeare's Richard—kingliness. When Richard appears, a "blushing discontented sun from out the fiery portal of the east", on the walls of Flint Castle, York cries:

> Yet looks he like a king: behold, his eye,
> As bright as is the eagle's, lightens forth
> Controlling majesty. (III, iii, 68–70)

At Stratford the words were ludicrous in their inappropriateness, and the opening of the King's rebuke to Northumberland,

> We are amaz'd; and thus long have we stood
> To watch the fearful bending of thy knee, (III, iii, 72–3)

conveyed nothing of magnificence, no sense of a miraculous recovery of power, and hence no dramatic shock to the audience, as it should. This scene and that of the deposition require more than the "mockery king of snow" of Richard's own description, which was all that Redgrave gave us; and at the end, when even a snow king should harden into something able to command respect and sympathy, this Richard melted, rather, into a sodden and witless object too far gone even for pity.

Did this watering-down of Richard throw into special relief the early, vigorous years of Lancastrian rule, was it that the actors all found in the first part of *Henry IV* their most congenial roles, or is this play really the greatest of the four? Certainly it was the climax of the Stratford cycle, and one ceased to wonder why in the eighteenth century it was so much more popular than its sequel. What a piece of work indeed it is! Once the play is seen in proper perspective, with the King and his son at the centre, the double perfection of its structure is imposing. It is admirably laid out in plan: the two worlds, of action and of dissipation, between which the Prince must choose, and their two champions, Hotspur and Falstaff, are balanced with a nice exactness. Viewed in sequence, too, the play is beautifully proportioned, each scene making just the right contrast to its predecessor, and the climaxes and relaxations perfectly judged. After the opening scene has presented, weightily but concisely, the main themes of the play, the rival worlds of Hotspur and Falstaff are elaborated with unhurried ease. This exposition is rounded off by the interlude at Glendower's castle, at once a breathing-space for the audience before the 'working out' of the play is attacked, and an inspired evocation of that fateful pause before action, when destiny stands for a moment suspended. With admirable restraint the producer allowed this scene to take its own time and—as never before in my experience—it was given in full, with long and passionate speeches in Welsh for Glendower's daughter. For one listener, at least, there was no sense of flagging, but it might have been otherwise without Hugh Griffith's Glendower (Plate IIIB); no ranting pomposo, this, for all his occasional flamboyances, but the dangerous, enigmatical and compelling personality that alone can cast the spell the scene demands. And to the little skirl that dissolves both spell and scene, to Hotspur's banter, so inadequate a leave-taking and yet so charged with overtones of tenderness, Redgrave brought just the right wry lightness.

There follows, as node and climax of the play, the interview between Henry IV, the father, and his son, Prince Hal. This scene, which recapitulates the whole past history of the royal house and looks forward at least as far as Agincourt, is also the mid-point of Bolingbroke's career and so found Harry Andrews at his best. Faced with the task of protracting through three plays the decline of Bolingbroke from tempestuous youth to exhausted age, he tended to over-play the extremes, making the young man too rombustious, the old too drained of all vigour, but here at the centre performance and conception went hand in glove. Moreover the springing rhetoric of the scene exactly suited the actor. Though the comment that sprang immediately to mind was "What writing!" it might as well have been "What acting!" for the magnificence of the writing would not have been so manifest had it not found at Stratford an ideal interpreter. In this scene, too, the Prince's somewhat strained and gawky monotone in verse passages, later to cause misgivings, was the perfect foil to the wide-ranging splendour of the King's rebuke. From this turning-point the play speeds to its conclusion, but there is nothing scamped about the ending. Shakespeare quickens the pace by using short scenes and switching more rapidly from one centre of interest to another. Falstaff's appearances in the battle-scenes, for instance, are models of timing; by such means the various actions are drawn evenly together at the close, and the lines of the play 'tumble home' like those of a clipper.

In the other dimension, of plan and complexity, the play grows ever firmer and weightier the more strongly Falstaff and Hotspur are played, provided the two remain in balance. At Stratford both strength and trim were admirable. The keynote of Redgrave's Hotspur was vitality. Here was a man whose restless spirit never allowed him to be still. His hands were always busy pointing, emphasizing, demonstrating, or merely gesturing impatience that speech should be so slow to express his driving emotions; when he moved it was in starts and quick turns. Most effective perhaps of all was his continual half-conscious flexing of the knees, the instinctive action of one who spent most of his life in the saddle and the rest of it dreaming what he might do there. The adoption of an accent so marked and so strange on the ear as the Northumbrian was risky. It can hardly be justified by the text. The speech of a Tynesider might conceivably, though unfairly, be described as "thick", hardly as "tardy", which must imply some impediment. Yet the risk was abundantly justified, for the rough brogue exactly conveyed the harum-scarum quality of Hotspur's chivalry. Beside the unregulated bravado of this border raider the Prince's calm and conscious courage shone the more gallantly. The accent also gave warmth, homeliness, pathos even, to the scenes with Lady Percy, though in these the restlessness and the roughness were carried too far. Even border raiders do not conduct their love-making à l'apache.

First impressions of Anthony Quayle's Falstaff were not encouraging. He was over-padded and over-painted; the 'old mon' loomed too clearly in the clumsiness of his gait and the guyed expansiveness of his gestures; his voice, elegantly unctuous, suggested rather Oscar Wilde than 'Oldcastle'. These extravagances once digested, however, one could relish two qualities, courtliness and ruthlessness, that cannot emerge when, as so often, Falstaff is played as a hobble-dehoy, a roaring boy or jolly Squire Western. Quayle's was very much a gentleman decayed, and this gives point both to his desire to live soft at any cost and to his adroit toadying of superiors. Falstaff's ruthlessness, most evident in his contempt for the ragamuffins he has pressed and his cynical dismissal of them when he has left them to be cut to pieces at Shrewsbury, ensures that the audience, however fascinated and delighted, shall never finally commit themselves to his party, and that his eventual rejection shall seem not an outrage but strict justice. With this preparation Quayle was able to play the rejection scene at full strength, foregoing none of the pathos that can be wrung from the utter dashing of Falstaff's hopes, yet with the new King's honour and dignity never in jeopardy. With these rarer qualities went, in ample measure, the animal vigour and complete irrepressibility that are indispensable in any reading of the part. These were epitomized in the technique of his recovery when put down by the Prince and Poins. For a moment he would stand between them like a cornered rat, head settled into hunched shoulders and his body pinched and withdrawn, while beneath bushy brows his eyes shifted from one to the other of his captors, measuring, calculating, seeking a way out. Then suddenly the idea would come, his whole person would expand, and he would overwhelm them with a tidal wave of confidence and explanations. The same richness, the same power was there in the set speeches whether delivered, like the Honour catechism, with a quiet, sly relish or, like the praise of sack, with lip-smacking exuberance. The final impression of Falstaff, as of Hotspur, was of an almost explosive force.

With two such supporters it might be expected that Prince Hal would be eclipsed; in fact they merely established him the more firmly, as they were designed to do. With an eye perhaps to the sequel, perhaps to the qualities of his actor, Richard Burton, the Director had emphasized Hal's essential kingliness at the expense of the youthful frivolity that at first should overlie it. His salvation was assured from the start, and though he threw himself with energy into the diversions of his corrupters it was never with abandon. His first entrance has already been described, slow, brooding, disillusioned, with a deeper and more personal reflectiveness, it seemed, than mere animal sadness after a debauch. The sense of sobriety and self-knowledge was reinforced in the speech that ends the scene—"I know you all". Hal had turned to watch Falstaff leave the stage; for a moment he stood looking after him; then his head moved slowly to regard the audience over his shoulder, and the speech followed, with a curious simplicity and tonelessness, and yet with a suggestion of strong emotion held in check. How far the effect was deliberate I am not sure; it is perhaps unfair to suspect that it was partly due to imitation of Sir Laurence Olivier, one of whose mannerisms is precisely this of the voice held uneasily in leash, capable at any moment of a sudden leap in an incalculable direction. However arrived at, it saved the speech from any Machiavellian taint. It expressed inexperience, valiantly steeling

PLATE III

A. *Richard II*, Shakespeare Memorial Theatre, Stratford-upon-Avon, 1951.
Production by ANTHONY QUAYLE; Costumes and Unit Setting for the
History Plays by TANYA MOISEIWITSCH. THE OPENING SCENE

B. *Henry IV, Part I*, Shakespeare Memorial Theatre, 1951.
Production by JOHN KIDD. GLENDOWER AND HIS ALLIES

PLATE IV

Henry IV, Part II, Shakespeare Memorial Theatre, 1951.
Production by MICHAEL REDGRAVE.
IN SHALLOW'S ORCHARD

PLATE V

A. *Henry IV, Part II.* THE REJECTION OF FALSTAFF

B. *Henry V*, Shakespeare Memorial Theatre, 1951. Production by
ANTHONY QUAYLE. THE CONSPIRATORS UNMASKED.

itself to a dangerous trial in order to gain knowledge and strength, and so won immediate sympathy instead of revulsion.

Hal's essential sobriety was again emphasized—hardly legitimately—in an unorthodox reading of the "play extempore". It is usual for Hal, on taking over the part of the King from Falstaff, to continue in the same clowning vein. So indeed he did at Stratford, but for a moment only; once launched on his diatribe against the "old fat man", he dropped the banter on the instant and his indictment was made with savage earnestness. As a single stage effect it was extremely powerful—the hooting spectators suddenly chilled into silence as they realize that the fun has somehow taken a wrong turning. But if we take the play, still more the two plays of *Henry IV*, as a whole, it is clearly an error of judgement so far to anticipate the rejection of Falstaff, and a failure of consistency thus early to puncture his complacency and set him desperately pleading that the Prince should not banish him. Of course Hal's rejoinder, "I do, I will", is laden with irony, but irony loses its point if those on the stage are let into the secret as well as the audience. The effect here is greatest if even the Prince does not seem to realize how true his words will prove.

If this scene of Part I, and the Prince's first soliloquy, are played as at Stratford, they bar in advance the whole *raison d'être* of Part II. Even if the play extempore is given its normal light-hearted interpretation (it is hard to imagine an alternative presentation for the soliloquy) it is still clear that by the end of Part I Hal has worked out his salvation and there is nothing for him to do in a second part but go the same progress again. Critics have defended the integrity of the double play on the Aristotelian grounds that a dramatic action must have a beginning, a middle and an end: Hal's delinquency is clearly the beginning, his rejection of Falstaff the end; *ergo* Parts I and II comprise a single action. The trouble is that *Henry IV* has two beginnings and two ends, for the Prince as plainly breaks with Falstaff in Part I as in Part II, and to give the sequel any point at all he has to be inexplicably plunged back to the start, as if in some cosmic game of snakes and ladders. True, there is only one middle in the two plays, for Part II, that ramshackle rag-bag of a piece, has none. It is oddly enough the soliloquy and the play extempore, the chief agents in proving the sequel redundant, that are most patently designed as preparations for it. I can only assume that in the course of composition what was intended for an introduction grew to absorb the whole subject; nor, I think, would Shakespeare have attempted to spin it out over a second play if the success of the first had not made a sequel commercially a most attractive proposition.

For *2 Henry IV* has pot-boiler written all over it. There is so little for Hal, the reputed hero, to do, that after a subdued appearance in Act II, as little more than an onlooker at Falstaff's debaucheries, he is dropped again entirely until the end of the play. He is then brought on only to re-enact in an extended and to my mind weakened version the scene of altercation and reconciliation with his father, and to set a ceremonial seal on the rejection of Falstaff to which he had committed himself ten acts earlier. The theme of rebellion, too, has petered out with the death of Hotspur and Worcester and Northumberland's politic withdrawal. The creation of a new brood of traitors (admittedly foreshadowed in Part I) is as factitious as their contemptuous dismissal when they have served their turn. The gap is filled by an enormous extension of Falstaff, and by the glorious irrelevancy of the Gloucestershire scenes. It is on these sideshows that Shakespeare lavishes his attention, with the result that they become completely out of balance and the play, as a 'History', is distorted. Falstaff, the airy embodiment of resilience and breezy opportunism, becomes a disturbingly actual old man, an ugly *memento senescere*. Instead of the nimble comedy of Part I, whose elements are volte-face and comic peripateia, puns, verbal flourishes, and non-sequiturs, we have a satirical analysis, Jonsonian in its concentration and pungency, of human frailties and fatuities. Reviewers have said that it was the over-playing of these scenes and roles at Stratford that disrupted the proper effect of the play, but it is difficult to see how they could have been soft-pedalled. Pistol, certainly, was exaggerated, but it was not the fact of exaggeration, but its character that was disturbing. When will producers cease to treat Pistol as a fantastic? He is the common man who tries to weave romance about himself with tags from the stage successes that have enchanted him, and his counterpart to-day would be an addict of 'westerns' and gangster films. William Squire's Silence was a monstrous exaggeration, a looming, lugubrious codfish with vaguely flapping fins (Plate IV); yet the loud expressionless chanting that would suddenly break from him with deliciously comic effect brought release and relief to the scene rather than disruption. It is not caricature but sober realism that bursts this play. Falstaff, Doll, Shallow are a grim antimasque that, in defiance of theatrical convention, refuses to be dislodged by the play proper, and while they hold the stage it is impossible to believe in kingly nobility or the natural attractiveness of order.

The performance of *Henry V* suffered by comparison with Glen Byam Shaw's production of the play at the Old Vic earlier in the year, already noticed in *Shakespeare Survey*, 5. At almost every point—the most notable exception being the scene of the three conspirators (Plate VB), presented at Stratford with rare concentration—the Old Vic led, for the simple reason that the play had there no strings to it and could be left to unroll without constraint its extraordinary variety of turns—romance and philosophy, high comedy and slapstick, melodrama, music-hall, epic. Thus unbuttoned it has a size and an immediacy that as the peroration to a political treatise it must forgo, a sparkle and verve that are lost when it is trimmed to fit a tetralogy. It is perhaps doubtful whether Richard Burton could have mustered the authority that Harry must have if the play is to stand on its own legs. As the copy-book king and leader promised in the preceding plays he was perfectly sufficient, and had no difficulty in winning the sympathy of the audience with the easy camaraderie that had made the early scenes on Gadshill and in Cheapside so attractive; but he gave no hint of greatness. At the Old Vic Clunes, in dismissing the French ambassadors, had conveyed an agonized yet undaunted awareness of the bitter struggle that must follow; Burton showed little more than pique. Burton worked up the Crispin's Day speech to a conventional fortissimo at "We few, we happy few"; Clunes at this point was suddenly intimate, a brother-in-arms sharing a radiant promise with his comrades. The greater stature of Clunes's performance had the curious effect of persuading us to look not so much at the central figure as, with him, at the whole human panorama of the play.

I missed, too, the earthiness of Livesey's Chorus at the Old Vic. This Chorus can be played in one of two ways: as something outside the play, a guide, conducting the spectators up to the play and encouraging them to grapple with it; or as an integral part of the play, its figure-head or emblem, not interpreting the action but setting the tone as a dumb-show might do. Redgrave was of course committed to the second alternative, for the irruption at this late stage of an interpreter would be incongruous in a tetralogy that has already afforded, in Rumour, a precedent for a Prologue. As Prologue Redgrave was forced to sacrifice everything to magnificence and forgo the humour and cajolery that made Livesey so persuasive an introducer.

One more complaint, about the transposition of Falstaff's page and Mrs Quickly's drawer—but no; it would be wrong to end on such a note. At Stratford we were given performances of the two parts of *Henry IV* that we shall be lucky to see bettered in our lifetime, and an experiment that required courage to mount and was of absorbing interest to watch. That the results were largely negative is immaterial; it is often from such negative results that knowledge makes its greatest advances. Now that *Richard II*, the two parts of *Henry IV*, and *Henry V* have proved themselves (despite critics and producers) to be plays, they may become more frequent, and more welcome, in the theatre.

FESTIVAL SHAKESPEARE IN
THE WEST END

BY

GEORGE RYLANDS

"*Antony and Cleopatra* is an attempt at serious drama. To say that there is plenty of bogus characterization in it—Enobarbus for instance—is merely to say that it is by Shakespear. But the contrast between Caesar and Antony is true human drama; and Caesar himself is deeper than the usual Shakespearean stage king." Thus Bernard Shaw in 1897, after "an afternoon of lacerating anguish, spent partly in contemplating Miss Achurch's overpowering experiments in rhetoric, and partly in wishing I had never been born". He had already endured the production at Manchester, where Janet Achurch's magnificent voice and audacious but discordant conception of Shakespeare's music suggested that she had been "excited by the Hallelujah Chorus to dance on the keyboard of a great organ with all the stops pulled out". Janet Achurch had created Ibsen's heroines for the English intelligentsia—unapproachable as Nora and Mrs Alving—and for Cleopatra, having no gift for comedy, "she substituted Brynhild-cum-Nora Helmer in an Ibsen-and-Wagner pie". What a contrast with the production seven years earlier in which Lily Langtry played Egypt! "She is (in Dio's phrase) Cleopatra περικαλλεστάτη γυναικῶν", wrote A. B. Walkley, "but λαμπρά τε ἀκουσθῆναι she cannot, with her thin, inflexible voice pretend to be. Nor will her plummet line suffice for the vasty deeps of one of the great Shakespearean heroines. She is best in her scenes of coquetry, but even that suggests the modern coquetry of Mayfair. One could not help wishing that Mr Wingfield had retained the Queen's invitation to Charmian: 'Let us to billiards'; for here was evidently a Cleopatra who had gone the round of the best country houses, and was doubtless an adept with the cue." Walkley was reminded of Hazlitt's criticism of the Cleopatra of his day: "Her manner bordered too much on the affected levity of a modern fine lady, and wanted the passion and dignity of the enamoured and haughty sovereign."

How, with these brief but significant records of failure in mind, are we to assess Vivien Leigh's performance in the part—which "is not playable by mortal woman" and was written for a boy? She was certainly nearer to Mrs Langtry than to Miss Achurch. She is περικαλλεστάτη γυναικῶν, and she can be a comedian. As certainly she cannot, like Janet Achurch, revel in the power of her voice and the steam pressure of her energy. Her plummet line hardly suffices for the vasty deeps of passion. Yet we remember her performances in Anouilh's *Antigone* and in Tenessee Williams's *Streetcar named Desire* and wonder whether her Cleopatra might not have had more variety, more intensity, bolder strikes and higher lights. Vivien Leigh never really let herself go. She played for safety and was justified in the event. For the first thing to record of this Festival of Britain presentation is that it was a popular success, a best-seller, which *Antony and Cleopatra* has seldom, if ever, been before. The fact that the two amorous protagonists were played by a married pair, twin stars of stage and screen, as famous in their day as Marcus Antonius and the Egyptian Queen in theirs, goes some way to account for it:

140

> the nobleness of life
> Is to do thus; when such a mutual pair
> And such a twain can do't.   (I, i, 36–8)

But the true explanation lies deeper. Laurence Olivier and his clever producer, Michael Benthall, sharing Dryden's nostalgia for heroism in a disillusioned age, played the tragedy as *All for Love or the World Well Lost*. The public prefer it so; and most of Shakespeare's critics have agreed with the public. Shaw knew better, as his Preface to *Caesar and Cleopatra* reveals: and Vivien Leigh played Shaw's Cleopatra with freedom and expression on alternate nights. Shakespeare's Roman Chronicle is, however, more realistic than tragic. As with *Hamlet* ten years earlier, he experiments and expends his talents in portraits and sketches from life, holding the mirror up to nature as far as, indeed more than, dramatic conventions and limitations allow. So that even Shaw, who thought Shakespeare a naive psychologist, can find "plenty of bogus characterization" in the play. But whereas in *Hamlet* the verse is easy, the prose abundant and idiomatic, the expression for the most part direct and natural, in *Antony and Cleopatra* the valiancy, audacity and extravagance of style dazzle and delude us. And as all theatre-goers are romantic we rejoice to be deluded, whether we are sighing lovers, soldiers full of strange oaths, capon-lined in the belly, or shrunk in the shank.

A similar interpretation, or idealization, we understand, achieved the same desired result, when Katharine Cornell and Godfrey Tearle were the protagonists in New York at the end of 1947. This production, played all out for glamour and romance, "broke the jinx which over the long years has dogged one of the marvels of dramatic literature". So wrote the distinguished critic, John Mason Brown, no less determined than everyone else (except Mark Antony) to shut his ears and eyes to the Cleopatra Shakespeare created.

The conversion of realism into romance necessitated, of course, some pretty high-handed treatment of the text. Michael Benthall's excisions were ruthless and his soldering-up expert. The Seleucus scene in Act v had to go. The great betrayal, when the Queen responds to the overtures conveyed by Thyreus, was sugared over. Cleopatra's suicide must appear to follow hard upon the death of her lord. A little juggling with the emphasis in this scene and that will persuade us that Egypt was never false of heart though presence or peril seemed her flame to qualify. The omission of the Ventidius scene, ironically juxtaposed by Shakespeare with the tipsy triumvirate on the pirate galley, spares Antony a sorry mark of shabbiness:

> Better to leave undone than by our deed
> Acquire too high a fame when him we serve's away.
> Caesar and Antony have ever won
> More in their officer than person....
> I could do more to do Antonius good
> But 'twould offend him; and in his offence
> Should my performance perish.   (III, i, 14–27)

Nothing in the life of the traitor Cawdor became him like the leaving it; the traitor Brutus was redeemed by death; it was the final tableau that we carried away from the St James's Theatre. Who will forget Vivien Leigh, robed and crowned in the habiliments of an Egyptian goddess, beauty on a monument smiling extremity out of act? The gipsy, the ribaudred nag, the boggler, the triple-turn'd whore, the fragment on Cneius Pompey's trencher, were all forgotten. There never was such a person anyway. The *femme fatale* of "the Romantic Agony", the Cleopatra of Gautier and Flaubert still exerts her spell and Shakespeare's boy player is suppressed.

Laurence Olivier sacrificed Antony to Cleopatra and "for his ordinary paid his heart". Only with Octavius Caesar was his true stature revealed; and with Eros, played mistakenly as a medieval squire, not as a freed slave. Robert Helpmann's Octavius made every pause and syllable tell, every flicker of his lid and finger; a cold-blooded youth who had never been a boy; and how formidable! This was Lucan's Julius:

> acer et indomitus, quo spes quoque ira vocasset,
> successus urguere suos, instare favori
> numinis, impellens quidquid sibi summa petenti
> obstaret gaudensque viam fecisse ruina.

And the Roman poet's comparison with Pompey held for Olivier's Antony. An oak laden with dedicated trophies, no longer clinging to the soil with strong roots but held by its own weight, ripe to fall at the first blast of the storm, yet worshipped in the midst of many forest trees still in their prime. *Stat magni nominis umbra.* This Antony was declined into the vale of years. The tone was light, the rhythms broken, the audience were presented with his profile or his back. It was an unselfish performance; warm and loving but the affection was domestic. There were moments when one even recalled the same players as Sir Peter and Lady Teazle, when the home life of Antony and Cleopatra, to reverse the famous comment of the Victorian era, was all too like that of our gracious Queen. However, for variety and pace, for colour and vitality the production was splendid and delightful; crowned with beauty at the close and rewarded with popular success.

The dividing and the scissoring of *Antony and Cleopatra*, a tragedy wrongly supposed to be formless, achieved the purpose which the protagonists and the producer clearly intended. In the production of *The Winter's Tale*, the substitution of three movements for two was less justifiable and more far-reaching in its effects. Shakespeare ended his first part with the bear's dinner and the prophetic words of the Old Shepherd: "Now bless thyself: thou mettest with things dying, I with things new-born.... This is fairy gold,... 'Tis a lucky day, boy; and we'll do good deeds on't." Then comes Father Time, against whose scythe nothing can make defence save breed, and turns his glass, and we slide over sixteen years. After a moment of prosy exposition we hear Autolycus singing of the lark and the daffodil; the sweet of the year grows ancient,

> Not yet on summer's death, nor on the birth
> Of trembling winter—. (IV, iv, 80–1)

Perdita is "no shepherdess but Flora Peering in April's front". It is a play of times and seasons; of brave day sunk in hideous night, of summer's green all girded up in sheaves, of sable curls silvered o'er, of young people standing on the top of happy hours.

> Shall I compare thee to a summer's day?
> Thou art more lovely and more temperate:
> Rough winds do shake the darling buds of May,
> And summer's lease hath all too short a date. (Sonnet XVIII)

Shakespeare looks back more than twenty years to his first sonnets. But we must not pause after the sheep-shearing. The shadows lengthen as we steal away with the young lovers to Sicilia, where reconciliations and Aristotelian recognitions and a *coup de théâtre* conspire that the prince and princess may live happily ever after. In the Romances, as every schoolboy knows, the sins of the fathers are redeemed by the children, by the heroines whose divine property it is to have mercy and to forgive. If the constancy and love of the young people are the means to an end, the means are surely no less important than that end. Peter Brook and John Gielgud sacrificed Perdita and Florizel, as Laurence Olivier sacrificed Mark Antony. The tragi-comedy was divided into three. The first movement (Sicilia) ended with the self-dedication of Leontes to expiation and remorse; and Diana Wynyard made the movement Hermione's with a faultless performance, stronger and richer than that she had previously given at Stratford. In the second movement (Bohemia) George Rose as Autolycus—pungent as garlic, sharp as vinegar, keen as mustard—dressed the Arcadian salad with gallic dexterity and gust. In the third (Sicilia Once More) Leontes, ably supported by Flora Robson's Paulina, came completely if belatedly into his own. Where then were Cinderella and Prince Charming? Alas, the tender juvenals could not compete with what Moth calls their tough seniors! (Antigonus was made real and true by Lewis Casson.) They certainly looked their parts and spoke very nicely, but, as Gwendolen said of the name Jack, they had positively no vibrations. Virginia McKenna was as pretty as a picture and obviously the daughter of the statuesque Hermione. *O matre pulchra filia pulchrior?* No, not quite. One can only do justice to Diana Wynyard's Hermione in the words of Donne:

> No Spring nor Summer beauty hath such grace
> As I have seen in one Autumnal face.

The whole production had in fact too deep an autumnal tone, culminating in a third movement *Adagio lamentoso e molto sostenuto*. Edmund Kean's Richard II, we remember, was described by Hazlitt as a violin solo. In the expiatory passion of Leontes and the ritual resurrection of the Queen, with Paulina as High Priestess, the linked sweetness was a touch too long drawn out. The tears which rose in the hearts of the audience and gathered in the eyes of Gielgud (like Parson Evans he has "a great dispositions to cry") were more idly Tennysonian than significant of any divine despair. In De Gourmont's words, "he who weeps for the death of Ophelia has no aesthetic sense", and we suspect playing that has a palpable design upon our heart-strings. It was, nevertheless, a very lovely suite of chamber music, worthy of a statue which outdid "that rare Italian master, Julio Romano", and the allegro passage between the four eloquent gentlemen, which critics and dons deprecate, was, as it always is, when skilfully played, extremely diverting.

If Michael Benthall decided to turn the realism of *Antony and Cleopatra* into romance, Peter Brook perhaps hoped to make the romance of *The Winter's Tale* more real. At any rate, when the play opened, John Gielgud was at pains to convey the jealous disposition of a tyrant "with doubts a long time smothering in his stomach" and to follow Shakespeare's original, Robert Greene, rather than Shakespeare. "In *The Winter's Tale*", wrote Bridges, "the jealousy of Leontes is senseless, whereas in the original story an adequate motive is develop'd." (A wise critic, Lascelles Abercrombie, pencils in the margin of my copy: "as jealousy often is".) "It may be", Bridges continues, "that Shakespeare wish'd to portray this passion in odious nakedness without reason or rein, as might be proper in a low comedy, where its absurdity would be

143

ridiculed away: but if so, his scheme was as artistically bad as any third-rate melodrama of to-day." Greene, less innocent than the late Poet Laureate, was aware that jealousy is not confined to low comedy and cannot be dismissed as absurd.

Among al the Passions wherewith humane mindes are perplexed, there is none that so galleth with restlesse despight, as the infectious soare of Iealousie....Yea, who so is payned with this restlesse torment doubteth all, dystrusteth him-selfe, is alwayes frosen with feare, and fired with suspition, having that wherein consisteth all his joy to be the breeder of his miserie.

As Greene on this occasion was writing a novel not a drama, he rightly concerned himself with motivation. Bellaria (Hermione) used Egistus (Polixenes)

so familiarly, that her countenance bewraied how her minde was affected towardes him: oftentimes comming her selfe into his bed chamber, to see that nothing should be amis to mislike him...there grew such a secret uniting of their affections, that the one could not be well without the company of the other.

In the novel, this behaviour induces a certain melancholy passion in Pandosto, until "doubtfull thoughtes *a long time* smoothering in his stomacke began *at last* to kindle in his minde a secret mistrust, which increased by suspition, grewe *at last* to be a flaming Iealousie". Now an actor cannot hope, and cannot be expected, to convey all these "at lasts" in some 120 lines, a few minutes after the curtain is up. And surely Shakespeare, the cunning dramatist, never supposed that he could. He is in fact writing melodrama, as Bridges detected; a tragical-comical-poetical melodrama à la Fletcher; and he takes his cue from another sentence in Greene:

The young sonne was nursd up in the house to the great joy and content of the parents. Fortune envious of such happy success, willing to shew some signe of her inconstancie, turn'd her wheele and darknd their bright sun of prosperitie, with the mistie clouds of mishap and misery.

Jove, as Horace tells us, sometimes thunders from an azure sky, the melancholy fit falls sudden from heaven like a weeping cloud. A poetic drama is a hurdle race and a pistol shot releases the runners. So it is with *Lear*. Leontes is a victim of daemonic possession. He is struck down in a flash of summer lightning, and thenceforward all is dark, dark, dark, beneath the blaze of noon. Had John Gielgud dared an effect of this kind, playing for wonder and sympathy rather than for the suspension of disbelief, he would, in my judgement, have dominated the first movement with greater tragic power. The whole play would have gained in intensity and passion. We must however con Shakespeare's text in Act I, ii, to assess the difficulties. For some thirty lines Leontes is importunate with Polixenes to stay and then appeals to Hermione for support. In her dialogue with Polixenes he takes no part. Is he on the rack—spying on her jealously (as Gielgud played it), or is he absorbed in Mamillius? Surely the significant words which bring him back into the scene are these—Hermione's conclusion:

> The offences we have made you do we'll answer,
> If you first sinn'd with us and that with us
> You did continue fault and that you slipp'd not
> With any but with us.
>
> (I, ii, 83–6)

PLATE VI

B. *The Winter's Tale.* "What you do
still betters what is done"

A. *The Winter's Tale,* Phoenix Theatre, London, 1951.
"Chide me, dear stone"

Production by Peter Brook; Costumes and Settings by Sophie Fedorovitch.

PLATE VII

A. *Antony and Cleopatra*, St James's Theatre, London, 1951. Production by MICHAEL BENTHALL. Costumes by AUDREY CRUDDAS; Settings by ROGER FURSE. "THE SOLDIER'S POLE IS FALLEN"

B. *Antony and Cleopatra*. "YOU THAT WILL FIGHT, FOLLOW ME CLOSE"

PLATE VIII

A. *Othello*, St James's Theatre, London, 1951. Production by ORSON WELLES; Decor by MOTLEY. "SOFT YOU, A WORD OR TWO BEFORE YOU GO"

B. *Othello*, Theatre of Olomouc, Czechoslovakia, 1951

Offences, sinn'd, slipp'd. Does Leontes overhear these words—and only these? His question "Is he won yet?" with its sequent "At my request he would not" might suggest that the surface is ruffled. What follows makes the scales fall from his eyes. Hermione has *twice* said well. The first time was when she plighted her troth and gave her hand to her future husband; the second now when she gives it again, winning "for some while a friend". And on the word she takes Polixenes' hand, as once she took her husband's. The gesture plunges Leontes into the abysm of hell. "Can such things be And overcome us like a summer's cloud?"

Both Olivier and Gielgud were blest in their designers. Roger Furse's monument surmounted by a Sphinx opened *Caesar and Cleopatra* and returned to complete the cycle when Egypt died upon her throne. A revolving stage, skilfully exploited, ensured continuity and pace. Most important of all we felt the contrast between Rome and Alexandria. We crossed and re-crossed *Mare Nostrum.* Sophie Fedorovitch observed the structure of the Elizabethan playhouse for the settings of *The Winter's Tale,* and Peter Brook's groupings followed suit. The sudden rejection of Hermione from a "window-stage" as she played with her son in the courtyard below was remarkably effective. The tempest which flap-dragon'd the vessel of Antigonus turned into a whirl of snow through whose flakes Father Time materialized—and melted away. The skies cleared to an open stage dressed with sunburnt rustics in their rye straw hats and all their pastoral "gear and tackle and trim".

Comparisons are odious. Both productions were more than worthy of the Festival and in both (although we quarrel with the Act divisions) Shakespeare was respected and understood. The palm goes to *The Winter's Tale* because the whole company led by Gielgud were more responsive to the quality of the style, to the movement of the verse, the complexity of the syntax, the pregnancy of the metaphor. Laurence Olivier and Vivien Leigh were adequately supported but—Helpmann apart—without distinction. Helpmann's outstanding performance conveyed Shakespeare's intention that the play be presented not only as a love story but as an imperial theme. Shaw, who allows that the conflict between Caesar and Antony is true human drama, would have applauded. In the same way George Rose's Autolycus was a corrective, an antidote of realism. As a sly and greedy confidence man, he just stopped short of nastiness and tricked us against our will. Enobarbus should exercise the same corrective function in *Antony and Cleopatra* but Norman Wooland was surprisingly ineffectual.

The Orson Welles *Othello* was so unusual that it must be recorded as an epilogue to the above. He disproved the axiom that the whole is greater than the part. His text was not cut but carbonadoed. The omissions and telescopings were hair-raising. Brabantio was over-played and Roderigo insufferably guyed. Iago was replaced by Jonson's Mosca and Peter Finch took such words as were left to him with miraculous speed. His function, indefatigably performed, was to stoke the blast furnace of Othello's dynamic personality. The dynamo, in the event, was more formidable before it began to rotate than when running at full power. However, when all has been said, Orson Welles gave as memorable and magnetic an impersonation of a Shakespearian role as has been seen for several decades. He bestrode the world like a Colossus and bore the palm alone. His production was unusual, more inspired by screen than stage. Depth, weight, pace, and naked simplicity were the keynotes, with a great front curtain which swept to and fro, so that before a scene had clearly ended another was in motion. "It is not growing like a tree In bulk doth make man better be", says Jonson. Orson Welles's bulk was immense, his movement conjured up antres vast and deserts idle. But his speech, most unexpectedly, was often delicate and musical and always just. He has an ear for Shakespeare. If the organ notes of the Farewell and the Pontic Sea passages were wanting, the address to the Senate could not have been bettered. Critics disparaged Gudrun Ure's Desdemona, while (rightly) praising the Emilia of Maxine Audley—a part in which no actress should fail. But Desdemona, although out of tune in the first part, was transformed from the moment of the Moor's brutal blow and moved us painfully as the loving wife who answers Emilia's "How do you, madam?" with the words "Faith, half asleep". Her powers of endurance when suffocated by Welles, trussed in a sheet and left to hang head downwards, deserve the striking of a special medal.

In conclusion, it can be said for once that the stars in their courses (save Orson Welles) did not fight against Shakespeare. Have the last few seasons at Stratford set an example and taught London a lesson? They differed from one another in glory, for that is the secret of stardom. If Olivier did not burn the great sphere he moved in but stood darkling, it was to lend light to the fleeting planet, the more than moon, who drew up tears to drown us in her sphere. "The skies are painted with unnumber'd sparks They are all fire and every one doth shine": yet in the number Orson Welles knows but one,

> That unassailable holds on his rank,
> Unshaked of motion,

and that one is he. Gielgud, on the contrary, as is his custom, was content to be the centre of a star-cluster in the spangled heavens; one of a galaxy proclaiming their great Original in the utterance "The hand that made us was divine".

THE YEAR'S CONTRIBUTIONS TO SHAKESPEARIAN STUDY

1. CRITICAL STUDIES

reviewed by M. C. BRADBROOK

"And is there a difference between the various years?" asked Hjalmer Ekdal. The answer is undoubtedly yes. In spite of the really alarming growth in Shakespearian studies—there is a book or article on Shakespeare for every day of the year—every year has a characteristic flavour. In *Shakespeare Survey*, 1, Miss Ellis-Fermor observed "the contemplation of Shakespeare as an artist and as a poet", and she looked for a crucial change in the direction of criticism within the next few years. The next year she laid the emphasis upon the development of Shakespeare's art and thought, and in *Shakespeare Survey*, 3 she said:

> The contributions of the last three years make two things clear: first that the stream of general studies is setting steadily in the direction of interpretation and...second, that the increasing tendency (at the time of writing) is to a close and, when necessary, an abstract habit of thought which nevertheless acknowledges the fundamentally unabstract nature of dramatic art. (p. 137.)

The critical studies of 1951 bear out these views. Shakespeare the artist and poet is the subject of the majority of works, and Shakespeare is interpreted in terms of speech and style. The language of the plays looks like being the central interest for some years to come. As in the 1920's Shakespearian study depended upon an increased awareness of the power of theatrical conditions, and in the 1930's was concerned chiefly with problems of imagery, so the writers of to-day are instinctively looking for poetic and dramatic patterns, but with a closer sense than the critics of the 1930's employed of the way in which these were shaped by Elizabethan habits of thought and of writing.

Preoccupation with style inevitably means the return to more general studies, rather than a concentrated examination of particular plays; and this is demonstrated in half a dozen books. First of all might be considered two which in many respects are sharply contrasted, *The Meaning of Shakespeare* by the late President of Swarthmore College, and *A Shakespeare Primer* by Peter Alexander.[1] The first is very large, very leisurely and very expensive; the second is very modest, very concentrated, and designed for the young student. They have in common vigour, enthusiasm and a power to draw upon the critic's total literary experience which can be evoked only by reading deeply felt, and long pondered. Both are ripe books: both transmit direct experience: they are not 'about' Shakespeare, they present him. At the same time, Goddard invokes Dostoievsky, Alexander whips in references to Proust, Henry James, Chekhov, Mozart or Molière.

Both writers, it may be said, are not afraid of being provocative, though their methods of provocation and their interest differ widely. When Goddard begins "Shakespeare is like life..."

[1] H. G. Goddard, *The Meaning of Shakespeare* (Chicago University Press; London: Cambridge University Press, 1951). Peter Alexander, *A Shakespeare Primer* (James Nisbet, 1951), reviewed on p. 158.

he is asking for a recoil which, from a certain type of student, he can depend upon receiving. Shakespeare is like life, he continues, in being Protean. So many readers, so many interpretations; but all interpretations, provided they are deep and sincere, are valid. Art is essentially ambiguous. Shakespeare's own integrity lay in his shaping spirit of imagination, in his selective power. This can be seen by an examination of the works in chronological sequence, when the foreshadowing of later work in early plays reveals the growth of the artist.

This Goddard proceeds to demonstrate. He is not concerned with the "historic background" as such (indeed he has some hard things to say about historic critics), but such a note as that on the meaning of "affection" (p. 201) reveals that he has a full historic sense of the words. Even Shakespeare himself might have queried the statement that Agincourt represented "the first victory of massed yeomen over knights"—for he had heard of Creçy and the Black Prince. In matters of general interpretation, Goddard is equally dashing, and holds that Katharine the shrew was the real victor of the contest, that *Cymbeline* is a species of allegory, that Henry V is an unreformed character: "What it all adds up to is that the Battle of Agincourt was the royal equivalent of the Gadshill robbery. If Shakespeare did not mean it, it means itself" (p. 260). But all must concede that in his readiness to adopt a variety of approaches, to look for the informing core of the play within the play itself, Goddard is right; his warm and generous writing should rouse both the learned and the simple towards a fuller enjoyment.

The editions of *Macbeth* and *Love's Labour's Lost*,[1] on the other hand, which have appeared in the New Arden Shakespeare, are very fully annotated and they illustrate the critical development of thought by their clear contrast with the older editions. Kenneth Muir has much to say on the imagery and themes of *Macbeth*, and Richard David makes clear the changed opinion of *Love's Labour's Lost* which developed from the work of Granville-Barker.

Two small books, both from the Oxford University Press,[2] raise large questions concerning the nature of dramatic art. D. G. James is writing mainly from the philosophical point of view, Arthur Sewell from the social and theatrical. But in each case, there is an attempt to penetrate through the examination of particular works to the level at which true generalizations spring, to gain perspective and to explore the presuppositions which lay behind the composition of the plays.

James's essay is highly compressed; it is written from and assumes knowledge of the Elizabethan age, and of the later Middle Ages also. Bacon and Shakespeare are seen as alike in their rejection of dogmatism: "Nowhere in Bacon's writing do we find certainty of touch, the fully formed idea, the fashioned conclusion." They are contrasted in their approach to knowledge: Bacon exempts poetry, like religion, from reason; it is a "dream of learning" which submits the shows of things to the desires of the mind. In Shakespeare's works, as James believes, we have "a rational treatment by the greatest man who has appeared in our civilization of human conduct and human destiny", but no theory and no philosophy. The imagination is an instrument of poetic discovery; poetry "represents a great labour of knowledge: not indeed of understanding, but of perception". The labour to *see* is part of the life of reason, and this is

---

[1] Kenneth Muir, ed. *Macbeth*, The Arden Shakespeare (Methuen, 1951). R. W. David, ed. *Love's Labour's Lost*, The Arden Shakespeare (Methuen, 1951).

[2] D. G. James, *The Dream of Learning*: An essay on *The Advancement of Learning, Hamlet* and *King Lear* (Oxford: Clarendon Press, 1951). Arthur Sewell, *Character and Society in Shakespeare* (Oxford: Clarendon Press, 1951).

illustrated by an examination of *Hamlet* and *King Lear*. In Hamlet Shakespeare portrayed the sceptical intellect; the hero is in a state of philosophic anxiety—of *Angst*—which is equal in importance to his emotional state. This interpretation throws great weight on the soliloquies, particularly the third, which James reads as a meditation of immortality. *King Lear* depicts "not the mind of Lear but the world's savagery as it overwhelms it". Evil has a monopoly of action; goodness is rendered helpless, even at the cost of such improbabilities in the fable as the sustained disguises of Kent and Edgar, which keep them so long concealed from those they love. The shows of things are emphatically not subject to desires of the mind. In this play the conflict of good and evil is presented in elemental terms, but though there is an element of allegory, this is a "hidden method personal to (Shakespeare's) needs". In a subtle passage which corrects by implication a good many critical pronouncements of the extreme school of symbolist critics James observes:

What we have...in these great tragedies is a state of affairs in which any conceptual schemes, any mere significances, never quite break out from the presented situations; they are strictly implicit; they are held, if only barely, in solution; and they are not precipitated in our apprehension of the plays...the state...is one of involvement, not of explication.... What is exhibited is charged with meaning: but it does not *carry* it. (p. 88.)

This is a secular imagination: James can detect no clear signs of Christian doctrine: the questioning is ultimate, the answer in *Lear* is given in terms of pure being—in the figure of Cordelia. The reading of these two great plays is instrumental to a wider view of Shakespeare's art; and though for some the total impression may be a somewhat too Coleridgean Shakespeare, the value, sincerity and power of James's view remain.

Sewell's approach to the great tragedies is not far removed from James's; for him, too, "character and moral vision must be apprehended together, and...when character is understood separately from moral vision it is in fact not understood at all" (p. 59). In each tragedy there is a conflict between the metaphysical vision and the world of everyday. "We impoverish poetic drama if we suppose that the creation of a character such as Lear is no more than 'the study of a man'.... Of course our concern is with a man, is with Lear: but our concern with him is this—the manner in which, even in his madness, he addresses himself to the universe, and the manner in which, in that address, the universe is seen anew" (pp. 84-5). The rehabilitation of the study of character which is here advocated depends upon a sense of drama; each character is 'real' only in the sense in which other people are real to us, not that in which we are real to ourselves: he is known only within the confines of the play, and only as he forms part of a larger order created by all the characters of the play. In the comedies this order is social; in the tragedies it is metaphysical. Within the limits proper to dramatic art even a minor character may enjoy individuality—

enrich, diversify and individually quicken the comprehensive view. Of that view he is the product but in that view he is also an agent. The minor character is not merely a deduction from the theme of the play, related by a kind of dramatic geometry to the whole pattern. In him, as in a single brush stroke in a picture, a moment of vision, a new angle of attitude transforms to however small an extent, and lights up, the whole matter. (p. 20.)

Each play embodies a specific vision, a specific address to the world; and in the greater plays each character has also his specific address to the world, which is given in terms of his personal idiom, his characteristic style. "Othello's world is the universe itself, which he all but creates... the poetic aggrandizement of himself, and as he addresses it he creates it."

Character can thus be studied only in terms of the total dramatic context, and in terms of the style. "An ideal form of character-presentation in poetic drama is that in which from moment to moment the character is realized within the particular situation and from that situation through him is distilled and concentrated poetic truth" (p. 22).

The sensitive and exact application of his theory which proceeds together with the statement of it constitutes the special felicity of Sewell's work. To say "Iago has that kind of actuality that comes from an audience" may sound post-Stoll platitude: it is the implication that counts. Here is aesthetics and 'practical criticism' blended in a manner which is not often met with. Without attempting a complete survey of all the works, he discusses representative comedies and histories, the great tragedies and the romances. I find the last chapters the least illuminating, and in his treatment of the romances Sewell seems to me to be flagging and to rely more upon other critics. But in its rare combination of lucidity and depth this is a memorable work, one to be taken slowly, and to be "chewed and digested". Whilst the historic argument in support of his case is not directly made by Sewell—in this he differs from James—the concept of character which he puts forward could readily be restated in terms of Elizabethan thought and might be applied to other Elizabethan dramatists besides Shakespeare.

With Wolfgang Clemen's welcome appearance in an English guise, the work which he originally produced in 1936 as *Shakespeares Bilder* is brought up to date and presented in lucid and sensitive terms to a wide public by means of admirable translation.[1] Clemen, while acknowledging his debt to Miss Spurgeon and to Wilson Knight, has his own way of approaching the problem of Shakespeare's imagery, which is to study it in relation to the general development of the style.

This study seeks to show how manifold and various are the conditions and qualifications determining the form and nature of each image, and how many factors are to be considered in order to grasp fully the real character of the imagery of a play....An isolated image, an image viewed outside of its context, is only half the image....It appears as a cell in the organism of the play, linked with it in many ways. (pp. 2–3.)

Accordingly the plays are considered in chronological order, and the approach to each one determined by the specific modifications of style which it displays. In *Richard II*, which Clemen rightly considers one of the great turning points of Shakespeare's art, imagery is linked closely with character drawing and becomes for the first time fully 'symphonic' as distinct from merely iterative. The account of the imagery of Othello and Iago should be compared with Sewell's account of these two characters: there is a remarkable measure of agreement. *King Lear* is the play in which "an attempt to interpret...solely on the basis of its imagery—a risky undertaking —would have the greatest chance of success" (p. 133), and in his consideration of the tragedies— which forms the middle section of his book—Clemen shows how the pattern of imagery gives

---

[1] Wolfgang Clemen, *The Development of Shakespeare's Imagery* (Methuen, 1951).

a shape to the play which lies below the level of character, even while it intensifies the distinctiveness of certain individuals—for example *Hamlet* is examined in terms of the contrast between the hero and all the other characters. There is no attempt in this work to be absolutely inclusive: *Macbeth* is not considered at any length and the romances receive rather cursory treatment. Perhaps there is a compensating gain in life and vivacity. Much of what Clemen has to say has become matter of general agreement in the sixteen years that have elapsed since his book was written: much might be amplified if he were to consider the original texts instead of sticking to the Globe text, which of course obliterates many images by course of modernization and editorial selection. But his work remains among the most moderate and sensitive statements of the subject and one which perhaps should first of all be put into the hands of the young student.

Wilson Knight, whose work did so much twenty years ago to kindle and stimulate an interest in imagery, has republished *The Imperial Theme*, the second volume of his original trilogy.[1] This contains essays on *Julius Caesar, Hamlet, Macbeth, Coriolanus* and *Antony and Cleopatra*, some of them among the best things that their author has written. In a lively introduction he makes a plea for interpretation rather than criticism, that is for imaginative and intuitive rather than historic or scholarly reading. It is sad that the two should appear to him to be so utterly incompatible. "Here our whole educational tradition is at fault: it stands itself with great composure, it is true, and much dignity, on its head." Dryasdust is a well-known figure and has been any time these six hundred years, but there are times when one is tempted to say: 'Would that the educational system could produce nothing worse!'

G. I. Duthie[2] is modestly catering for that same educational public in his little book. He is concerned to give the general reader an account of the trends of modern Shakespearian studies: how formidable a task this is only those who have attempted the sifting can appreciate. After disposing of the naturalistic theory of character, Duthie gives a chapter to the Elizabethan concepts of Hierarchy, Order and the Chain of Being—the Lovejoy Layer-cake, it might be called, or unmysterious universe. Tamburlaine he regards as the first successful rebel against this view of things.

Chapters on comedy as critical and subtle restatement of Order, on history according to Tillyard, and on tragedy with special reference to *Macbeth* and *Coriolanus* are related to the initial concepts: there are also a chapter on *Troilus and Cressida*, in which issue is joined with Wilson Knight, and a final chapter on *Cymbeline*. It will be seen that Duthie has solved the problem of compression partly by selecting his topics and partly by selecting his plays. This is quite essential if the author is limited to two hundred small pages; and though the final result may appear rather eclectic, I cannot really see how it could be otherwise.

Ifor Evans[3] surveys the body of Shakespeare's plays (for he excludes the poems) from the point of view of the language in its dramatic effectiveness. He passes through the whole corpus in chronological order, and with a scene-by-scene commentary upon the dramatic power of the verse, illustrated by frequent quotation. He is not concerned with the historic or rhetorical aspects of the language which have recently been so much studied, but attempts rather to convey his own enjoyment of the poetry to the general reader.

[1] G. Wilson Knight, *The Imperial Theme*. Third edition with a new preface (Methuen, 1951).
[2] G. I. Duthie, *Shakespeare* (Hutchinson's University Library, 1951).
[3] B. Ifor Evans, *The Language of Shakespeare's Plays* (Methuen, 1952).

G. B. Harrison, in his volume on *Shakespeare's Tragedies*,[1] employs a similar method to illustrate the general theory of tragedy which he puts forward in his first chapter. "The first gift essential to a tragic dramatist is the sense of *lachrimae rerum*, that is, a profound moral sense", and this Shakespeare pre-eminently possessed. The second quality is a sense of *mortalia*, the ability to feel the pathos in human suffering: the third is craftsmanship. Harrison sees English critics as divided into philosophers or vocal readers. He himself would wish, I think, to be included in the second class:

> ...we read him more for his own sake than for his judgements which do not always add very much to our understanding or to our sensibilities, but we are glad of his good company: for he reminds us that great literature is a comment on life and not dead matter to be anatomized and dissected by specialists. (pp. 27–8.)

The unfortunate historic critics are receiving brickbats from all quarters at the moment.

Augustus Ralli is emphatically of the same way of thought. In a collection of essays entitled *Poetry and Faith* he lustily attacks our present decayed civilization[2]—"The pure money maker is as far beyond education as he is beyond good and evil"—and defends the Imagination. He writes on Dante, Virgil and Homer as well as on Shakespeare. In the plays he encounters above all a "world of social joys", of love and friendship. The key to Shakespeare's world he takes to be kindly relations, the sense of community.

Ralli sees the function of the imagination as education for action; the function of the poet he defines much as Philip Sidney defined it. He is not afraid of the great platitudes, the unfashionable models—such as Saintsbury—and the frank prejudices of the Victorian.

Several generations younger, aggressively mathematical, and occasionally inventing a symbolic language of his own, W. Empson comes somersaulting in, doing his Charlie Chaplin act again. *The Structure of Complex Words*[3] presents a general theory of language based on its essential ambiguities, the significances of what the Elizabethans would call amplifying and diminishing, and in fact all the equipment of a new rhetoric calculated to make even Miss Rosemond Tuve look like milk for babes. In the middle of the general theory are embedded essays upon *Lear*, *Timon*, *Othello* and *Measure for Measure*. Some of this material is developed from Empson's earlier works and the method is certainly familiar. The lightning-quick movements, the careful humility of colloquialism, and the deliberate impertinence of esoteric knowledge lightly tossed off: innocent prodding of giants, and sudden profound bows to Miss Maud Bodkin; this cult of the clown might earn for the author the title of the wisest fool in Christendom, if he did not take every opportunity to cock a snook at theology.

Empson's way is to take a single concept—Folly in *Lear*, the Honesty of *Othello*, Sense in *Measure for Measure*—and to work outwards from this centre upon the meaning of the play. The history of some words is followed up for a considerable period—e.g. he pursues Sense as far as Jane Austen—but the main purpose is of course not historical. Those who have read Empson will know what to expect: the dazzling ingenuities, the felicitous irrelevances, the maddening apparatus and unsystematic richness of one of the best-equipped minds of our time which

---

[1] G. B. Harrison, *Shakespeare's Tragedies* (Routledge and Kegan Paul, 1951).
[2] Augustus Ralli, *Poetry and Faith* (The Bodley Head, 1951).
[3] W. Empson, *The Structure of Complex Words* (Chatto and Windus, 1951).

happens to be quite devoid of the principle of organization. It is always surprising to find how much Empson knows that hardly anyone else has heard of, and how staggeringly unfamiliar he is with things that everybody else seems to have known from the cradle.

As an example, perhaps the comment on Lear's "I am even the natural fool of fortune" may serve:

Natural in the sense 'imbecile' is insisted on by *fool*, the other half of the stock term (they define each other, like 'look-see'), and yet the main sense of "natural" carries so crucial a conflict for the play that it still rises here. It surely means something good, at any rate in Lear's intention; the wicked are unnatural, but Lear has found his way back to unsophisticated nature, like the *fool*. Yet taking the phrase as a whole, it says that fortune keeps making a fool of him; that is, he keeps having bad luck because nature has a spite against him. (p. 145.)

In his highly personal way, Empson is writing upon the same stuff as the historic students of the language, although American journals are constantly enlivened by his combats with the more traditional of them. Academically he is himself a subject of much controversy and some veneration (which he must find extremely entertaining): his particular judgements will be discussed and quarrelled with, but I suspect that his theories will be still-born.

F. R. Leavis, in *The Common Pursuit*,[1] publishes a collection of his essays from the periodical *Scrutiny*, including one on *Othello*, one on *Measure for Measure* and one on 'The Later Plays'. He is concerned with *Othello* as a character study, but Iago he regards, as Sewell does, as an instrument of the plot. Othello's self-dramatizing is Leavis's main theme: he wrote the essay some years ago, and is mainly concerned with a deliberate rebuttal of Stoll as the representative of academic critics. The essay on *Measure for Measure* is concerned with the structure of the play, and is again dated some years ago. The study of 'The Later Plays' depends upon the criticism of other critics. In each case Leavis is concerned with making a general critical judgement upon the temper of the play, through analysis of key passages.

Two American scholars have produced full-length studies of single plays. C. T. Prouty is concerned with *Much Ado about Nothing*[2] as a preliminary to studies of the other two great comedies, which he hopes eventually to write upon. The first half of his book presents the sources, both dramatic and non-dramatic, which were open to Shakespeare: the second deals with Shakespeare's modification of the plot and of the leading characters. The match of Hero and Claudio has been turned into a realistic *mariage de convenance*, while Benedick and Beatrice are interested in genuine feelings instead of the conventional relationships that society took account of. "For one couple, love is a business arrangement, for the other, a real emotion. But the play is not a *drame à thèse*, it is essentially high comedy wherein the frailty of human pretensions is humorously revealed" (pp. 63–4). By an examination of the original material Prouty demonstrates the reasonable and consistent nature of the alterations, and ideas which may lie in the background but which cannot be traced to any one literary antecedent, such as the concept of the Disdainful Woman applied by Hero to Beatrice.

---

[1] F. R. Leavis, *The Common Pursuit* (Chatto and Windus, 1952).
[2] C. T. Prouty, *The Sources of 'Much Ado about Nothing'. A Critical Study* (New Haven: Yale University Press; London: Oxford University Press, 1950).

In *Scourge and Minister* G. R. Elliott gives a close line-by-line commentary upon *Hamlet*.[1] He sees the Prince as a Christian Humanist, utterly opposed to revenge: sensitive, subtle, the ideal gentleman and prince, but "very proud"; his deepest motives are the true ones, and both he and Claudius evade what they know only too well to be their duty. Hamlet's hesitation in following up the rout of Claudius in the play scene is such a relapse; and in the prayer scene that follows we see "prince and king offending against heaven—against the spirit of just charity, of charitable justice" (p. 110), for the ideal revenge which Hamlet proposes is "not only blackly primitive, but pettily domestic, irrelevant to his Denmark's needs". Hamlet's need to control his terrific vital energy means that in the first half of the play he is caught often enough at a disadvantage: Elliott sees him not as a thinker exclusively but as a man of action. The value of his study lies in the detailed commentary, in which the significance of a line, a word or an implied gesture is fully brought out. It might be called infra-red reading and is certainly too packed for the stage, where some selection and some throwing away is inevitable.

From Spain comes a small book, *Shakespeare para Españoles*,[2] which surveys the works in chronological order, with brief biographical and critical notes upon the background of each. The story of Shakespeare's life as told here is not perhaps one with which all would agree, but the critical comments and the translations of Shakespeare's verse into Spanish will be found of general interest.

2. SHAKESPEARE'S LIFE, TIMES AND STAGE

reviewed by CLIFFORD LEECH

New fragments of information, conjectures and odd fancies are still abundant concerning the details of Shakespeare's life, but the longer and perhaps now more valuable studies are concerned with helping us to see the dramatist in relation to his fellow-writers and the general current of Elizabethan thought and feeling. To such studies Lawrence Babb[3] has notably contributed in his account of melancholy as it was presented by the scientific writers and the dramatists of the time. He has shown that the tradition derived from Galen presented melancholy as a dreaded disease: in the medical literature this attitude was dominant, but simultaneously, through Aristotle's influence, melancholy was seen as a privileged condition, the almost inevitable mark of the highly endowed. This opposition is at its clearest in Milton's companion poems: *L'Allegro* presents the Galenic picture of melancholy, *Il Penseroso* the Aristotelian. And love, intimately associated with melancholy, was a disease to be cured, and yet, through the inheritance of the Courtly Love tradition, was an honourable state. The more the age is studied, the more such contradictions seem to abound. This book should increase our reluctance to see any seventeenth-century drama as embodying a thesis: even Ford, in many respects closer than his fellows to the medical writers, presents Giovanni not merely as a pathological case but also as a man raised

[1] G. R. Elliott, *Scourge and Minister. A Study of 'Hamlet'* (Duke University Press; London: Cambridge University Press, 1951).

[2] Charles David Ley, *Shakespeare para Españoles* (Madrid: Revista de Occidente, 1951).

[3] *The Elizabethan Malady. A Study of Melancholia in English Literature from 1580 to 1642* (East Lansing: Michigan State College Press, 1951).

above his fellows, demanding horrified respect. Babb's study has cleared a way through a dense Renaissance thicket, though it is odd to read that "Angelo is not treated as a criminal in *Measure for Measure*"; and when he states that "Shakespeare does not take lovesickness very seriously" he is surely overlooking the dark comedies and perhaps *Othello*.

The first half of Miss M. C. Bradbrook's new book[1] has many good things on characteristic Elizabethan attitudes and on their ever-changing condition. She relates the plays to the non-dramatic poems of the time, and admirably places *Venus* and *Lucrece* in the history of Shakespeare's development. Her later chapters survey Shakespeare's plays up to 1600. Wise and striking comments are to be found, as when she sees *Titus* as a formal pageant, very different from "a brawling headlong play like *Lust's Dominion*", but in her judgements on the comedies and histories she is perhaps over-anxious to discount 'modern' reactions. Some of her most vigorous writing is devoted to bringing out the complications in *All's Well*, but in a full treatment of this play there might also be considered the idea of love as a disease (as noted by Babb), the Elizabethan condemnation of ambition, and the way in which Parolles in his exposure comes to win something of our liking. In her account of the histories Miss Bradbrook may give a too simply favourable portrait of Prince Hal: his first soliloquy argues that a clouded youth will give him a political advantage when he falsifies men's hopes, not that "my disguise of riotous living will become as potent a source of knowledge as magic could be", and Warwick's defence of him in Part II, which she accepts as truth, is hardly compatible with his manifest enjoyment of low company.

J. A. K. Thomson[2] has given us an orderly book, proceeding from the more particular to the more general observations. His first section goes through the poems and plays, noting the classical references and their probable sources, and taking a more cautious view of Shakespeare's classical reading than, for example, T. W. Baldwin. He then considers Shakespeare's relations with his more "learned" contemporaries, agreeing with Dover Wilson on the "upstart crow", identifying the Rival Poet with Chapman, and demonstrating the anti-medieval portrayal of the Greek characters in *Troilus*. Finally, he considers the Greek and the Shakespearian tragic styles, inevitably noting the stronger "particularity" of Shakespeare's manner but finding a basic similarity in *Weltanschauung*: there was, he thinks, in Plutarch a channel of communication through which the Greek idea found its way to Shakespearian tragedy. In this last section Thomson provides a healthy corrective to many recent interpretations, and it may therefore seem ungrateful to suggest that in Shakespeare the tragic attitude is more precariously based than would appear from this book.

Mrs Catherine Ing's[3] concern is only incidentally with Shakespeare—indeed, with him she is inclined to the casually pious gesture, as when she speaks of "the mature human Mariana, with her vocation for wifehood"—but she has done much to clarify our ideas of verse-structure in the lyrics of his time. We have a useful account of Elizabethan theories of prosody and of the distinction between the madrigal and the air. She comments on pitch and quantity, on stress

---

[1] *Shakespeare and Elizabethan Poetry. A Study of his Earlier Work in Relation to the Poetry of the Time* (Chatto and Windus, 1951).

[2] *Shakespeare and the Classics* (Allen and Unwin, 1952).

[3] *Elizabethan Lyrics. A Study in the development of English metres and their relation to poetic effect* (Chatto and Windus, 1951).

and assonance, but ultimately sees duration as the structural element in the lyric. It is true, of course, that poetry, being a structure in time, cannot be analysed without reference to time values; but, just as architecture, though a structure in space, depends for its structural effect not merely on its spatial dimensions but on the materials employed within that space, so temporal elements in poetry do not give the whole structure: the stress, the pitch, the very character of the sounds employed help to constitute the materials which partly determine the structure. Here Mrs Ing seems to have been carried too far by her argument, but this in no way invalidates her sensitive comments on individual lyrics: her chapter on Campion is perhaps her best.

Articles on Elizabethan thought patterns have been contributed by L. A. Cormican,[1] Heinrich Straumann,[2] Hermann Heuer,[3] Hardin Craig,[4] and D. L. Clark.[5] Cormican, continuing his study of 'Medieval Idiom in Shakespeare',[6] has shown that the medieval background gave a sense of depth to Shakespeare's tragedies: what the characters did and became had distant reverberations, and were inescapably seen in relation to Adam's sin and Christ's passion. He shrewdly comments that Cleopatra's anticipation of an immediate Heaven would be "full of irony" for an Elizabethan audience. What he neglects, perhaps, is that the "medieval idiom" is persistent but weakening in the early seventeenth century: Shakespeare is almost won over by his own Cleopatra. A rather artificial separation is made between 'Shakespearian tragedy' and dramas of the Renaissance like *Richard III*, *Tamburlaine* and *Titus*, and Cormican leaves untouched the problem why it was only at the last gasp of medievalism that tragedy came to flourish. Straumann runs over the development of drama from the cycles to *Gorboduc*, and the comments on tragedy made by sixteenth-century critics. Heuer's article is a study of the notion of spiritual order in Shakespeare, dependent largely on L. C. Knights, E. M. W. Tillyard and Theodore Spencer: its most interesting feature is its evidence that the present political atmosphere in Western Germany encourages this approach to Shakespeare, which underlines his condemnation of the destructive, the immoderate, the demonic. Craig is concerned with the Jacobean popularity of the "Galenic psychology of the passions": he insists that "Shakespeare never illustrates psychological principles by his plots but merely illuminates his plots by the use of psychological principles" (which perhaps leaves us with the question why Shakespeare chose the plots he did), and that in Shakespearian as in ancient tragedy it is the conquest of reason by emotion that precipitates disaster. Clark briefly surveys the study of rhetoric in Renaissance times, and shows how it strengthened the impulse to didacticism.

A number of short studies have related particular plays to the intellectual background. Roy W. Battenhouse[7] has convincingly put forward the view that the Ghost in *Hamlet* comes not from a Catholic Purgatory but from a pagan underworld. It is certainly true that no purgatorial spirit should be so concerned with revenge, or so ready to see Claudius as irredeemably sinful.

[1] 'Medieval Idiom in Shakespeare, (II) Shakespeare and the Medieval Ethic', *Scrutiny*, XVII (March 1951), 298–317.

[2] 'Zur Auffassung vom Wesen der Tragödie in der Englischen Literatur vor Shakespeare', *Eumusia: Festgabe für Ernst Howald zum sechzigsten Geburtstag* (Zürich: Eugen Rentsch Verlag, 1947), pp. 140–53.

[3] 'Der Geist und seine Ordnung bei Shakespeare', *Shakespeare-Jahrbuch*, LXXXIV–LXXXVI (1950), 40–63.

[4] 'Shakespeare and Elizabethan Psychology: Status of the Subject', *Shakespeare-Studien: Festschrift für Heinrich Mutschmann* (Marburg: N. G. Elwert Verlag, 1951), pp. 48–55.

[5] 'Ancient Rhetoric and English Renaissance Literature', *Shakespeare Quarterly*, II (July 1951), 195–204.

[6] His first article on this subject was noted in *Shakespeare Survey*, 5 (1952).

[7] 'The Ghost in Hamlet: A Catholic "Linchpin"?', *Studies in Philology*, XLVIII (April 1951), 161–92.

That the Ghost is a thing of night, driven away by cock-crow, is forcibly underlined by the words of Marcellus in I, i on the cock's crowing all night long in Advent. Battenhouse in places presses his argument too hard: he contends that a soul in Purgatory should ask for prayers and that Hamlet never himself mentions Purgatory, but Catholic doctrines could not be too explicitly presented in 1601. But one is persuaded that this is a Senecan ghost, given some Christian colouring in the references to the sacraments and St Patrick. This article excellently brings out the blurred edges in the Christian and pagan feelings of the time. Henry J. Webb[1] has defended Shakespeare's knowledge of military affairs against J. W. Draper. An Elizabethan audience, he says, would feel that "Whatever Othello has been in the past, he appears at the very beginning of the play as a man who has begun to disintegrate as an officer". D. S. Brewer[2] has noted that the medieval tradition presenting Brutus as a murderer was modified in the 1587 additions to *The Mirror for Magistrates*, and that in Shakespeare the medieval and Renaissance attitudes to Caesar's death are presented side by side. Miss Lily B. Campbell[3] has suggested that the "king-becoming graces" listed by Malcolm in *Macbeth*, IV, iii, are derived from *Basilikon Doron* and that the whole scene "is directed to expounding the pet political ideas of Shakespeare's king": if so, it is odd that at one point Macduff is ready to cast off his allegiance to Malcolm, whose alleged vices should, according to James, in no way affect his right. Walther Fischer[4] has urged that the political ideas in the history plays are incidentally and fragmentarily introduced, and has entered a caveat against relating them to more recent political developments.

Life and times are both the concern of F. E. Halliday's remarkable compilation:[5] here in alphabetical order is a list of Shakespeare's poems and plays and the characters in them, of his friends and acquaintances and many others of his contemporaries, of the theatres of the time and many of the plays produced in them, of the companies, of printers, actors, scholars and critics. In general, the statements in this book are cautiously made, though one pauses before the statement (in the article on 'Interpolations') that Merlin's prophecy "is undoubtedly interpolated nonsense". The assertion that, according to Dover Wilson, *The Famous Victories* is "an abridgement of Shakespeare's trilogy" is not accurate, nor can we be sure that Tarlton played in it. Halliday makes no claim to completeness, and his selection of material is judiciously done. But it is hardly true that the "most important plays" of the Elizabethan-Jacobean theatre are listed. Halliday seems, for the most part, to include only those plays with some Shakespearian connexion: *The Duchess of Malfi*, for example, is included apparently for the sake of its cast-list, *The White Devil* is omitted; none of the major plays of Chapman, Middleton or Ford is given a separate entry, but *The Iron Age* is included for its connexion with *Troilus*. Halliday's work overlaps with that of W. H. Thomson[6] in that both give us a list of Shakespeare's characters. But Thomson's field is more limited than his title would suggest: he is concerned only with the English historical plays and *Macbeth*. Quotations in the text have their authors indicated, but there are no precise references.

[1] 'The Military Background in *Othello*', *Philological Quarterly*, XXX (January 1951), 40–52.
[2] 'Brutus' Crime: A Footnote to *Julius Caesar*', *Review of English Studies*, n.s. III (January 1952), 51–4.
[3] 'Political Ideas in *Macbeth*, IV, iii', *Shakespeare Quarterly*, II (October 1951), 281–6.
[4] 'Zur Frage der Staatsauffassung in Shakespeares Königsdramen', *Shakespeare-Studien*, pp. 64–79.
[5] *A Shakespeare Companion 1550–1950* (Duckworth, 1952).
[6] *Shakespeare's Characters: A Historical Dictionary* (Altrincham: John Sherratt and Son, 1951).

Among other contributions to our knowledge of Shakespeare's time, we may note Miss Hilda M. Hulme's 'A Warwickshire Word-list',[1] which is compiled from the accounts of twenty-five parishes and in a few instances throws light on Shakespeare's word-usage; the account, by Charles J. Sisson and Arthur Brown,[2] of the pirate Danseker based on a Chancery suit of 1611 and on pamphlets of the time; and J. B. Leishman's 'L'Allegro and Il Penseroso in their Relation to Seventeenth-Century Poetry'.[3] Leishman notes how Milton takes over words, phrases, images from earlier poets, including Shakespeare, and, by precise placing and economical expression, achieves a sense of finality.

In the field of Shakespeare biography, this year's most signal contribution has come from Peter Alexander.[4] He gives, straightforwardly and with authority, the established facts of the life, the circumstances of performance, the provenance of the texts. As elsewhere, Alexander here refuses to accept Malone's interpretation of Greene's attack, and assigns some ten plays (including the early Hamlet) to the period ending 1592. He proceeds to a critical survey of the plays, giving briefly, but without over-simplification, a personal view of the characteristic Shakespearian effect in each dramatic kind. History and tragedy are distinguished, he suggests, in that at the end of the one our interest is carried on into the national future, at the end of the other the future hardly touches us, our interest is conterminous with the hero's existence. This distinction, sound as in general it appears, would surely put Julius Caesar among the histories: the developing antagonism of Antony and Octavius takes from the death of Brutus the tragic finality that it has for Alexander. There are good words on the juxtaposition of contrasted feelings in both histories and comedies (we are warned not to extract from them "a nebulous edification"), but perhaps this characteristic may have endured into the time of the tragedies and the romances. Alexander distinguishes between these last two kinds, saying that a romance shows virtue finally rewarded in the way that in actuality is not impossible, while tragedy shows virtue robbed of every support, denied all reward, existing bare and self-dependent. The tragedy and the romance are complementary pictures, but no explanation is offered for the order in which Shakespeare gave them to us. Alexander is surely right in insisting on the fineness of temper in a Shakespearian tragic hero, but his interpretation of Hamlet's soliloquy in IV, iv depends on a Hamlet notably deficient in self-knowledge: 'honour', as the character sees it, demands that he accomplish his revenge, but for Alexander it is Hamlet's 'honour' that will not let him kill a defenceless man.

Several writers have argued concerning this or that detail of Shakespeare's life. Alan Keen[5] sees him as a singing-boy with Houghton in 1578, returning to Stratford in 1581 after Houghton's death, as a player with Sir Thomas Hesketh at Rufford Old Hall from 1585 to Hesketh's death in 1588, writing The Phoenix and the Turtle in 1587 to celebrate the marriage of John Salisbury of Lleweni, joining Strange's Men in 1589, and then returning to Shropshire in 1590–1 to practise

---

[1] *Modern Language Review*, XLVI (July and October 1951), 321–30.

[2] '"The Great Danseker", Literary Significance of a Chancery Suit', *ibid.* 339–48. James G. McManaway, *ibid.* XLVII (April 1952), 202–3, has noted that one of the pamphlets mentioned by Sisson and Brown was quickly reprinted in an abbreviated form.

[3] *Essays and Studies* (1951), pp. 1–36.

[4] *A Shakespeare Primer* (Nisbet, 1951).

[5] '"In the Quick Forge and Working-house of Thought..." Lancashire and Shropshire and the Young Shakespeare', *Bulletin of the John Rylands Library*, XXXIII (March 1951), 256–70.

his new craft of play-writing. There is little evidence for all this: we hear of an oral tradition at Rufford that Shakespeare was there as a young man; it appears that Hesketh had a company of players; there are a number of Shropshire words in the plays.[1] Karl Wentersdorf[2] argues shrewdly that Shakespeare was a member of the Queen's Men before 1592. Accepting the view that he was with Pembroke's in 1592–3, Wentersdorf suggests that this company was originally the section of the old Queen's Men that split off under Dutton's leadership in 1588–9: in difficult times they had turned to a new patron. The article is closely reasoned, and leaves one at least prepared to entertain the theory. Leslie Hotson,[3] who grows yet more confident that the *Sonnets* were written in 1589, finds a reference in Sonnet LXVI to an intensification of censorship which reached its peak in that year, and identifies the 'painful warrior' of Sonnet XXV with Drake, whose 1589 expedition was considered a failure. The Rival Poet can now, we are told, be Marlowe. W. Schrickx[4] believes that Shakespeare was Southampton's tutor "from 1591 onwards", and that, when Shakespeare refers to the moon (which he regarded "with an unfavourable eye"), a satiric glance at Chapman is to be inferred. Miss Janet Spens,[5] challenging Dover Wilson's argument that Greene's attack implied plagiarism,[6] claims that the words suggest general thieving, such as a playwright might charge a player with, not the stealing of a particular play: Chettle's reference to Shakespeare's 'honesty' means only that he was 'an honourable gentleman'. In reply, Dover Wilson[7] underlines Chettle's use of the word 'up-rightness', and points out that at least one contemporary understood the charge to be one of 'purloining'. Roy Walker[8] and Sidney Thomas[9] have joined in this controversy, the former noting borrowings from *James IV* in *Richard II* and *Hamlet* and suggesting that there were earlier examples of this practice, the latter adducing a use of "other mens feathers" with clear reference to plagiarism and one of "mine owne Feathers" in relation to authentic writing. Percy Simpson and I. A. Shapiro[10] have disagreed concerning Shapiro's inquiry into the Mermaid Club legend,[11] Simpson stressing the account given by Aubrey, Shapiro noting the manifest inaccuracies in Aubrey's statement. Cecil G. Gray[12] has traced the names of the first three complainants in the Blackfriars suit among landowners in Essex. Frank Simpson[13] has reproduced drawings of New

---

[1] Keen also adduces some further, hardly convincing parallels between the plays and the MS. annotations in his copy of Hall.

[2] 'Shakespeares Erster Truppe. Ein Beitrag zur Aufklärung des Problems der sog. "verlorenen Jahre"', *Shakespeare-Jahrbuch*, LXXXIV–LXXXVI (1950), 114–30.

[3] 'More Light on Shakespeare's Sonnets', *Shakespeare Quarterly*, II (April 1951), 111–18.

[4] 'Solar Symbolism and Related Imagery in Shakespeare. Some Possible Inferences', *Revue Belge de Philologie et d'Histoire*, XXIX (1951), 112–28.

[5] 'Dr Dover Wilson and "The Upstart Crow"', *Times Literary Supplement*, 15 June 1951.

[6] Noted in *Shakespeare Survey*, 5.

[7] '"The Upstart Crow"', *Times Literary Supplement*, 29 June 1951.   [8] *Ibid.* 10 August 1951.

[9] 'Greene's Attack on Shakespeare', *Modern Language Notes*, LXVI (November 1951), 483–4.

[10] '"The Mermaid Club" An Answer and a Rejoinder', *Modern Language Review*, XLVI (January 1951), 58–63. Subsequently Simpson has listed the seven MS. copies of Beaumont's verse-letter to Jonson (*ibid.* XLVI (July and October 1951), 435–6).   [11] Noted in *Shakespeare Survey*, 4 (1951).

[12] 'Shakespeare's Co-Plaintiffs in the Blackfriars Lawsuit of 1615', *Notes and Queries*, CXCVI (10 November 1951), 490–1.

[13] 'New Place. The Only Representation of Shakespeare's House from an Unpublished Manuscript', *Shakespeare Survey*, 5 (1952), 55–7.

Place and the Stratford bust made by George Vertue in 1737: they are now among the Portland papers deposited in the British Museum.

Karl Wentersdorf[1] has reconsidered the chronology of the plays on general grounds, and discussed whether metrical tests can be used as contributory evidence in dating. He puts *Titus* in 1588–9, many of the plays a year earlier than Chambers, *The Merry Wives* 1596–7, *Timon* 1604–5, *Pericles* 1607–8 (before *Coriolanus*). He works out a 'metrical index' for each play (an average of the percentage of lines with extra syllables, the percentage of overflows, the percentage of unsplit lines with pauses, and the percentage of split lines), and finds that there is, in general, a gradual increase in this index. Though one may not accept all Wentersdorf's dates or his judgement of the tone of certain plays, his metrical tests seem in general to confirm our notion of the sequence in which the plays were written. The date of *Twelfth Night* is considered by Raymond Chapman,[2] who feels we cannot disregard the strong hint of Malvolio in de Witt's drawing of the Swan. De Witt's visit may have been at any time from 1596 to 1598: if it was in the earlier year, Langley at the Swan may have been presenting a version, called perhaps *Love's Labour's Won*, which was later revised.

Slightly touching Shakespeare's biography are an historical romance by Carlo Villa,[3] who attributes the plays to Michelagnolo Florio, a cousin of John Florio and the adopted son of John Shakespeare of Stratford; an article by Conrad V. Emde Boas,[4] who finds the patron-poet-mistress relationship mirrored in Rosalind/Ganymede-Orlando-Phoebe, in Viola/Cesario-Orsino-Olivia, and in Sebastian-Antonio-Olivia; and a note by John W. Draper,[5] suggesting that the two references to 'the Sophy' in *Twelfth Night* reflect interest in the Shirleys' expedition to Persia and were inserted in an endeavour to assist Essex, the patron of the Shirleys, "by calling attention to the Sherleys' glamorous career".

Of writings on the stage, the most considerable is the *Oxford Companion* edited by Miss Phyllis Hartnoll.[6] The primary concern of this book is with playhouses rather than plays, with actors rather than dramatists, and more space has been given to the last two centuries than to earlier times. However, there are useful accounts of medieval and Elizabethan plays and stages, though the article on the Morality Play is over-brief and gratuitously patronizing, and it is odd to read that de Witt's drawing shows no canopy over the stage. It would probably have been better to eschew literary criticism in the sections on individual dramatists: in such limited space a critical comment is bound to seem, at the best, facile. However, the book will certainly be a 'companion' and much of its writing is authoritative summary.

G. L. Hosking[7] has written an account of Alleyn's life and times, which aims at giving, in

---

[1] 'Shakespearean Chronology and the Metrical Tests', *Shakespeare-Studien*, pp. 161–93.

[2] '"Twelfth Night" and the Swan Theatre', *Notes and Queries*, CXCVI (27 October 1951), 468–70.

[3] *Parigi vale bene una messa!* (Milan: Editrice Storica, 1951). The novel is followed by the abstract of a lecture, in which the case for authorship is argued: dates given are not always accurate, and Villa is not well versed in recent views on the provenance of the Folio texts.

[4] 'The Connection between Shakespeare's Sonnets and his "Travesti-Double"-Plays', *International Journal of Sexology*, November 1950. The most interesting point made here is that Shakespeare, as the father of boy-and-girl twins, must have known that such twins are no more alike than other brothers and sisters.

[5] 'Shakespeare and Abbas the Great', *Philological Quarterly*, XXX (October 1951), 419–25.

[6] *The Oxford Companion to the Theatre* (Cumberlege, 1951).

[7] *The Life and Times of Edward Alleyn* (Cape, 1952).

the most discursive way, a picture of the conditions in which he lived. The book has many unascribed quotations, and the chapter-headings have often only a chance-relationship to the medleys that follow them. Inaccuracies are frequent: we are told at one moment that the sharer-system dated from the building of the Globe, at another that there were sharers in 1594; "most of Shakespeare's later and best plays" are said to have been first performed at the Blackfriars; the account of *Faustus* shows no acquaintance with Sir Walter Greg's work on the text.

The model of the Globe made for the English Seminar at the University of Basel has been described by H. Lüdeke.[1] In general this model follows the plan of J. C. Adams, but Lüdeke assumes that in the Globe, as apparently in de Witt's drawing of the Swan, there were steps leading to the first gallery from the yard: Adams assumes a staircase leading to the gallery from the theatre entrance. The 'ingressus' of de Witt has, however, been differently interpreted by R. C. Bald,[2] who suggests that the theatre entrances were at the sides fairly close to the stage (below the external staircases indicated in Hollar's view) and that there were stairs leading from these entrances down to the yard, which Adams has argued was below ground-level. Bald gives interesting confirmatory evidence from the later (Restoration–nineteenth century) practice of having the pit-entrance close to the stage. The use of the different acting-areas is queried by Richard Flatter,[3] who inquires for the evidence on which Adams bases his statement that from 1599 to 1610 "Shakespeare mounts 43 per cent of all his scenes on the outer stage alone...almost 20 per cent are intended for the study alone, and 10 per cent for the upper-stage alone". William Empson[4] thinks that the closet-scene in *Hamlet* was originally intended for the upper stage, and that the inner stage was to be used for the King's study in the following scene. In Q2, he points out, the Queen enters the King's study after the closet-scene, but in the Folio the King enters to Gertrude immediately after Hamlet drags out the body of Polonius. Empson believes that the Quarto indicates Shakespeare's intended staging, but that the players persuaded him to have the closet-scene on the inner stage. He would prefer it presented above, as he feels that Hamlet's jealousy and obscenity should not be too prominently exhibited. This may depend on a too literal approach to the Elizabethan stage: because the King is here in private, it does not seem to follow that he must be in the 'study'. Perhaps, too, Empson here exhibits a too delicate approach to the disturbing things in Shakespeare. Another point of staging has been raised by Richard Flatter,[5] who suggests that the show of kings in *Macbeth* was written with a royal performance in mind, and that the eighth king carried the glass, in which James was able to see himself. Peter Ure[6] has objected that the dumb-show has a much more important function than to serve as a courtly compliment, and that the glass was clearly a magic, prospective glass in which Macbeth was to see James's descendants. C. B. Purdom,[7] while agreeing that more than a courtly compliment is involved, has approved Flatter's suggestion and announced his intention to use it in his Crosby Hall production. One is constrained to wonder how, if

---

[1] 'Shakespeares Globus-Theater. Nach den neuesten Ergebnissen der Forschung', *Shakespeare-Jahrbuch*, LXXXIV–LXXXVI (1950), 131–9.

[2] 'The Entrance to the Elizabethan Theatre', *Shakespeare Quarterly*, III (January 1952), 17–20.

[3] 'Outer, Inner, or Upper Stage?' *ibid.* II (April 1951), 171.

[4] 'The Staging of "Hamlet"', *Times Literary Supplement*, 23 November 1951.

[5] 'The Dumb-show in "Macbeth"', *ibid.* 23 March 1951.

[6] 'The Dumb-show in "Macbeth"', *ibid.* 6 April 1951.

[7] 'The Dumb-show in "Macbeth"', *ibid.* 20 April 1951.

James was to see himself, Macbeth was simultaneously to see him and "many more" in the glass, and how clear the whole contrivance would be to other spectators.

The Elizabethan audience has been again considered. Moody E. Prior[1] remarks that the audience has for long been used to explain away things in the drama not acceptable to current taste, but there has been little consistency in the various pictures of the audience, and a commentator will often make different deductions from different plays. Prior has particularly noted the absurdity of speaking of the audience's insensitiveness to physical suffering, in connexion with Gloucester's blinding, when it is clearly necessary for Shakespeare's purpose in the scene that they should be sensitive to it. G. M. Young's British Academy lecture[2] reminds us that members of the Inns of Court formed one, doubtless important, element in Shakespeare's varied audience. I. J. Semper[3] has given an account of MS. 4787 in the Folger Library, which records a controversy of 1618 on whether or not Catholic priests should attend plays. There is evidence that priests did not infrequently attend, and the prohibition issued in 1618 by William Harrison, Archpriest of England, was revoked.

R. B. le Page[4] has questioned the validity of J. W. Draper's mechanical tests for the speed of utterance in the Elizabethan playhouse. These tests depend on the use of elisions: le Page points out that we cannot be sure where elisions were used in dramatic speech, and that speed depends on the mood and temper of the verse rather than on its mechanical structure. Draper[5] has now used these tests for *Macbeth*, but le Page's objections have thrown considerable doubt on the basis of the argument.

The disputed performances of *Hamlet* and *Richard II* on the *Dragon* in 1607 have been the subject of new controversy. G. Blakemore Evans[6] has announced the discovery of a slightly varied form of the log-entries in an article signed 'Ambrose Gunthio' and called 'A Running Commentary on the Hamlet of 1603': it appeared in the *European Magazine* for August 1825–January 1826. Sydney Race[7] has suggested that 'Gunthio' was Collier, who he thinks was also responsible for other articles in the *European Magazine*. F. S. Boas[8] has pointed out that, when Rundall printed the entries in 1849, he used Elizabethan spelling: he must therefore either have been quoting from a manuscript and not from 'Gunthio', or have shared in the deception with Collier. Evans,[9] returning to the matter, throws doubt on the possibility that 'Gunthio' was Collier, for the author of the article seems insufficiently versed in Elizabethan stage conditions. The affair remains a problem, but the new evidence has strengthened the believers' case.

---

[1] 'The Elizabethan Audience and the Plays of Shakespeare', *Modern Philology*, XLIX (November 1951), 101–23.

[2] 'Shakespeare and the Termers', *Proceedings of the British Academy 1947*, pp. 81–99. This lecture was noted in *Shakespeare Survey*, 2 (1949), on its separate publication.

[3] 'The Jacobean Theater through the Eyes of Catholic Clerics', *Shakespeare Quarterly*, III (January 1952), 48–51.

[4] 'The Dramatic Delivery of Shakespeare's Verse', *English Studies*, XXXII (April 1951), 63–8.

[5] 'Scene-Tempo in "Macbeth"', *Shakespeare-Studien*, pp. 56–63.

[6] 'The Authenticity of Keeling's Journal Entries on "Hamlet" and "Richard II"', *Notes and Queries*, CXCVI (21 July 1951), 313–15.

[7] 'The Authenticity of Keeling's Journal Entries on "Hamlet" and "Richard II"', *ibid.* CXCVI (24 November 1951), 513–15.

[8] 'A Performance of "Hamlet"', *Times Literary Supplement*, 7 March 1952.

[9] 'The Authenticity of the Keeling Journal Entries Reasserted', *Notes and Queries*, CXCVII (15 March 1952), 127–8.

James G. McManaway[1] has printed the Lord Chamberlain's warrant of 12 March 1630–1 now in the Folger Library: it was previously printed, from the transcript in the Lord Chamberlain's books, in the Variorum of 1821 and in the *Malone Society Collections*. He points out that the schedule of plays performed by the King's Men at Hampton Court and at the Cockpit in Whitehall in 1630–1 (printed by Bentley) was clearly attached to the Folger document.

More recent performances of Shakespeare have provoked free and copious comment. Murray W. Bundy[2] has described the very full account of Edwin Booth's performance of *Hamlet* made by Charles W. Clarke in 1870. This document, 'perhaps the fullest record of any Shakespearian production before the advent of the motion picture and the sound track', will eventually be deposited in the Folger Library. C. B. Purdom[3] has described the stage and production methods used for his performance of *Macbeth* at Crosby Hall on 14–19 May 1951. There was a platform-stage, with a large balcony, an inner stage, and a staircase. Among the points noted by Purdom are the greater stillness possible on a platform-stage, the need for the verse to be recognizably verse and for the rhyme to be emphasized, and the need for the audience to be directly addressed except in 'straight dialogue'. For the show of kings he used the business suggested by Flatter. Purdom's production was intended to show the play as "essentially... Macbeth's contemplation of his own life, a vision of events, not a repetition of them". One who has regretfully not seen this production must wonder how far such a view of the play could be communicated through performance.[4]

3. TEXTUAL STUDIES

reviewed by JAMES G. McMANAWAY

Textual and bibliographical studies of Shakespeare were more numerous and more important than usual in 1951–2. The major publication of the year is surely the second volume of *A Bibliography of English Printed Drama to the Restoration*[5] by Sir Walter Greg. This is one of the works

[1] 'A New Shakespeare Document', *Shakespeare Quarterly*, II (April 1951), 119–22.

[2] 'A Record of Edwin Booth's *Hamlet*', *ibid*. pp. 99–102.

[3] *The Crosby Hall "Macbeth"* (Dent, 1951).

[4] Among other comments on recent performances the following are to be noted: Audrey Williamson, *Theatre of Two Decades* (Rockliff, 1951), including a number of Shakespeare productions in her descriptive record of the English theatre in recent years; Richard David, 'Shakespeare in the Waterloo Road', *Shakespeare Survey*, 5 (1952), 121–8, reviewing Old Vic productions; Alice Venezky, 'Current Shakespearian Productions in England and France', *Shakespeare Quarterly*, II (October 1951), 335–42, noting particularly the performances of the history-cycle at Stratford in 1951; Wolfgang Stroedel, 'Theaterschau 1947–50', *Shakespeare-Jahrbuch*, LXXXIV–LXXXVI (1950), 229–36, reviewing performances in Germany, where the comedies seem now more popular even than *Hamlet*; D. de Gruyter and Wayne Hayward, 'Shakespeare on the Flemish Stage of Belgium, 1876–1951', *Shakespeare Survey*, 5 (1952), 106–10, giving brief comment and a chart of productions; Orhan Burian, 'Shakespeare in Turkey', *Shakespeare Quarterly*, II (April 1951), 127–8, providing information concerning Ankara and Istanbul; Fritz Budde, 'Shakespeare und die Frage der Raumbühne', *Shakespeare-Studien*, pp. 21–47, referring to the performances of the 'Marburgen Festspiele' of 1928–39 in illustration of his somewhat romantic notions of Shakespeare staging. The 'Shakespeare Number' of *Theatre* (26 April 1952) reviews productions in many places, and vigorously exhibits our growing respect for Elizabethan stage-methods.

[5] Oxford University Press, for the Bibliographical Society, 1951.

for which must be reserved the adjective 'monumental'. Of direct interest to Shakespearians are the entries relating to *Othello*, first printed in 1622, and the plays which were published for the first time in 1623 in the First Folio. But the *Bibliography* is too well known and too widely used to need praise. It is not inappropriate at this point to return thanks for the reissuing of Greg's *The Editorial Problem in Shakespeare*,[1] which has long been out of print. The second edition contains a few corrections in the text and nine pages of prefatory matter in which the author takes account of a decade of textual studies.

"Contrary to what appears to be a general opinion in universities", writes Douglas Southall Freeman in *George Washington: A Biography*, "it [the history of the American Revolution] is a field that should be replowed and tilled for nearly the whole of its wide area". The remark is equally applicable to the subject of the text of Shakespeare. The exact nature of the manuscripts from which Shakespeare's plays were printed in the early quartos and the First Folio is very imperfectly apprehended even "in universities". Nor is there general comprehension of the various ways in which the text of a particular play was exposed to contamination in the process of transmission from the pen of the author to the printed page. The general public may be forgiven for expressing wonder that there are certain entire plays and portions of others which we shall never recover in the exact form Shakespeare gave them in his fair copies.

The lay reader—or scholar (and unfortunately his name is legion)—who questions the need of further textual studies of Shakespeare on the grounds that the currently standard texts give us as much Shakespeare as we need or are capable of and in a sufficiently accurate text is advised to read 'Restoring Shakespeare: The Modern Editor's Task'[2] by Peter Alexander, who comes to the task fresh from the editing of *The Complete Works*.[3] With shy humour and considerable point, he describes a number of typical cruxes in the text and reveals how editors and commentators, after discovering the nature of the corruption, have restored the true reading. And though the victories of the moderns may be less renowned than those of the ancients (as Theobald, for example, with his "a babled o' green fields"), they have done, and are still doing, much to contribute to the reader's ease and enjoyment. "Those who are oblivious of their debts, and yet exclaim against their benefactors, should be condemned to read their Shakespeare only in the original texts" (p. 2).

It is not alone those seized with the *furor editoris*, if I may be permitted the phrase, who are giving thought to the editing of Shakespeare. In an essay full of insight,[4] Georges Bonnard describes the plight of the Continental reader with a good knowledge of spoken English who is confronted with an old-spelling—or even partially modernized—text and the usual textual apparatus and footnotes. In confusion and frustration he is likely to put the book aside and turn again to one of the translations from which he had hoped to escape. Bonnard's requirements are so reasonable that surely some enterprising publisher will bring out an edition that meets them. He does not say, as well he might, that many English and American readers would find enormous satisfaction in the use of such an edition.

Another kind of editorial activity than that described by Alexander is illustrated in 'An Approach to the Problem of *Pericles*'[5] by Philip Edwards. In reading it, one senses the excitement

[1] Oxford: the Clarendon Press, 1951.
[2] *Shakespeare Survey*, 5 (1952), 1–9.
[3] London and Glasgow: Collins, 1951.
[4] *Shakespeare Survey*, 5 (1952), 10–15.
[5] *Ibid.* pp. 25–49.

which drives bibliographers and textual critics to "live laborious days", for despite the modest wording of his title and the tentativeness with which he states his conclusions, Edwards has come very near to the solution of the chief problems of *Pericles*, if indeed he has not found it. *Pericles* was printed three times in quarto format in Shakespeare's lifetime and thrice more by 1635, yet it was not included in the First or Second Folios. It is a moving play, as all who have witnessed a performance can testify. Its kinship with the Romances in theme and situation is very close, and many of its lines, particularly in Acts III–V, are right Shakespeare. The problem is further complicated by the existence of a prose history of Pericles, published in 1609, which claims to give the story as it had been acted by Shakespeare's company. It has been generally assumed that Shakespeare had a collaborator or that he revised, at least in part, another man's play. In the absence of objective evidence and another text with which to compare the First Quarto of *Pericles* (1609), for it alone has any authority, scholars have been guided by taste and their subjective impressions.

Using several of the techniques of modern analytical bibliography, Edwards finds that three different compositors were engaged in setting the type, notes their habits of spelling and punctuation, and ascertains their varying abilities to set prose and blank verse, and, especially, to deal with the lineation of hypermetrical verse. Next he tabulates the pages set by each compositor, checking his results against the evidence of the running-titles. After this, he is ready to discuss the nature of the copy used in printing the Quarto. This, he believes, was a memorial reconstruction of a play written wholly by Shakespeare. Taking the capacities of the three compositors into account, he is then able to suggest boldly that the qualitative differences between Acts I and II on the one hand and Acts III–V on the other are traceable to the two agents who reconstructed the text. As to Wilkins's novel, it too is a report of a performance of Shakespeare's play, eked out with passages borrowed from Twine's earlier prose history. So on occasion a modern editor can confidently lift a short passage from Wilkins to fill a gap in the reported texts of agents *A* and *B*. We are left to infer that difficulty about the copyright made it impossible to include *Pericles* in the First Folio.

On the evidence in hand, Edwards has been brilliantly successful. It is to be regretted that he had not the space to publish all his detailed evidence. In my opinion he is wrong in suggesting that the type was set in two different shops, even though one compositor used one sort of type and put 37 lines on a page while the other two set 35 lines in a different sort. The distribution of work among the three men is such that they must all have worked in the same shop.

The most valuable contribution of modern scholarship to the study of Shakespeare is the painstaking effort to discover exactly what kind of manuscript or printed copy lies behind the early Quartos and Folios, so as to determine the precise authority of each line and eventually to produce a perfect text. Not, alas, the text that Shakespeare intended in his fair copy or even the text, cut and adapted, that one might have heard in a letter-perfect performance at the Globe or Blackfriars. But something far less precious, and yet a text that would be preferred above anything now in print, namely, one in which proper allowance has been made for the idiosyncrasies of scribes, compositors, and proof readers and for the contamination of superior copy by inferior. Philip Edwards's paper is a good example of this kind of scholarship. In a series of articles aimed in the same direction, some of which will win fuller acceptance than others, Alice Walker has compared the Quarto and Folio texts of a number of plays with startling results.

She reasons[1] by analogy from *Richard III*, the Folio text of which was printed, except for two passages, from a copy of Q6 corrected by reference to a theatrical manuscript. The text of the two exceptions was set directly from leaves abstracted from a copy of Q3 that bore prompt notes and had at some time been inserted in the prompt-book to supply a deficiency. Apparently Jaggard strongly preferred to have his men supplied with printed copy rather than manuscript, if we may judge by what was done with this play and with *Lear*. Did the same thing happen, Miss Walker inquires, to *2 Henry IV*, *Othello* and *Hamlet*?

In the case of *2 Henry IV*, the Quarto gives every indication of having been printed from Shakespeare's foul papers, in which certain cuts had been marked. The text of the Folio supplies the omissions and differs in other respects so much that M. A. Shaaber, the Variorum editor, argues for the use of a manuscript based on the prompt-book. It is Miss Walker's opinion that the Folio's errors in speech tags could not have originated in the prompt-book or a transcript of it. Though differing somewhat from those in the Quarto, they bear them a peculiarly close relationship. And so it is with certain unusual spellings. Her conclusion is that the Quarto was printed from foul papers and the Folio from a copy of this text which had been collated with a fair copy of the foul papers. The suggestion that this fair copy was made by a person unknown, in which some passages were tidied up, and which served as the basis for the prompt-book and the players' parts, I find difficult to accept. The process is too complicated. The copy for the Quarto was legitimately obtained, and when a scene was inadvertently omitted by the printer someone was scrupulous to have an expensive cancel inserted to supply the deficiency. If the foul papers were in such shape that an intermediary transcript had to be made (see p. 223) before it was safe to proceed with the original prompt-book, why were these later sent to the printer of the Quarto instead of this hypothetical transcript? And how did the printer manage to produce so good a text as we find here? Granting that the Folio contains erroneous speech tags and duplicates some unusual readings in the Quarto, may it not be well to assume that a copy of the Quarto, whose text was known to have been curtailed, was amplified by reference to the prompt-book itself, with insufficient attention to the corrections of minor errors, inconsistencies, and irregularities?

Continuing her attack upon received opinions about the group of plays for which there seem to be two substantive texts, Miss Walker turns next to *Othello*.[2] Collation has driven her to the conclusion that the "well-recognized inferiority of the Quarto text was due not to scribal errors but to memorial contamination" (p. 16), which is not to be charged against the actors but was rather "the work of a book-keeper who relied on his knowledge of the play as acted and on his invention where memory failed" (p. 24). She is persuaded by the frequency of common errors, the orthographical evidence, and variant readings that a copy of the Quarto was corrected by reference to a manuscript which she refrains from identifying; admitting that there is no positive bibliographical proof that the Folio was set, at least in part, from the Quarto, she yet urges that in no other way can we account for the preservation of "so many common accidental features". Some of the instances she cites are difficult to explain otherwise. While, however, her challenge cannot be ignored, her explanation will not be widely accepted unless a more detailed study reveals bibliographical dependence of the one text upon the other.

[1] 'Quarto "Copy" and the 1623 Folio of *2 Henry IV*', *Review of English Studies*, n.s., II (July 1951), 217–25.
[2] 'The 1622 Quarto and the First Folio Texts of *Othello*', *Shakespeare Survey*, 5 (1952), 16–24.

The third play for which Miss Walker attempts to discover new textual relationships is *Hamlet*.[1] Here again she starts with the assumption that printed copy for the Folio was supplied by Jaggard whenever possible. But before attacking the supposedly independent authority of the Second Quarto and Folio texts, her ultimate objective, she reminds us of certain typographical resemblances between the first two Quartos and insists that the latter was set from a corrected copy of the former to the end of the first act, and thereafter from manuscript. This is decidedly iconoclastic. Turning finally to the Folio, Miss Walker questions its independent authority because in a score of words there is almost complete identity between the Second Quarto and Folio readings, not to mention frequent agreement in pointing. It seems incredible to her that a compositor working from Shakespeare's foul papers in the former should so frequently preserve the same accidentals (to use Greg's term) as have likewise survived the process of copying the foul papers and (1) preparing the prompt-book, (2) transcribing this for the Folio, and (3) setting it in type. How much simpler if a copy of the Second Quarto was corrected from the prompt-book and used in printing the Folio text! The simplicity Miss Walker attains is to be distrusted. As an example of the new difficulties resulting from acceptance of her thesis, consider her explanation of the inferior readings found in the Folio. These have hitherto been attributed to the debasement that is unavoidable when a text is transcribed or printed; Miss Walker would place the chief responsibility on Jaggard's compositors but assigns part of it to a book-keeper, who in "renewing" a prompt-book that must surely have been worn out between 1602 and 1622 "admitted into the new prompt-book what was customarily spoken on the stage instead of what was originally set down in the 'parts'" (p. 336). Before agreeing, we must remind ourselves that there is no historical evidence whatever that the *Hamlet* prompt-book needed replacement; then we must decide whether to allow three staggering assumptions: (1) that if the old prompt-book were replaced by a new one the scribe would go to the trouble of assembling and copying out the players' parts instead of transcribing the tattered original; (2) that these players' parts had been modified (by the actors?) so as to include gags and other debasements; and (3) that the book-keeper would prefer and write down his own recollections of what had been spoken on the stage rather than follow his copy, thus introducing "the anticipations, recollections and interpolations which require explanation in the F. text" (p. 336).

To do justice, it must be added that Miss Walker admits not having examined later quartos to see whether one of these might have been used in printing the Folio, but she maintains this does not weaken her case that the Folio was printed from a corrected Quarto. Obviously, all the evidence must be examined again, for Miss Walker would persuade us that instead of being blessed with one Bad and two independent, substantive Good texts, we are plagued by the sudden realization that we hold a much less secure textual position.

The newly chosen editor of the 'McKerrow' Shakespeare, G. I. Duthie, continues his study of Good and Bad Quartos in an important article[2] about *Romeo and Juliet*, which he is preparing for the New Cambridge edition. His initial assumptions are that the First Quarto is a reported text, that back of the Second Quarto is a Shakespearian manuscript, and that a few passages in

---

[1] 'The Textual Problem of *Hamlet*: A Reconstruction', *Review of English Studies*, n.s., II (October 1951), 328–38.

[2] 'The Text of Shakespeare's *Romeo and Juliet*', *Studies in Bibliography* (Charlottesville: Bibliographical Society of the University of Virginia, 1951), IV, 3–29. The article is adapted from a paper read at the English Institute in September 1950.

the latter were printed directly from the former. These are shared by most Shakespearians. Duthie's contributions are threefold. First, he argues that not Shakespeare's foul papers but a transcript of them served as the basic copy for the Second Quarto. This not very fully substantiated opinion is buttressed by Duthie's second proposition, which is that the scribe kept his eye constantly on the First Quarto and, finding the text faithfully reported on leaves B3 and B4, simply tore them out and inserted them in the proper place in his transcript, taking care to cancel everything except the lines from I, ii, 57 to I, iii, 36. At several other places, and this is the third innovation, he noticed that the text of the First Quarto could be altered to agree with Shakespeare's manuscript by interlineation or marginal correction and again he removed leaves (the Prologue, D1, E1, and G3) from his copy of the Quarto, edited them, and inserted them in his transcript. Elsewhere this scribe relied exclusively on Shakespeare's foul papers, and the Second Quarto, printed from his transcript, is the only authoritative text. In the main, Duthie's hypotheses provide the best explanation of the bibliographical and textual relationships between the two texts, but some may remain unconvinced that the copy of the Second Quarto did not consist of leaves from the First Quarto and Shakespeare's foul papers. His account of the use of italics in printing the Nurse's lines is less lucid than, for example, Sir Walter Greg's in *The Editorial Problem in Shakespeare*, a book to which he does not refer.

Of equal interest is Duthie's discussion of how an editor should prepare the text of this play. A thoughtful consideration of it should be compulsory for everyone engaged in editorial work in this period and will be enlightening to everyone who wants to read Shakespeare in the best possible text.

The second play in the new and revised Arden edition is *Love's Labour's Lost*,[1] which confronts Richard David, the editor, with two major problems in the wording of the title-page of the earliest surviving quarto: "As it was presented before her Highnes this last Christmas. Newly corrected and augmented...1598." Following Dover Wilson and others, David believes that the play was first written about 1594 or 1595; that a Bad Quarto (earlier than 1598) has failed to survive; and that Shakespeare revised his text for the performance at Christmas of 1597, whereupon his foul papers (not the prompt-book) were sent to the publisher. He is inclined to the opinion that Shakespeare reworked an old play by an unknown author who had access to unpublished details of contemporary French history and that if a copy of the lost Bad Quarto could be found it would probably contain portions of the source play. This seems unnecessarily complicated, particularly with respect to a source play; news pamphlets in quantity were circulated in London with accounts of skirmishes, sieges, and the other exciting incidents of the French wars, and it is a safe assumption that even more tales travelled by word of mouth. David is certainly correct in thinking that the second and fifth acts show change of intention on Shakespeare's part, but his discussion of the duplications of text is less acceptable; they are probably alternate drafts written when Shakespeare was constructing the play in 1594. In general, the editor is surprisingly shy of matters bibliographical (cf. p. 104 for the note on IV, iii, 180) in an edition of such importance. There are several readings about which I do not agree. At V, ii, 808, for instance, "rackt" in the Quarto is surely a misreading of a manuscript 'răcke'—"You must be purged to[o], your sinnes are rancke". Like Wilson and Miss Yates, David goes too far, in my opinion, in reading into the play an extensive attack on the so-called School of Night.

[1] London: Methuen, 1951.

There is now a considerable literature on the subject of memorial reconstruction, and the results of research based on this theory are of first importance, not only in evaluating the authority of a given text, but also in reconstructing the story of Shakespeare's development as a dramatist. It makes a great deal of difference whether *The First Part of the Contention* and *The True Tragedy* are (1) source plays used by Shakespeare in writing the second and third parts of *Henry VI*, or (2) first drafts, or (3) imperfect memorial reconstructions of the 'Good' texts printed in the First Folio. Confident acceptance of the implications of the theory of Good and Bad Quartos has resulted in the denial that Shakespeare began his career by revising other men's plays or even by collaborating, and the assertion that his earliest efforts may have been penned in 1587 or 1588 instead of 1590 or later. It is not to be expected that there would be complete agreement. Dover Wilson's edition of *Titus Andronicus* assumes the participation of George Peele, and his article on 'Malone and the Upstart Crow'[1] revives, mistakenly I think, the charge that Shakespeare was a borrower—or worse—in his dealings with Robert Greene. Another manifestation of dissent is William Bracy's monograph, *The Merry Wives of Windsor: The History and Transmission of Shakespeare's Text*.[2] Bracy rejects utterly Greg's thesis of memorial reconstruction as stated in 1910 and since modified, and maintains that the Quarto is an abridgement prepared (not by Shakespeare but by a "practical adapter-reviser of the company") for stage use by a company of limited size on a provincial tour. He boldly avers that "the reporter theory is completely supererogatory in explaining any of the textual phenomena" (p. 96).

It is a good thing for received opinion to be challenged occasionally, but this particular challenge might be taken more seriously if one could be sure that Bracy always understands the significance of the evidence he is dealing with. Does he realize that legitimate ownership of copyright, secured by normal entry of a title in the Stationers' Register, is no guarantee of the authority of the text so entered—that such a text is not necessarily the one licensed by the Master of the Revels or performed by Shakespeare's company (p. 71)? Does he understand the significance of the bibliographical evidence that certain passages in some of the Good Quartos were printed directly from Bad Quartos (p. 63)? He finds it convenient to assume that, since playhouse manuscripts were not highly prized in those days for their literary merit, they were handled so carelessly as to permit all manner of textual corruption (p. 63); this is to ignore their monetary value and the evidence that the acting companies guarded their manuscripts jealously. There is still much to be learned about *Merry Wives*, and Bracy's questioning of conservative opinion is welcome; his initial study of the play is insufficiently documented, however, and is thesis-ridden.

In the first of three notes[3] which at once establish Shakespeare's dependence upon *The Herball* of John Gerard and restore Shakespeare's meaning that had been lost in the verbiage of commentators, J. W. Lever finds confirmation that *Love's Labour's Lost* was "newly corrected and augmented", as the title-page of the 1598 Quarto asserts. What is sung of

> Lady-smocks all silver white
> And cuckow-buds of yellow hue   (v, ii, 905–6)

---

[1] *Shakespeare Survey*, 4 (1951), 56–8.
[2] Columbia, Missouri, 1952. University of Missouri Studies, xxv, no. 1.
[3] 'Three Notes on Shakespeare's Plays', *Review of English Studies*, n.s., III, 117–29.

could not have been written before the publication of *The Herball* (entered in the Stationers' Register, 6 June 1597).

The tendency to push back the date of Shakespeare's early plays is illustrated in two articles by Karl Wentersdorf. In 'Shakespeares erste Truppe',[1] he traces the career of the Queen's Men and the Earl of Pembroke's Men, concluding that the section of the former which Dutton headed had secured Pembroke's patronage by Christmas 1593. Turning to the plays which are known to have been written for the Queen's Men and for Pembroke's, and particularly to the piracies which were printed about 1594, Wentersdorf finds further confirmation. Then he points out that Robert Greene's anger in 1592 was directed against actors as well as against the upstart Crow; and, recalling Greene's sale of *Orlando Furioso* a second time when the first purchasers, the Queen's, were on tour, he maintains that Greene naturally had the Queen's Men in mind. These, he thinks, had turned from Greene to Shakespeare. Therefore Shakespeare must have been writing for them before becoming a Pembroke's man in 1593. If so, the extraordinary way in which he later made use of *King Leir*, *The Troublesome Reign of King John*, and *The Famous Victories of Henry V* may be explained in terms of Shakespeare's early familiarity with them. Wentersdorf does not go quite so far as to suggest that the interest was proprietary, but the possibility exists, as I hinted three years ago.

The related study[2] is an examination of the evidence for the dating of Shakespeare's plays and a reappraisal of the value of metrical tests. As might be expected, Wentersdorf assigns dates which are often two or three years earlier than those of Chambers. One of Wentersdorf's purposes is to modify the application of the metrical tests, in which he expresses confidence. He maintains that a curve drawn to represent metrical irregularities of the history plays and another curve for those in the tragedies and comedies would, in general, show steady progression and put each play close to where other evidence assigns it. His calculations include extra syllables, overflows, or run-on lines, pauses in unsplit lines, and split lines, i.e. those divided between two or more speakers. The curves reveal a remarkably regular increase in metrical freedom.

The false dating of several Shakespeare Quartos by Thomas Pavier and William Jaggard was proved in 1908 and 1910, but the controversialists of those years would have welcomed the discovery recently made by Allan H. Stevenson.[3] At the Huntington Library he has found a leaf in the Church copy of *Henry V* (dated "1608") with a watermark dated 1617 or 1619, and in the Church copy of *Sir John Oldcastle* (dated "1600") a leaf dated 1608. The value of the discovery at this late date is, as Stevenson says good humouredly, largely sentimental; but it enables him to make several acute observations about intrusive watermarks. For a revolutionary discovery, one should read Stevenson's other article in the same volume (pp. 57–91), 'Watermarks Are Twins'. The fact that watermarks were, and are, made in pairs is a commonplace among paper-makers and historians of paper-making, but English and American bibliographers have been unaware of it, though, as Stevenson demonstrates, it may be used to advantage.

One of the more recalcitrant plays in the canon is *Troilus and Cressida*. In recent years we have learned the truth about the cancelled leaves in the First Folio, the relationship of the Quarto and

[1] *Shakespeare-Jahrbuch*, LXXXIV–LXXXVI (1950), 114–30.
[2] 'Shakespearean Chronology and the Metrical Tests' in *Shakespeare-Studien, Festschrift für Heinrich Mutschmann* (Marburg: N. G. Elwert Verlag, 1952), pp. 161–93.
[3] 'Shakespearian Dated Watermarks', *Studies in Bibliography*, IV (1951–2), 159–64.

Folio texts, and the nature of the change in quality of the Folio text that begins with the fourth page and continues to the end of the play. But how was Jaggard able to resume the printing of the play after once having had to abandon it? Sir Walter Greg supplies the answer[1] and prints in tabular form the variants that occur in the first three pages in the Folio and also those that are found in the later pages. When Henry Walley, who had entered *Troilus* in the Stationers' Register in 1609 in defiance of the grand possessors, refused to come to terms with Jaggard, the latter discontinued printing the play and substituted *Timon*. Walley's continued stubbornness drove Jaggard to the discovery that he already had a sort of claim to ownership of the copy by virtue of being the successor to the late James Roberts, who had registered *Troilus* conditionally in 1603. Furthermore, Jaggard had the good fortune to come into possession of (or gain access to) a manuscript of the play that differed markedly from the Quarto and had a hitherto unprinted Prologue. His legal position thus fortified, Jaggard resumed printing, inserted the Prologue, altered the Quarto text to conform to his manuscript, and included some forty or fifty lines missing from Walley's quarto.

The Fourth Folio was printed in three sections, as M. A. Shaaber and M. W. Black noted a decade ago, and probably in three different shops. The identity of all three printers was unknown until last year, when F. T. Bowers identified[2] the ornamental initials in the first section as the property of Robert Roberts.

There has been little occasion to study the Fourth Folio, and so several of its bibliographical peculiarities have gone unnoticed or unexplained. Giles Dawson now brings them to public attention.[3] The first is a series of incorrect signatures in the second section of the book. Another irregularity is the printing of leaf L 1, pp. 123–4, in 8-point type to squeeze in one page of text that had been carelessly overlooked by the compositor. All known copies of the Fourth Folio share these irregularities.

The most important aberration, noted inadequately as long ago as 1880[4] but subsequently neglected, is the reprinting of no fewer than seventeen sheets (Dawson estimates that half as many more may exist in copies that have not been examined). These are easily recognized, because the side-rules and foot-rules which help enclose the columns of text elsewhere in the volume have been omitted. Dawson conjectures that long after 1685 the owner of the unsold stock of sheets discovered a shortage, which interestingly enough occurs in the second section of the volume, and found it to his advantage to have certain sheets reprinted. Only six (four in the Folger Library and two in the New York Public Library) of the sixty-six copies examined or reported on contain the reprinted sheets.

Some of the more puzzling discrepancies between the Quarto and Folio texts of *The Merry Wives* are found in the masque which ends the play. John H. Long proposes,[5] as a solution, that the Quarto gives the substance of the masque as originally written and performed, while the

---

[1] 'The Printing of Shakespeare's *Troilus and Cressida* in the First Folio', *Papers of the Bibliographical Society of America*, XLV (1951), 273–82.

[2] 'Robert Roberts: A Printer of Shakespeare's Fourth Folio', *Shakespeare Quarterly*, II (1951), 241–6.

[3] 'Some Bibliographical Irregularities in the Shakespeare Fourth Folio', *Studies in Bibliography*, IV (1951–2), 93–103.

[4] In *Contributions to a Catalogue of the Lenox Library, No. 5, Works of Shakespeare, Etc.* (New York, 1880), p. 41.

[5] 'Another Masque for *The Merry Wives of Windsor*', *Shakespeare Quarterly*, III (January 1952), 39–43.

Folio has the text as it was altered for a revival at Windsor Castle early in 1604. The earlier version, popular in form and vulgar in tone, actually resolves the plot, according to Long, better than the formal revision and should be substituted in modern texts.

The Shakespeare Association (London) continues its series of collotype facsimiles of Shakespeare Quartos with the publication of *Hamlet* (1603)[1] from the British Museum copy. Now for the first time scholars can collate the two extant copies of this First Quarto, for the Huntington Library copy is already available in facsimile. Sir Walter Greg's Introductory Note gives the history of the two copies and notes the variant readings in the two states of both formes of sheet B. It is interesting that an eighteenth-century hand has twice corrected "weasel(l)" to "Owsle (Owstle)" on G1, lines 25 and 26 (III, ii, 396–7), for the same emendation occurs in both of the prompt-books of John Ward, grandfather to Mrs Siddons, and in a Folger Library copy of *Hamlet* (1703) partly marked for prompt use.

[1] *Hamlet, First Quarto, 1603*. Shakespeare Quarto Facsimiles No. 7. London: The Shakespeare Association and Sidgwick and Jackson, 1951.

BOOKS RECEIVED

ALEXANDER, PETER. *A Shakespeare Primer* (London: James Nisbet, 1951).

BRADBROOK, M. C. *Shakespeare and Elizabethan Poetry; A Study of his Earlier Work in Relation to the Poetry of the Time* (London: Chatto and Windus, 1951).

CLEMEN, W. H. *The Development of Shakespeare's Imagery* (London: Methuen, 1951).

CRAIG, HARDIN. *An Introduction to Shakespeare: Eight Plays, Selected Sonnets* (Chicago: Scott, Foresman and Co., 1952).

CRANE, MILTON. *Shakespeare's Prose* (University of Chicago Press; London: Cambridge University Press, 1951).

DUTHIE, G. I. *Shakespeare* (London: Hutchinson's University Library, 1951).

ELLIOTT, G. R. *Scourge and Minister* (Durham, North Carolina: Duke University Press; London: Cambridge University Press, 1951).

EMPSON, WILLIAM. *The Structure of Complex Words* (London: Chatto and Windus, 1951).

Essays and Studies, 1951 (Published for the English Association by John Murray, London).

EVANS, B. IFOR. *The Language of Shakespeare's Plays* (London: Methuen, 1952).

GODDARD, HAROLD C. *The Meaning of Shakespeare* (University of Chicago Press; London: Cambridge University Press, 1951).

GREG, W. W. *Jonson's Masque of Gipsies in the Burley, Belvoir and Windsor Versions. An Attempt at Reconstruction* (Published for the British Academy by Geoffrey Cumberlege, Oxford University Press, 1952).

HALLIDAY, F. E. *A Shakespeare Companion* (London: Duckworth, 1952).

HARRISON, G. B. *Shakespeare's Tragedies* (London: Routledge and Kegan Paul, 1951).

HARTNOLL, PHYLLIS. *The Oxford Companion to the Theatre* (London: Oxford University Press, 1951).

HOSKING, G. L. *The Life and Times of Edward Alleyn* (London: Cape, 1952).

ING, CATHERINE. *Elizabethan Lyrics: A Study in the Development of English Metres and their Relation to Poetic Effect* (London: Chatto and Windus, 1951).

JAMES, D. G. *The Dream of Learning: An Essay on The Advancement of Learning, Hamlet and King Lear* (Oxford: At the Clarendon Press, 1951).

KNIGHT, G. WILSON. *The Imperial Theme*. Third edition (London: Methuen, 1951).

LEY, CHARLES DAVID. *Shakespeare Para Españoles* (Madrid: Revista de Occidente, 1951).

Proceedings of the British Academy, vol. XXXIII, 1947 and vol. XXXIV, 1948 (Published for the British Academy by Geoffrey Cumberlege, Oxford University Press).

PROUTY, CHARLES T. *The Sources of Much Ado about Nothing* (New Haven, Connecticut: Yale University Press; London: Oxford University Press, 1950).

PURDOM, C. B. *The Crosby Hall Macbeth* (London: Dent, for The Shakespeare Stage Society, 1951).

RALLI, AUGUSTUS. *Poetry and Faith* (London: The Bodley Head, 1951).

SEWELL, ARTHUR. *Character and Society in Shakespeare* (Oxford: Clarendon Press, 1951).

Shakespeare Quarterly, vol. II (New York: Shakespeare Association of America, 1951).

SHAKESPEARE, WILLIAM. *Hamlet*. First Quarto, 1603. Shakespeare Quarto Facsimiles No. 7. Introduction by W. W. Greg (London: The Shakespeare Association and Sidgwick and Jackson, 1951).

SHAKESPEARE, WILLIAM. *Love's Labours Lost*. The Arden Edition of the Works of William Shakespeare. Edited by R. W. David. Based on the Edition of H. C. Hart (London: Methuen, 1951).

SHAKESPEARE, WILLIAM. *Macbeth*. Introduction by Sir Lewis Casson (London: The Folio Society, 1950).

SHAKESPEARE, WILLIAM. *The Taming of the Shrew*. The Penguin Shakespeare. Edited by G. B. Harrison (London: Penguin Books, 1951).

Studies in Bibliography. Papers of the Bibliographical Society of the University of Virginia, vols. I–IV, 1948–51. Edited by Fredson Bowers (Charlottesville, Virginia).

THOMSON, J. A. K. *Shakespeare and the Classics* (London: George Allen and Unwin, 1952).

THOMSON, W. H. *Shakespeare's Characters: A Historical Dictionary* (Altrincham: John Sherratt and Son, 1951).

VILLA, CARLO. *Parigi vale bene una messa! William Shakespeare e il poeta valtellinese Michelagnolo Florio* (Milano: Editrice Storica, 1951).

WILLIAMSON, AUDREY. *Theatre of Two Decades* (London: Rockliff Publishing Corporation, 1951).

INDEX

INDEX

Bradley, A. C., 2
  Interpretation of Falstaff, 12–13
Brennan, Dennis, 119
Brewer, D. S., 157
Bricker, Herschel L., 124
Bridges, Robert, 143–4
Briggs, W. D., 3
British Museum, 62, 160, 172
Britten, Benjamin, 123
Brook, Peter, production of *The Winter's Tale* reviewed, 142–5
Brooke, Arthur, *Romeus and Juliet*, 58
Brooke, C. F. Tucker, 3, 6, 14, 39, 58
Brown, Arthur, 158
Brown, Gilmore, 124
Brown, John Mason, 141
Budde, Fritz, 163 n.
Bull, Richard, 61
Bundy, Murray W., 163
Burgersdijk, L. J., 122
Burian, Orhan, 163 n.
Burton, Richard, 136–7, 138

Cain, H. E., 15 n., 24 n.
Calderón de la Barca, Pedro, 25, 106
Cambyses (1569), 72, 74 n.
Camden, William, editions of his works in the Huntington Library, 57
Campbell, Lily B., 10, 57, 157
  Shakespeare's 'Histories' reviewed, 10
Campion, Thomas, 60, 156
Canada, report on Shakespeare in, 118
Candoni, Luigi, 121
Capgrave, John, 59
Capon, William, 66
Carter, John, sketches of Trinity Hall, 69–70, 71, 72 n.
Casson, Christopher, 119
Casson, Lewis, 143
Caxton, William, printer, 56, 63
Chambers, R. W., 5, 7, 63 n.
Chambers, Sir E. K., 14, 39, 73 n., 74 n., 75, 160, 170
Chao's Bridge, a Chinese story, 112–13
Chapman, George, 9, 78 n., 155, 157, 159
Chapman, Raymond, 160
Charles I, King, 56
Charles, Nicholas, 70
Charlton, H. B., 6, 7, 13
Chaucer, Geoffrey, *Canterbury Tales*, 56, 59
Chester Plays, 60
Chettle, Henry, 159

Chih-mo, Hsu, 115, 116
Chronology of Shakespeare's plays, *see under* Shakespeare
Church, Elihu Dwight, his library, 54
Churchill, G. B., 3
Clark, A. M., 74 n.
Clark, Cumberland, 33 n.
Clark, D. L., 156
Clarke, Charles W., 163
Clemen, Wolfgang, 6, 11
  The Development of Shakespeare's Imagery reviewed, 150–1
Clunes, Alec, 138
Cœur de Lion, romance, 37
Cole, George Watson, 54, 55
Coleridge, S. T., 17, 87, 149
Collier, John P., 58, 60, 63 n., 162
Collins, J. C. Churton, 3
Coltellacci, Giulio, 121
Constable, Henry, *Sonnets to Diana*, 88
Contention of York and Lancaster, The, 4–5
  First Part, 58, 169
Coprario, Giovanni, 60
Cormican, L. A., 156
Cornell, Katharine, 141
Courthope, W. J., 2, 5
Courtney, T. P., 1
Craig, Hardin, 4, 8, 11, 156
Crane, Francis, 54
Crane, Ralph, 60
Crespo, José María Blanco, translation of *Hamlet*, 107–9
Crosse, Samuel, actor, 74 n.
Cunliffe, J. W., 12
Cupid's Cabinet Unlocked, 58
Czechoslovakia, report on Shakespeare in, 118–19

Danby, J. F., 10
Daniel, Samuel, 9
  Civil Wars, 4, 35 n.
  Cleopatra, its possible reference to Shakespeare's *Antony and Cleopatra*, 91–3
Dante Alighieri, 152
Dasent, J. R., 73 n.
Davenant, Sir William, 58
Davenport, Thomas, *Drinking Academy*, 60
David, Gerard, 59
David, Richard, 148, 163 n.
  Edition of *Love's Labours Lost* reviewed, 168
Davies, Robertson, 118
Dawson, Giles, 171
Dean, L. F., 10

INDEX

Defoe, Daniel, editions of his works in the Huntington Library, 57
Dekker, Thomas, 74 n.
 Editions of his works in the Huntington Library, 57
 A Knight's Conjuring, 74 n.
Delannoy, Marcel, 120
Denmark, report on Shakespeare in, 119
Devlin, William, 124
Devonshire, William Cavendish, Duke of (1790–1858), his library, 54
De Witt, Johannes, Swan Theatre drawing, 160, 161
Dio Cassius, 93 n., 140
Doheny, Mrs E. L., 61
Donne, John, 60, 143
Doran, Madeleine, 5, 11
Doren, Mark Van, 11
Dowden, E., 1, 3
Drake, Sir Francis, 159
Draper, J. W., 15 n., 157, 160, 162
Droeshout, Martin, portrait of Shakespeare, 61
Dryden, John, 141
Du Bartas, Guillaume, 82, 83, 88 n., 89 n.
Dudley, Robert, Earl of Leicester, his company of actors, 65, 73 n., 74 n.
Duff, E. Gordon, 63 n.
Duthie, D. W., 4
Duthie, G. I., 14, 151, 167–8
Dutton, John, actor, 159, 170

Ebisch, W., and Schücking, L. L., *Shakespeare Bibliography*, 3
Economidis, J., 120
Edmonds, C. K., 55, 63 n.
Edward III, see *Raigne of King Edward the Third*
Edward IV, King, 60
Edward VI, King, 66
Edwards, Hilton, 119
Edwards, Philip, 'An Approach to the Problem of *Pericles*' reviewed, 164–5
Egerton, Sir John, 55
Egerton, Sir Thomas, 54
 his library, 59–60
Eggen, Arne, 123
Eickhoff, Louise, 48 n.
Eire, report on Shakespeare in, 119
Eliot, George, 1
Eliot, John, his life, 79
 Ortho-Epia Gallica described, 79; Shakespeare's knowledge and use of it, 80–90
 Survey or Topographical Description of France, 89 n.

Eliot, T. S., 105
Elizabeth I, Queen, 60, 64, 68, 106
Ellesmere, Francis Egerton, 1st Earl of, 63 n.
Elliott, G. R., 154
Ellis-Fermor, Una, 10, 75, 147
Elson, J., 11
Empson, William, 161
 The Structure of Complex Words reviewed, 152–3
Eschenburg, —, 120
Essex, Robert Devereux, second Earl of, 1, 6–7, 160
Etienne, Claude, 117
Euripides, 25
Evans, B. Ifor, 151
Evans, G. Blakemore, 162

Faire Em, 58
Falk, Sawyer, 124
Family papers in the Huntington Library, 60
Famous Victories of Henry the Fifth, The, 4, 36, 37, 71, 157, 170
Farley, Frederick, 122
Farnham, Willard, 13
Farrand, Max, 55, 62
Farrant, Richard, 65
Feuillerat, A., 73 n.
Finch, Peter, 145
Finkel, Simon, 121
Firth, Kenneth, 122
Fischer, Walter, 157
Fitton, Doris, 117
Flatter, Richard, 120, 161, 163
Flaubert, Gustave, 142
Fleay, F. G., 39, 75, 78 n.
Fletcher, John, 6, 57, 144
Florio, John (Giovanni), 88, 160
 First Fruites, 73 n.
Florio, Michelagnolo, 160
Fogle, French R., 63 n.
Folger Shakespeare Library, 162, 163, 171, 172
Ford, John, 154–5, 157
Forsett, Edward, *Paedantius*, 60
Fothergill, G., 73 n.
Foxe, John, *Acts and Monuments*, 73 n.
Frangcon-Davies, Gwen, 123
Freeman, Douglas S., 164
Frings, Cardinal, 120
Froissart, Jean, 4, 39
Fry, Mary Isabel, 57, 63 n.
Furness, H. H., 2
Furnivall, F. J., 5
Furse, Roger, 145

INDEX

INDEX

Homer, 152

Homilies, Tudor, their influence on Shakespeare, 7

Hosking, G. L., 160–1

Hotson, Leslie, 80, 88 n., 159

Houghton, Alexander, 158

Howgego, J. L., 73 n.

Huisman, Jacqueline, 118

Huisman, Jacques, 118

Hulme, Hilda M., 158

Hunt, Althea, 124

Huntingdon, Henry Hastings, third Earl of, papers in the Huntington Library, 60

Huntington, Collis P., 53

Huntington, Henry Edwards, the growth of his library, 53–5, 61–2, 63 n.

Huntington Library, California, 170; its growth and collections of Shakespeariana and early books described, 53–63

Ibsen, Henrik, 25, 140, 147

I-che, Teng, 114

Imagery in Shakespeare's plays, *see under* Shakespeare; image-clusters in *Edward III*, 43–4

Ing, Catherine, *Elizabethan Lyrics* reviewed, 155–6

Ireland, W. H., 60

Ishanturayeva, Sara, 125

Israel, report on Shakespeare in, 121

Italy, report on Shakespeare in, 121

Jackson, William A., 61

Jaggard, William, printer of the First Folio, 167, 170, 171

James I, King, 106, 161–2
  Basilikon Doron, 157

James, D. G., *The Dream of Learning* reviewed, 148–9

Jefford, Barbara, 132

Jodelle, Etienne, 93 n.

John, Ivor B., 35 n.

Johnson, Dr Samuel, 104–5

Jones, Margo, 124

Jonson, Ben, 57, 61, 72
  Sejanus his Fall, 54
  Gypsies Metamorphosed, 60

Karl, Joseph, 121

Karthaios, K., 120

Kean, Charles, 50

Kean, Edmund, 143

Keen, Alan, 11, 158–9

Keith, Ian, 124

Keller, W., 6

Kemble, John Philip, 54

Kenny, Thomas, 5

Kidd, John, production of *1 Henry IV* reviewed, 134–7

King Leir, 170

King, Lucille, 7

Kingsford, C. L., 4, 7

Kirschbaum, L., 5

Kittredge, G. L., 13, 14, 48 n.

Klatzkin, Raphael, 121

Knell, —, actor, 74 n.

Knight, Charles, 61

Knight, G. Wilson, 6, 8–9, 35 n., 150, 151

Knights, L. C., 12, 156

Knowlton, E. C., 15 n.

Koefoed, H. A., 48 n.

Kokoschka, —, 120

Kraus, Werner, 117

Kyd, Thomas, 72, 74 n.
  The Spanish Tragedy, 71, 72, 74 n.

Lambley, Kathleen, 80

Laneham (Lanam), John, actor, 74 n.

Langham, Michael, 118

Langland, William, *Piers Plowman*, 59

Langley, Francis, 160

Langsam, G. G., 10

Langtry, Lily, 140

Larpent, John, 59–60

Larum for London, A, 48 n.

Laurence, Michael, 119

Law, R. A., 11, 13, 17, 21

Lawes, Henry, 55

Lawrence, W. J., 74 n.

Leavis, F. R., 153

Legge, Thomas, *Richardus Tertius*, 60

Leicester, Earl of, *see* Dudley, Robert

Leigh, Vivien, 123, 140, 141–2, 145

Leishman, J. B., 158

Lever, J. W., 169

Lewis, C. S., 101

Ley, Charles David, 154

Liebermann, F., 4

Libraries (*see also under* Huntington Library)
  Bodleian, 62
  British Museum, 62, 160, 172
  Folger, 162, 163, 171, 172
  New York Public Library, 171

Lindabury, R. V., 6

Lindsay, Jack, 79, 80, 85

Linthicum, M. Channing, 93 n.

Livesey, Roger, 138, 139

Locrine, 34 n.

INDEX

Palmer, John, 10–11
Parallel passages as evidence for authorship, 43–7
Parish, William A., 63 n.
Partridge, A. C., 6
Pasternak, Boris, 125
Pater, Walter, 12
Patrick, D. L., 4
Paul, J., 33 n.
Pavier, Thomas, printer, 170
Payne, B. Iden, 124
Peel, Albert, 60
Peele, George, 39, 40, 72, 169
    Edward I, 36
Pembroke, Mary Herbert, Countess of, 93
Penry, John, *Journal*, 60
Percy, William, *Comedies and Pastorals*, 60
Pereson, Edward, 67, 68, 69, 74 n.
Pereson, John, 69
Petit-Dutaillis, C., 10
Phillips, Edward, 57
Phipson, E., 48 n.
Pierson, Thomas, 74
Pilotto, Camillo, 121
Pivec, Jan, 118
Platt, A., 39
Plutarch's *Lives, see* North, Sir Thomas
Pollard, A. F., 3
Pollard, A. W., 5, 58
    with Redgrave, G. R., *Short-Title Catalogue: 1475–
    1640* books in Huntington Library, 56, 57, 61
Pomfret, John E., 63 n.
Porter, Henry, *Two Angry Women of Abington*, 88 n.
Prescott, W. C., 61
Price, H. T., 4, 5, 34 n.
Prick of Conscience, The, 59
Priestley, J. B., 13
Printing, Elizabethan, in relation to textual problems in
    Shakespeare's plays, 165–72
Prior, Moody E., 162
Productions of Shakespeare's plays:
    in the United Kingdom during 1951, 126–8
    Festival of Britain productions reviewed, 140–6
    recent performances abroad, 117–25
    Stratford and Birmingham productions of history
    plays discussed, 49–52, 129–39
Prokofieff, Sergei, 125
Prophecies in Shakespeare's history plays, *see under*
    Shakespeare
Prouty, C. T., 5, 153
Purdom, C. B., 161, 163
Pushkin, Alexander, 125

Quasimodo, Salvatore, 121
Quayle, Anthony, 136
    Production of *Richard II* reviewed, 129, 132–4
    Production of *Henry V* reviewed, 138–9
Quiller-Couch, Sir A. C., 13

Rabelais, François, 79
Race, Sydney, 162
Raigne of King Edward the Third, The, 34 n.; imagery
    and authorship, 39–48
Raleigh, Sir Walter (*ob.* 1618), 9
Raleigh, Sir Walter (1861–1922), 2
Ralli, Augustus, 152
Ravenscroft, Thomas, *Brief discourse...on measurable
    music,* 55
Redgrave, G. R., *see* Pollard, A. W.
Redgrave, Michael, 132, 134, 135–6, 138–9
    Production of *2 Henry IV* reviewed, 137–8
Reese, Gertrude C., 9
Reinhardt-Thimig, Frau, 117
Reyher, Paul, 4, 10, 26, 33 n., 34 n.
Reynolds, Sir Joshua, 61
Ricci, Renzo, 121
Roberts, James, printer, 171
Roberts, Robert, printer, 171
Robertson, J. M., 78 n.
Robson, Flora, 143
Rolle, Richard, 59
Roman de la Rose, 101
Rose, George, 143, 145
Rose, Harry, 59
Rossiter, A. P., 10, 11, 29, 33 n., 34 n., 35 n.
Rothe, H., 124
Rowe, Nicholas, 58, 77, 81
Rubow, Paul V., 119
Rundall, —, 162

Sackfull of Newes, A, 64
Sackville, Thomas, *see* Norton, Thomas
Saintsbury, George, 39, 152
Salisbury, John, 159
Salvini, Guido, 121
Santuccio, Gianni, 121
Sanvic, Romain, 117
Sarrazin, Gregor, 11
Saudek, E. A., 118–19
Schad, Robert O., 63 n.
Schalla, —, 120
Schelling, F. E., 2, 3
Schlegel, A. W., 1
Schrickx, W., 159

INDEX

INDEX

INDEX